The Play of Mirrors

iLAS **Translations from Latin America Series**

The Play of Mirrors
The Representation of Self as Mirrored in the Other

by Sylvia Caiuby Novaes
Translated by Izabel Murat Burbridge

University of Texas Press, Austin
Institute of Latin American Studies

Library of Congress Cataloging-in-Publication Data

Novaes, Sylvia Caiuby, 1949–
   [Jogo de espelhos. English]
   The play of mirrors : the representation of self as mirrored in the other /
by Sylvia Caiuby Novaes : translated by Izabel Murat Burbridge.
      p.   cm. — (Translations from Latin America Series)
   Includes bibliographical references and index.
   ISBN 0-292-71196-4 (pbk. : alk. paper)
   1. Bororo Indians—Psychology. 2. Bororo Indians—Ethnic identity.
3. Bororo Indians—Social conditions. 4. Self-perception—Brazil—Mato Grosso (State) 5. Identity (Psychological—Brazil—Mato Grosso (State)
6. Salesians—Missions—Brazil—Mato Grosso (State) 7. Culture—Brazil—Mato Grosso—Semiotic models. I. Series.
F2520.1.B75N6513 1997
   155.2'.089'984—dc21   97-13918

In memory of my father, Orlando Caiuby Novaes,
for his care, encouragement, and admiration.

To the Bororo men and women, old and young,
themselves heroes of a lengthy battle.

First, all those mirrors. Whenever you see a mirror—it's only human—you want to look at yourself. But here you can't. You look at the position in space where the mirror will say "You are here, and you are you," you look, craning, twisting, but nothing works, because Lavoisier's mirrors, whether concave or convex, disappoint you, mock you. You step back, find yourself for a moment, but move a little and you are lost. This catoptric theater was contrived to take away your identity and make you feel unsure not only of yourself but also of the very objects standing between you and the mirrors.

—Umberto Eco, *Foucault's Pendulum*

CONTENTS

Preface ix

Acknowledgments xix

1. Contemporary Anthropology and Studies of Identity and Social Change 1

2. Identity in the Broad Sense: The Other as Model 17

3. Literature as Mirror: Different Views of Social Change in Bororo Society 26

4. Self-Image as Formed in the Play of Mirrors: Structural Distance and Reference Values 45

5. The Salesian Missions in Mato Grosso 65

6. The Salesians and the Progressive Church: The Reshaping of an Image 102

7. Missionaries and Indians: Identification Created through Martyrdom 120

Notes 145

Bibliography 155

Index 163

Photos

Baraedu ku kuri. Pantomime in which the Bororo imitate
non-Indians   22–23

Otávio Kodo Kodo, a Bororo nurse's aide   57

Bororo village next to Salesian mission, early 1900s   76

The Salesians have educated Bororo youth from the beginning
of their missionary work   81

Bororo girl with spinning wheel   87

Father Giovanni Balzola, first director of the Salesian mission
to the Bororo   90

Soccer team of Bororo boys   96

Father Balzola and the Reverend Malan surrounded by Bororo
youths   96

The Salesians boosted male and female labor   98–99

Young Bororo newlyweds received their trousseau from the
missionaries   109

Father Ochoa and Bororo Indians performing the funeral ritual   112

At the Meruri outpatient ward, Father Rodolfo Lunkenbein
watches the vaccination of adults and children   121

The Bororo give Salesian nuns the ornamented bones of Father
Lunkenbein   126

Bororo village at the Meruri Salesian mission   140

Tables

1. Father Albisetti's 1935 Census   101

2. Identification Mechanisms   134

3. Salesian Censuses of the Bororo Population   136

Preface

Establishing the Issue

This book addresses the representation of self, that is, the self-image built by a society or a specific group within a society and how the investigation of self can lead to an understanding of the actions of groups or societies as they relate with other groups or societies. My approach is primarily anthropological, but I incorporate contributions from other disciplines, such as psychology, psychoanalysis, linguistics, and semiotics.

The representation of self is associated with one's representation of the other and the representation of various others in given contexts. An interdependent relationship is established between the image of the self and the image of these various others.

In 1975 Hartmann analyzed the documentary value of the iconography of Brazilian Indians produced by painters and drafters who integrated "scientific expeditions organized to disclose to the world the immense Brazilian territory" (1975: 5). Despite focusing specifically on the graphic image produced by artists—rather than on their mental representation, which is my goal—she showed how this picture revealed "cultural differences between Indians and non-Indians expressed in terms of barbarism, a concept that included nudity, body malformations and cannibalism," in addition to traces left by touches of "innocence that romanticism added to human groups marginalized by civilization" (1975: 7–8). Her analysis of the iconographic records, she claimed, revealed a great similarity between graphic representation and language. Although the kaleidoscopic flow of impressions affecting these artists is subjected to frequent modifications, "when reproducing the image on paper they have already opted for an organized impression of reality, which is in itself quite jumbled and transmits the result of this choice . . . following their culture and the categories of this culture" (1975: 18–19).

I also start from the premise that "reality presents itself as a kaleidoscope of objects and living beings within a status of dynamic relations" (1975: 19). I try to show how this reality is perceived historically by those who participate in it and how this perception can be changed by elements combined in a given context. I try to demonstrate how this reality differs depending on the observer's viewpoint. Thus, the relationships among societies or even among various groups in the same society cannot be adequately analyzed from a unidirectional viewpoint that prioritizes the perspective of one of the groups or societies involved in these relationships.

Though I have tried to address different social groups and segments, my empirical focus is on the representation of self in the Indian societies of contemporary Brazil, specifically, the Bororo, whom I have been researching since 1970. A few of my conclusions may be generally applied to the so-called sociological (though certainly not demographic) minority groups such as Afro-Brazilians, Indians, and women.

If a few generalized conclusions can be drawn for present-day Brazil's Indian societies, others apply only to the Bororo and to the groups with which they have been in contact, for example, the Xavante and the Salesian missionaries.

My objective is to show that the representation of self leads to a better understanding of the conduct of a group of individuals or even a society in terms of their actual behavior. Depending on the context in which this representation of self is evoked, however, variations occur in the elements to be considered and in the range of this representation and the effective actions that may result therefrom. Therefore, a distinction must be made between identity, self-image, and the notion of the person. These three concepts provide the main theme for the book.

Identity, Self-Image, and the Notion of the Person

In 1976, as he ended a seminar on the issue of identity, Lévi-Strauss seemed to have definitively concluded all discussions of this theme. According to him, anthropologists should consider identity as "a sort of virtual focus to which we must refer to explain a certain number of things, but without which there is never a real existence" (1977: 332). Seemingly, the great master of anthropology, who had made such significant contributions to the analysis of mythology and kinship systems, did not regard identity as an issue worth investing in: "I ask myself to what extent does this postulated unity correspond, in any way, to something real" (1977: 331).

Lévi-Strauss's pronouncements could have led to the ending of all studies on the issue of identity. The literature produced at the end of this century, however, reveals significant excitement surrounding the subject.

In a certain way, Lévi-Strauss was right when he affirmed that identity was a virtual focus devoid of a corresponding reality. His statement was even more accurate with regard to the identity of human beings, who are endowed with the greatest powers of differentiation and individualization. No one is exactly like anyone else; thus, the human sciences cannot apply a mathematical concept of identity—a relationship of equality applicable to all values of the concerned variables. Nor are we dealing with insects, that is, standardized and interchangeable units adapted to functions from which they cannot disengage (i.e., maximum efficiency combined with minimum individuality). If identity is the constitution of sameness as a theme, and if this sameness is an attribute lacking in the relationship between men and women, then one must seek the domains and conditions under which this attribute is evoked.

Identity can be evoked only at the level of discourse, and it appears as a resource for the creation of a *group mind* (gathering us, Indians; us, women, us, Afro-Brazilians; us, homosexuals). This *us* refers to an identity (equality) that actually does not exist, but that constitutes an indispensable tool for our system of representation. This tool is indispensable because, based on the discovery or re-assertion—or even cultural creation—of its similarities, any group in a confrontational or minority status will be able to claim for itself a social and political space.

The concept of identity must thus be investigated and analyzed, not because anthropologists have stated its importance (as political science or sociology has emphasized the concept of social class, for example), but because it is vital to the contemporary social groups that claim an identity. Granted that identity is a condition growing out of certain historical and cultural elements rather than something given and verifiable, its efficiency as an instrument for action is temporary. Furthermore, the greater its association with an emotional condition of social life, the greater its power. It is the anthropologist's task to verify how this identity has been constructed and in which contexts it is evoked.

I believe that this collective *us*, that is, this "broad" identity, is invoked every time a group demands greater social visibility in light of its historical obliteration. To a great extent, the Brazilian political scenario that began in the mid-1970s has been set up by groups that articulate themselves to effectively enter the scene, thus becoming more socially visible.

Who are these groups? Which claims crystallize themselves in the construction of group identity? If we restrict ourselves to examining contemporary Brazilian society, we will see that there are many such groups. Although they have existed as organized units for a long time, some of these groups became politically more active as a result of the new political freedom of the late 1970s. Groups of homosexuals, for example, engaged in militant action "with the purpose of rethinking homosexual identity and fighting social prejudice in all its manifestations" (Fry and MacRae, 1983: 31).

In other places, such as the United States and some European countries, this search for greater social visibility began in the late 1960s. "Typification, visually recognizable images and self-presentation, is not just something wished on gay people but produced by them, both in the pre-political gay subcultures and in the radical gay movement since 1968" (Dyer, 1983: 3). In the foreword to her photographic essay "Lesbian Photography: Seeing through Our Own Eyes," J. Biren, a lesbian photographer, writes, "Part of defining ourselves is the creation of a common language—oral, written and visual . . . Without a visual identity we have no community, no support network, no movement. Making ourselves visible [which has fundamental importance for homosexuals, since there are no biological, sexual, or racial traces that differentiate them] is a political act. Making ourselves visible is a continual process" (1983: 81). The same occurred with sociological minority groups that started organizing more effectively in Brazil at that time. The Afro-Brazilian movement, the feminist movement, and the Indian movement itself became more prominent in large cities.

What traits do these movements share that permit us to address them, at least in theory, from the same analytical standpoint? Identity allows the creation of a *group* mind leading to effective, if brief, political action. This phenomenon implies the constitution of a *sameness* created by the manipulation of diacritical cultural signs. These signs, although expressed within the original context of one of these groups, do not have, as signs, the same meaning they originally had. Identity springs from the constitution of political subjects. In this sense, the possibility of creating a collective female, a collective Indian, a collective homosexual necessarily implies disregard for the differences that establish the distance between these various groups gathered under a single political name. Therefore, it is not as members of a specific society—Terena, Bororo, Guarani—that native peoples address the government or the national society to claim their rights. The native movement, as I shall demonstrate in chapter 2, appropriates a broad category—"Indians"—external to each of the participating societies and tries to manipulate certain diacritical signs that belong in the imaginary of Brazilian society's conjectures about who, in fact, the "Indians" are.

The feminist movement also addresses society from a broad category, "we, women," and within this context it does not propose to state the numerous differences between the various groups in this category: heterosexual women, homosexual women, middle-class and working-class homemakers, professional women, nonprofessional women, and so on. Maria Célia Paoli states:

as they constituted themselves as a political subject, women began
to build a discourse about themselves, in which they, controver-
sially, identified the meaning of feminine as an image and, principally, women's relationships within a specific oppressive
situation. . . . This debate is especially important because it discovers, in an intermittent and painful manner, a specific space for the
oppressed woman while acknowledging a specific submission that
may prompt the desire to rupture this condition. The emergence of
a condition common to all women, regardless of class distinction
and opportunity differences, promotes unquestionable recognition,
which is rendered as theme particularly in the submission of their
sexuality to family and reproduction. (1985: 67–69)

Thus the concept of identity functions at the level of a macrosocial
structure and constitutes a phenomenon that necessarily involves considerations of a sociopolitical, historical, and semiotic nature. Identity
is evoked every time a group claims the political space of difference.
These demonstrations do not have a specific interlocutor. The groups
address either society in general or an abstract entity such as "the
government." It is within this broad context of recognizing similarities
and differences that the articulation between *power* and *culture* becomes discernible. This articulation involves a desire to recover autonomy and the roads leading to it, which necessarily include the paths
of culture. After all, it is precisely in the cultural domain that these
groups (whether they be women or Indians) recover their autonomy and
reassert their difference.[1]

Through the concept of identity we can perceive what is common to
such heterogeneous claims as those originating from movements set up
by the so-called sociological minority groups. If the concept of identity
is evoked before a broad and generic interlocutor such as society or the
government, *self-image* is necessarily a relational concept determined
by very specific concrete relationships that a society or social group
establishes with others. The concept of identity always presents the
same face; it is, to a certain extent, a concept that establishes attributes
because it operates from diacritical cultural signs. Self-image implies
extremely dynamic and multifaceted, nonfixed characteristics that
transform themselves depending on who the *other* is who serves as the
reference for the establishment of the imaged self. Self-image further
depends on how one's relationship with this other is transformed over
time. It is precisely this conception of self-image that enables me to
address it by using the play of mirrors metaphor in chapter 4.

As we shall see, the self-image concept implies a confrontation
between conflicting value systems that are evoked in the representation
of self both in the course of role playing before the other and in the

assessment of this same role playing. From this standpoint, it is important that a study of contact relationships be conducted when addressing the self-image of Indian societies. It is possible here to incorporate contributions from psychology, particularly with respect to the constitution of self-awareness and the importance of the *other* to the attainment of this awareness of self (chapter 1).

Finally, I address a concept that has been extensively incorporated into anthropological studies: the notion of the "person." This notion constitutes a category of representation, according to Mauss (1968), and is extremely important for understanding South American Indian societies.[2] If "to take the notion of the 'person' as a category means to take it as an instrument for organizing social life, i.e. as a collective construction that provides meaning to actual life" (Seeger et al., 1979: 6), then this category must certainly be present when the current situation involves the contact of two societies. The findings of studies conducted on the notion of "person" in Brazilian Indian societies were restricted to the internal cultural context of the society in question. These chiefly interpretative studies sought the exegesis of native texts and tried to reconstruct the development of this notion in a given society. It seems to me, however, that this category cannot be disregarded when the study focuses on historical relations that a society establishes with others or with other segments of the larger society. The study of contemporary Brazil's Indian societies must take into account not only the conceptions and cultural practices of these societies and of other social segments with which they come into contact, but also the economic, political, and historical reality of this national society into which they are inserted.

The utilization of processual analysis—as developed by Turner (1974b) and Van Velsen (1967),[3] who take into account the different actors involved in the social situations in question—as a theoretical reference for understanding the contact situation between two societies cannot be conceived as a unidirectional analysis focusing on only one of the sides. An analysis of greater sociological content, focused on the interaction of these two societies, would benefit greatly from the incorporation of cultural standards (from both societies) that guide and provide meaning to this contact experience (which is certainly different for each of the participating societies or agents). This analytical framework will allow me to demonstrate the relevance of the "play of mirrors" (chapter 4) for understanding the dynamics of the contact situation.

Mauss (1968) discussed both the various forms given in different societies to the concept of person and their implications in terms of religion, law, customs, social structure, and mentality. Authors who tried to study this contact situation and its resulting new realities, however, did not utilize the same approach as Mauss, possibly, because they opted for a more sociological approach and addressed the effects of contact on the social institutions of native societies (e.g., family and kinship system, chieftaincy, division of labor). From the ideological standpoint, they analyzed the situation unidirectionally while considering only the interests, characteristics, and motivations of the national society's agents who made contact with the native societies.

Of the authors who have studied Bororo society and addressed the issue of contact, not even the more recent ones, such as Crocker or Viertler, have tried to incorporate the category of person, following Mauss's, or have taken into account traditional Bororo cultural practices, which, most certainly, would clarify the Bororo's historical relationship with national society.[4]

Commonly referred to as "an encounter with the other," anthropology is the discipline usually selected not only for analyzing encounters but also for studying discrepancies among various cultures, the strategies, domination, and resistance that permeate the relationships established among different societies and even among different groups of the same society. This posture is not new; since the late nineteenth century, anthropologists have devoted themselves to this task. Several theoretical positions elucidating this theme have been developed by European, U.S., and Brazilian authors with a deep interest in the Brazilian reality. Scholars who identify with diffusionism, historical empiricism, acculturation, and interethnic friction demonstrate the different theoretical perspectives drawn on to analyze cultural contact and its resulting phenomena.

The studies on identity and social changes discussed in chapter 1 were first outlined in the late 1960s. These studies focused on the issue of cultural contact between two societies or between two segments of a same society. In 1969 Fredrik Barth published a collection entitled *Ethnic Groups and Boundaries: The Social Organization of Culture Difference*, with the objective of analyzing the factors involved in the persistence of ethnic groups in the face of confrontation with other groups. In 1969 Abner Cohen published a study that greatly influenced other investigations of identity. Cohen's and Barth's works were to become as significant for Brazilian anthropology as Linton's, Herskovits's, and Redfield's had been in the 1930s and the 1940s; these authors left their imprint on the Brazilian anthropological literature of the 1950s and the 1960s.[5]

More than twenty years after the publication of these studies, the approach that currently seems most relevant involves not only focusing on the cultural phenomena that result from the confrontation between different groups, but also checking how each of these groups creates representations of the other and of itself while incorporating these representations into concrete political action. This is the central issue of this book, and I attempt to present it from a historical perspective in chapters 5, 6, and 7. I also develop a critical review of authors who have devoted themselves to the theme of identity,[6] both in anthropology and sociology and in related fields such as linguistics, semiotics, psychology, and psychoanalysis. My ultimate objective is to check the relevance and pertinence of these writings as instruments for researching the process of identity construction in contemporary Indian societies that are in contact with national society and to check the process of resistance to the physical and cultural "decharacterization" to which they have been subjected.

In a 1981 article (republished in 1983), I discussed a topic that I had addressed in my master's thesis and that refers to the Bororo mode of constructing their notion of person. To think through the notion of person within this society, I tried to analyze three elements of Bororo material culture used in funeral ceremonies that enable the living to recover the dead by reorganizing elements that characterized them. The funeral is the most important of the numerous Bororo rituals and serves to reconcile the society of the living and to ensure, by means of the *aroe-maiwu* (social representative of the dead), the continuity of the social category to which the deceased belonged.

The different roles of individuals with respect to the various funeral rites—bone ornamentation, production of the mortuary gourd and bone basket, the braiding of mourners' hair—shows, by means of metonymical processes (such as hair braiding) or metaphorical processes (such as producing the mortuary gourd) how the Bororo conceptualize the attributes that characterize the person.

Here I analyze the Bororo's current self-image as well as their view of contact and of the sociocultural changes resulting from it. I investigate the relationship between how the Bororo handle their different contact situations and how they conceptualize their notion of person. I base my argument on empirical data collected during my research in various Bororo villages in the state of Mato Grosso since 1970. I have tried to focus on the relationship that the Bororo have established with Salesian missionaries since the late nineteenth century.

I obtained the historical data on the establishment of Salesian missions in Mato Grosso from Salesian publications and the records kept at the Inspetoria Salesiana (Salesian headquarters) in São Paulo. The missionaries' accounts of the early years of this contact explain how this relationship continues to develop and make sense of the encounters and disagreements it implies. These accounts are equally important for assessing the transformations in the relationship between the Salesians and the Bororo since the mid-1970s.

Given that self-image can be analyzed within the play-of-mirrors structure I propose in chapter 4, and that my analysis emphasizes the relationship between the Salesians and the Bororo, I demonstrate how the Bororo see themselves when the mirror reflects other population segments that affect the formation of their own self-image. Throughout this book I introduce data concerning the relationship between the Bororo and the Xavante and data in which the "other" is, in fact, the Bororo themselves in another time (the past) and space (under the tutelage of FUNAI rather than the Salesians).

A discourse encompassing anthropology, linguistics, semiotics, psychology, and psychoanalysis permeates this book. This discourse is not new to anthropologists, who, since Boas, have been trying to implement it—as I show in chapter 1. I hope that this book provides a new basis for this discourse. This, at any rate, is the challenge I propose to take on.

Acknowledgments

A book never results from a strictly personal experience. Its writing requires a long period devoted to investigating the scope of human science that is shared, even if involuntarily, by a large number of individuals. These people include family members, peers, institutions, and anyone who has contributed to turning a project into reality.

Between 1980 and 1989, I conducted research work funded by the Centro Nacional de Pesquisa (National Research Council—CNPq). The Centro de Trabalho Indigenista (Center for Native Work—CTI) funded all my field trips and placed at my disposal its project files. I received more than just material support from my friends at CTI. As I stress throughout the book, this publication evolved from my contact with Gilberto Azanha, Maria Elisa Ladeira, Maria Inês Ladeira, Virgínia Valladão, Vincent Carelli, Iara Ferraz, Sônia Lorenz, Aurélio Michiles, and many others whose work is directly involved with Indian societies.

Other important supporters include the Salesian missionaries, particularly Father Gonçalo Ochoa and Master (of Congregation) Mário Bordignon, who work in the Meruri River area and demonstrate a great love for the Bororo. I am very grateful to them and to Father Luiz Garcia de Oliveira, from Salesian headquarters in São Paulo, who granted me access to the records in the Largo Coração de Jesus Archives. Missionaries often do not appreciate or even show any particular interest in anthropologists' writings about them and their work. These two categories seem to resent one another, in a relationship that somewhat resembles the resentment between anthropologists and indigenists. During my field research and during their several visits to São Paulo, we were able to overcome our differences (or so I hope). I feel privileged to have the Salesians as my informants and judges and as part of a dialogue that is not accessible to very many scientists and researchers in other fields.

I was also able to count on the support of Eny Orlandi, a linguistics teacher at UNICAMP (Universidade de Campinas), as well as Ana

Almeida and Norberto Abreu e Silva Filho, both of whom teach at the Psychology Institute of the Universidade de São Paulo—USP. Certainly, they are not to blame if I have entered their respective fields and, as a result, am vulnerable. I thank them for having allowed me to face this challenge.

Luis Donizeti Benzi Grupioni was a great traveling companion in my visits to various Bororo villages in 1986. I thank him for the texts on the mission, which he discovered.

My colleagues at USP offered encouragement and suggestions. Maria Célia, Bruni, Maria Helena, Sérgio Adorno, Paula Montero, Leonel and Maria Lúcia Montes played an extremely important role in reintroducing me to sociology and political science while placing anthropology in the more ample context of the human sciences.

I could not possibly have written about the representation of self, the construction of identity and of self-image, had it not been for a very special mirror. Merces Grossi Violeta assisted me on personal attitudes toward issues that are reviewed from the sociocultural standpoint.

Thekla Hartmann was my wise MA and PhD adviser.

My artist cousins, Eduardo Caiuby Novaes, Fernanda Salata, and Robinson Salata, enabled me to explore illustrations and handle them as dense images that dispense with words.

My two daughters, Laura and Isabel, often traveled with me to the Bororo villages, and several times these trips constituted our vacation. Bel, then age nine, even read parts of the draft. She did so with a mixture of pride, bewilderment, and interest. Laura kept daily track of the number of pages I'd written.

My mother, Teresa Caiuby Novaes, tirelessly supported me by looking after my home and children. Dora Ilha and Dorita Leal Medeiros, my mother-in-law and sister-in-law, respectively, took care of the girls during school vacations. I am forever grateful to these three great mothers for their love and understanding.

Jorge Leal Medeiros, my longtime companion, has been a prized source of support in all the ways a good companion can be.

The translation was sponsored by the Anthropology Department of the University of São Paulo. I would like to thank my friend and translator, Izabel Murat Burbridge; Elizabeth Ewart, who revised some chapters; Fabio Morganti and Peter Gow for the translation of the Italian quotations; Vanessa Lea for the translation of French quotations; Inês de Castro for the reproduction of photographs; and my good friend Greg Urban, who encouraged me to have it published in English.

The Play of Mirrors

1.
Contemporary Anthropology and Studies of Identity and Social Change

> For anthropology to live, its object must die; it avenges
> itself, dying for having been discovered, and defies, by its
> death, the science that strives to seize it.
> —Baudrillard, *La précession des simulacres*

The Functionalist Approach and Acculturation Studies

Since World War II, social and historical changes have been taking place
at such an accelerated rate that they have begun to affect the scope of the
various humanistic disciplines. Within anthropology, the disappearance
of entire societies that were once independent units (such as the Indian
societies of North America, South America, Australia, and New Guinea)
and their incorporation into larger units, the appearance of new nations
in Africa, and the swift cultural changes that occur in the most diverse
societies have posed new problems.

It is no longer a matter of observing relatively isolated, culturally
stable societies on a reduced demographic scale, such as those Malinowski
and Radcliffe-Brown studied. Because the changes in these societies that
drew the interest of anthropologists frequently resulted from value
crises, growing depopulation, and so on, the social sciences were summoned to participate in these changes; they did not simply analyze the
process but also suggested guidelines for political, social, and administrative action. The so-called primitive world, a privileged laboratory that
anthropologists selected for their analyses, seemed to be the main victim
of this crisis.[1]

Lévi-Strauss attributes to this period the modern crisis of anthropology and the apparent paradox that characterizes it as a discipline from
which "one expects great syntheses and, at the same time, reasons for life
and hope" (1962: 19). Handling the paradox of a discipline that, on seeing
its object, that is, "primitive societies" (as the public knows them), runs

the risk of becoming "science without an object." How do we keep these transformations, which in theory motivate the increasing interest in "primitives" by simultaneously speeding up their extinction (1962: 21)?

Lévi-Strauss shows that this paradox is only apparent. The object of anthropology is not extinguishable, even if the peoples who constitute its subject matter are extinct, even if those "living peoples undergoing full demographic expansion pose against it [anthropology] a refusal of psychological and moral order" (1962: 23). To Lévi-Strauss, "dissimilarities among societies and groups will never disappear, save for reconstituting themselves in different ways," and this will be the domain of anthropology (1962: 26).[2] At any rate, it is in this dramatic context of change, social crisis, and extinction of societies that studies of acculturation (as they became known in the United States) or cultural change (the British phrase) begin to take shape in anthropology.[3]

What are the repercussions of these analyses by anthropologists who devoted themselves to the study of Indian societies in Brazil? Studies of the Tupi, in particular, to a certain extent applied this perspective best.[4] The scholars of acculturation were also concerned with the issues of intertribal acculturation, particularly in the regions of the Xingu and the Upper Negro Rivers (Galvão, 1959). Besides the writings of Baldus (1979 [1937]), which are not limited to this perspective, the literature on the Bororo includes an article by Saake (1953) and another by Huestis (1963).

Galvão presented one of the first retrospective analyses of the study of the acculturation of Indian groups in Brazil at the First Brazilian Meeting on Anthropology, in 1953. He showed that these studies not only focused on the changes (such as machete, hatchet, and horse) introduced by alien elements, but they also gained a new dimension that basically allowed them to address the change that resulted from contact with the farming population. In 1965 Schaden published a more detailed review of these analyses in the first chapter of a book meant to analyze the cultural change "of Indian tribes in their contact with the non-Indian world" (as the book's subtitle tells us).

In Brazil, England, and the United States, acculturation studies were heavily influenced by functionalism, even when they appeared as a reaction to it. They first studied the issue of cultural dynamics, which the classical functionalists had bypassed. Anthropologists felt it necessary to understand the processes of ongoing change in the Brazilian historical and cultural scenario while providing a foundation on which to base the actions of the foster agency, which at the time was the Serviço de Proteção dos Índios (Indian Protection Service—SPI). These analyses, permeated by a sociological perspective,[5] tried to capture the social process and the ongoing changes from the point of view of the minority society's institutions. Precisely because they wrote from this perspective, these scholars emphasized, for example, the population policies of the societies in contact with one another and the demographic effects of this contact: epidemics, depopulation, weakened marriage traditions, alterations in the sexual division of labor, and so on.

These authors by and large incorporated the functionalist perspective, which regarded society as a totality comprising interdependent parts, some of which played a more important role than others in the maintenance of the whole. Thus, in the case of resistance to contact, the religious domain played a major role because it remained immune to change for a longer period of time (Schaden, 1965).

Social change, however, is not a process that mechanically replaces elements of the original culture with others from the dominating culture in such a way that the original culture is gradually extinguished or completely loses its original characteristics. When they were not emphasizing the loss of cultural characteristics, these scholars were predicting a truly catastrophic future for Indians societies in Brazil. None of these authors were able to overcome this perspective; they all associated the changing processes in these societies with impending decadence or the loss of cultural characteristics and subsequent disintegration.

I do not wish to deny the historical process of domination of Indian societies, nor even the process of systematic extinction of many of these societies beginning with the country's colonization. The Tupinambá, Ofaié, Xetá, Oti, Guató, Laiane, and many other societies are dramatic examples and too well known to be disregarded. I wish only to remark that those Indian societies that were not extinguished by this historical process were wiped out by scholars who wrote about them. If two articles by Darcy Ribeiro—"Convívio e contaminação" (Coexistence and Contamination, 1956) and "Culturas e línguas indígenas do Brasil" (Indigenous Cultures and Languages of Brazil, 1957) show the dramatic fate of numerous Indian societies in Brazil in the early sixteenth century, they also "contaminated" the perspectives that anthropologists devised for the societies they surveyed. Various societies were "extinguished" by catastrophic prognoses.

All of these analyses feature an implicit or explicit conception of culture as a finished product, a stock of cultural traits that, like genetic stock, is passed down in the form of social inheritance to younger generations. Given that these traits do not have the same guarantee of preservation as genetic traits, however, they can be irretrievably lost. In this sense, the effects of contact could be considered only in terms of replacement of original cultural traits by those from the dominating culture—which immediately asserts the decharacterization of the original culture—or as a syncretic combination of these aspects—which also allows us to regard the original culture as decaying.

Geertz's "Ritual and Social Change: A Javanese Example" (1957) apparently did not influence those authors engaged in the study of acculturation at the time the article was published. The vision of change as a "progressive disintegration," which vision Geertz criticized in functionalist authors, prevailed in most of these studies and certainly in all the analyses of Bororo society, even those written in the 1980s (see, for example, Viertler and Crocker). Geertz claimed that the difficulties of the functionalist theory sprang from investigators' treatment of sociological and cultural processes as equal and from the difficulty of fitting historical data into the functionalist conceptual framework. He proposed that an analytical distinction be made between the social and the cultural aspects of human life: "Culture is the fabric of meaning in terms of which human beings interpret their experience and guide their action; social structure is the form of action that takes the actually existing network of social relations" (1957: 33).

This distinction allows investigators to address more adequately the issue of integration, which is necessarily different in the cultural and social domains. According to Geertz, this distinction precludes the implicit vision of cultural disintegration (which at times is explicit, as we shall see in those authors who study Bororo society) as inherent in every contact that leads to domination. Geertz's focus was the particular nature of the integration that characterized each of these domains: "By logico-meaningful integration, characteristic of culture, is meant . . . a unity of style, of logical implication, of meaning and value. By causal-functional integration, characteristic of the social system, is meant the kind of integration one finds in an organism, where all the parts are united in a single causal web; each part is an element in a reverberating causal ring which 'keeps the system going'" (1957: 34).

This perspective allows us to understand contact not as destruction of traditional ways of life but as a process that leads to the construction of a new lifestyle, with new strategies and alternatives, wherein culture has an essentially dynamic and adaptive dimension. Seen from this angle, the religious domain does not appear as a mere keeper of cohesion and social structure (in the conservative sense, as something that remains immune to change); it is deeply overlaid by the lay domain of social life and may be activated by political claims for more flexible or fairer standards of beliefs and values (see chapter 7).

The Javanese funeral rite showed that the rituals themselves were transformed into debate issues and clearly revealed existing political conflicts among the participants. Rituals therefore express not only patterns of meaning but also modes of social interaction.

According to Geertz, culture cannot be regarded as an epiphenomenon of social structure nor social structure as an epiphenomenon of culture.

If these domains are not seen as spheres with a certain degree of independence, change becomes unfeasible; that is, society and its culture are viewed as petrified, and any change can be understood only as a disintegrating factor. As Geertz wrote, culture is not merely "learned behavior" (which transforms it into a static phenomenon), and social structure does not necessarily imply a balanced interaction with no space for conflict (1957: 53).

Interethnic Friction, Identity, and Ethnicity

The pessimistic forecasts concerning the future of Brazil's Indian societies that characterized acculturation studies also characterized the studies conducted beginning in the early 1960s as part of the Investigation of Interethnic Areas in Brazil Project, headed by Brazilian anthropologist Roberto Cardoso de Oliveira. Inspired by Balandier's notion of "colonial situation," these studies focused on "an investigation of sociocultural change; however, by emphasizing the comprehension of the Indian in situ, Balandier expands the researcher's area of observation and immediately begins to investigate the inclusive, national, or colonial society as well" (Cardoso de Oliveira, 1965: 38).[6]

Despite their being based on a theoretical perspective that contradicted that of scholars analyzing acculturation processes, the investigations of interethnic friction were directed at understanding the mechanisms that enabled the Indians' unavoidable integration into national society.[7] Thus, the "extinction" of these societies was prompted by the same irreversible future reserved for them. And this future was identified with the one society sought. According to Cardoso de Oliveira, "From the moment Indian groups lose their isolation, with the consequent loss of social and biological balance, they will be able to recover only by means of their insertion into a process of regional development" (1968: 377).

When studying interethnic areas, "the fulcrum of analysis *should not be the aforementioned cultural heritage* but the relations established among the populations or societies in question" (1968: 341, my emphasis). According to Oliveira Filho (1988: 45), this theoretical directive brings together Cardoso de Oliveira's subsequent impressions and the approach suggested by Barth (1969).Those authors who, following Barth, devoted themselves to the investigation of interethnic identities, exhausted the cultural dimensions of this phenomenon and treated the issue from a nearly exclusively sociological standpoint.

Barth was interested in demonstrating that, despite the contact, mobility, and information that characterize the day-to-day lives of ethnic groups, they always remain involved with the broader society of which they are a part. The contributors to Barth's edited volume frequently cite the intense social interaction between different groups as leading to ethnic differences, the overstatement of these differences, and the persistence of borders between interacting groups.[8] To avoid the inventory of cultural traits of groups in contact that characterizes acculturation studies, Barth proposed the investigation of ethnic groups as a form of social organization (1969: 13). While focusing on that which was socially effective, Barth regarded ethnic groups as *organizational types* that include as members those who identified themselves or were identified as members.

Cardoso de Oliveira, using Barth's reflections, proposed a characterization of ethnic identity: "Contrastive identity seems to be constituted in the essence of ethnic identity. . . . It implies asserting *us* before the *other*. . . . It is an identity that springs from opposition. It is not self-asserted. In the case of ethnic identity, it is asserted by 'denying' the other identity, which it views 'ethnocentrically'" (1976: 5–6). His definition oversimplifies the concept, though he maintains it throughout the book. Many tribal groups have a self-denomination that may be translated as "people," "human being," and so on, thus excluding all those who don't belong in the group.[9] Nonetheless, tribal groups that live in close contact with other segments of society do not gather all these other segments under a single category; furthermore, in their daily relations with these segments, they cannot deny them by not treating them as "people."

Thus, I find it more interesting to use the self-image concept to contemplate the issue of contact. The images that a society builds of itself and of the segments it takes as parameters for reflecting itself are not fixed or perennial. They transform themselves continually as a result of changes in relations. They are images impregnated with values, many of which conflict. They are images that imply the simultaneity of confronting cultural systems; that is, there is no single movement that simply asserts or denies the other's identity. I find it unproductive to analyze contact without considering its cultural dimensions (ignored by Barth and Cardoso de Oliveira). This theoretical perspective may be responsible for the failure of the pessimistic forecasts of studies of interethnic friction.[10]

It is precisely in the field of culture and the relationship between culture and power that Indian societies manage to articulate their processes of resistance to the surrounding society. This symbolic capital enables them to constantly reinterpret domination and the elements imposed on them by the dominating society. It is precisely by considering reflections that involve the cultural domain that we are able to understand that differences between the native society and the surrounding society are continually reformulated rather than suppressed. Disregard for the cultural dimension also hinders the utilization of perspectives devised by anthropologists who studied identity and ethnicity (following in Cohen's and Barth's footsteps), when the analytical focus is on contemporary Indian societies.

A fine bibliographical retrospective of anthropological literature written by U.S. and European authors is found in Royce (1982). In Brazil, the principal anthropologist to address this issue was Cardoso de Oliveira (1976), who inspired a series of other works, most of which were published as articles.[11] Studies of ethnic identity and ethnicity appear to be more successful when they deal with the reality of different ethnic groups located in an urban context: from Cohen's first essays (1969) on the phenomenon of tribalization in modern Africa to the most recent essays about immigrant ethnic groups inserted in a wider urban context in which they participate actively, such as African Americans, Jews and Hispanics in New York, or Pakistanis in London (see Cohen, 1974).

Within these contexts, it is possible to analyze the ethnic group as an "organizational type" that allows its members improved performance within this wider context in which they interact directly. Therein, traditional customs and values constitute only the ethnic idiom through which these people articulate their new roles. The situation of most of Brazil's Indian societies that do not undergo the "retribalization" process because they are not "detribalized" is quite different.

The Dialogue among Anthropology, Psychology, and Linguistics

> Scientific development becomes the piecemeal process by which these items (facts, theories and methods) have been added, singly and in combination, to the ever growing stockpile that constitutes scientific technique and knowledge
> —Thomas S. Kuhn, *The Structure of Scientific Revolutions*

The various scientific branches did not develop independently. Until around the 1920s, the canons and objectives of scientific analysis, defined as such by the natural sciences, imbued the procedures as well as the theoretical and conceptual framework of the social sciences. Beginning then, a more fruitful dialogue was initiated among the several disciplines that set the understanding of human behavior as their goal, in terms of subjective experience, sociocultural practices, or individual behavior.

The representation of self (in an individual or a social group), the individual's self-perception as a social being, and the relationship among nature, culture, individual, and society have been not only the object of anthropological, psychological, and linguistic investigations but also themes that throughout history have promoted dialogue and confrontation between these various disciplines. The mutual influence of the three affects the development of each, and the concepts produced by each acquire a new dimension in other disciplines that appropriate their developments.

By observing behavior and then creating certain abstractions and generalizations about the universe of human experience, anthropologists (and sociologists), linguists, psychoanalysts, and psychologists have formulated concepts that have built a theoretical framework. This framework, even while emphasizing the perspective of a particular discipline, does not prevent the other sciences from pursuing paths in new directions.

Among the key concepts that have promoted dialogue among anthropology, psychology, and linguistics, the most important are—beginning with anthropology—*culture* (and its various meanings in the different schools of anthropology), *collective representation* (Durkheim), and a derivative of collective representation, the *notion of individual* (although conceived by Mauss in 1938, only recently important in anthropological literature and in the work of psychologists and linguists).

In the field of psychoanalysis, the most important concepts are *ambivalence, conflict,* and *the unconscious* as developed in Freud's works (but mainly in those in which he addresses "cultural issues"). In the field of psychology, the most important concepts are *self* and *alter,* taken from the works of George Mead, and *identity* (from Erikson).

Other equally important concepts include those utilized by other disciplines and further revised by linguistics, such as *sign, symbol, signifier, signified,* and the *unconscious nature of language* (from Saussure, Peirce, and Sapir). The concept of *simulacrum,* featured in more recent works by authors involved in semiotics (e.g., Barthes and Baudrillard) is also important for providing individuals with a clearer understanding of self-image and social representation.[12] These intertwined concepts, based as they are on perspectives specific to each of these disciplines, lead to a better knowledge of the diverse aspects of human behavior. As scientific concepts they are not perennial and unchangeable; although each has trod a specific trajectory within the discipline in which it has evolved, they were devised at a certain time, assimilated by other disciplines, and later reformulated. Furthermore, as concepts built on data obtained from the observation of behavior, they must be associated with the specific procedures utilized to collect the data and, obviously, kept within the theoretical framework in which they belong.

It is not my objective to present an exhaustive history of the discourse among these disciplines, nor to analyze everything and everyone that has contributed to it. I shall highlight only those moments and authors that explain the perspective that I intend to discuss in this book. My analysis, although anthropological, results from an approach that seeks nourishment from other disciplines.

Should we set out looking for the "ancestry" of the dialogue, we would certainly find a book by Freud that was explicitly intended to "bridge the gap between students of such subjects as social anthropology, philology and folklore on the one hand, and psycho-analysts on the other" (Freud, 1950: ix). Stimulated by the works of Wundt and Jung and using data gathered mainly by Frazer and Tylor, Freud recognized that the two themes addressed in his book—totems and taboos—did not receive the same treatment. He devoted his greatest attention to taboos and the possibility of analyzing them using the analogy with neurotic manifestations (through the concepts of ambivalence and conflict). It is precisely his views on totemism, however, that later echoed among the anthropologists of the time, particularly in England and the United States. Ambivalence and conflict, which are central to Freud's conception of the individual, and the symbolic interpretation of neurotic symptoms (and of customs related to taboos) were not assimilated by anthropologists who were contemporaries.[13]

Stimulated by the criticism of evolutionism, these anthropologists were more concerned with the methodological aspects of data collection and analysis and tried to demonstrate the nonplausibility of Freud's material and inferences. He treated hypothetical data as if they were historical data. In 1920, when Freud's book was translated into English, Kroeber published a review in which he indicated the impossibility of empirically demonstrating that the Oedipal complex was the first milestone of religion, ethics, the arts, and society itself, not to mention the origin of, for example, totemism and the incest taboo (Kroeber, 1952: 301). Anthropologists contraposed the concept of *culture* to a *universal human nature*, as devised by Freud, in which ontogenesis would necessarily be a review of philogenesis. Boas, who had been one of Wundt's students, proposed to his own students a series of research studies that might have jeopardized the Freudian conception of this universally determined human nature.

The studies of culture and personality conducted in the United States from the 1920s to the 1940s, especially those conducted by Ruth Benedict (1934) and Margaret Mead (1928, 1930, 1935), argued the plasticity of human behavior and the impossibility of considering biopsychological components, such as the libido, as elements in the scientific elucidation of the individual's development, regardless of the sociocultural context in which they were analyzed. For these anthropologists, culture prevailed over nature, and this dominance was precisely what yielded the substantially varied phases of an individual's life in different cultures and what caused society to present a specific cultural configuration.

In 1939 Kroeber reviewed his criticisms of *Totem and Taboo* but maintained his basic viewpoint: that Freud handled as historical data the hypothetical data he collected from an intuitive imagination. He could never have established the Oedipal complex as the great event that gives birth to culture, since "events are historical, and beginnings are historical, and human culture is appreciable historically" (1952: 306).

Kroeber resented Freud's indifference to Malinowski's observations about the matrilineal Trobiand family, in which the father was not an object of his son's ambivalent emotions. While acknowledging the universality of the incest taboo (which was continued in a masterly manner by Lévi-Strauss), however, Kroeber recognized that there must be, in the human condition itself and, therefore, in the human psyche, a factor underlying the reproduction of this phenomenon, in terms of time and space, in the most remote localities.[14] The studies of culture and personality presented a psychological perspective that derived, directly or indirectly, from Freud's works—whether in the form of an attack or the incorporation of his fundamental concepts, such as the relevance of childhood in the makeup of adult behavior..

In addition to Boas's historical particularism and the stimulating influence of psychoanalytical theories, investigations into culture and personality were closely related to the development of linguistics, chiefly in Sapir's writings. Language and linguists' reflections on language were to provide a paradigm for the analyses of cultural phenomena. Aberle (1957) pointed to a convergence in the works of Sapir and Benedict (and of various anthropologists of the time) that made it possible to demonstrate the importance of the linguistic model to cultural theory and the fragility of this model when it was shifted beyond its original limits. Aberle primarily criticized the reductionist solution adopted by the scholars of culture and personality, who perceived in the socialization standards the origin of cultural configurations. For these authors, cultural standards and language had to be regarded as learned, standardized behavior that was largely unconscious and selective. Aberle showed that individuals were not mere reproducers of the effective social order, but producers of this order. They were social agents whose practices, though understandable only within a historically outlined picture, were not necessarily homogeneous, as suggested by the evolutionist analyses.

Developments in linguistics and anthropology, especially Van Velsen's (1967) work related to the ethnography of speech and the situational analysis proposed, showed the importance of contextualization to the analysis of language and culture. It became increasingly more important to find out who communicated with whom, when, how, and about what. It was not a matter of leaving aside the value systems that guided a culture; it was a matter of seeing them as values that guided action but that were not to be taken as action itself. Otherwise, the individual would become a mere recipient of culture (an idea that permeates the configurationist studies conducted by Boas's students), and it would be impossible to explain why certain basic cultural values remained while others changed.

It was these analyses by functionalist anthropologists (whether English or U.S.), however, that introduced the concept of culture and the necessity of analyzing society in its entirety. They stand out as milestones in the great contribution of anthropology. In his critical review of anthropology in the first half of the twentieth century, Kroeber states, "culture—a society's customs, traditions, tools, and ways of thinking—plays the dominant part in shaping the development of human beings, and therefore ought to be the central concern of anthropology" (1952a: 139).

It is exactly this conception of culture as a set of traits, a finished product still very close to Tylor's classical definition of culture, however, that has led anthropologists to assume, in the discourse with other disciplines, the role of data supplier. It is up to psychologists to interpret these data by using the analogy between language and culture. Freud's generalizations, questioned by a data collection procedure—fieldwork— that was to alter the specificity characteristics of anthropological studies beginning in the 1920s, place the concept of culture in the most important position. In its original formulation, however, this concept still cannot generate a debate in which anthropology furnishes not only data but also interpretations. The anthropological "interpretation" is for all practical purposes limited to no longer describing culture (taking into consideration the manner in which it is conceived) as fragmented traits but as a consistent and well-articulated whole.

This same configuration of discourse among the three disciplines is maintained in the schools of thought that succeeded culture and personality studies, in the form of interdisciplinary projects completed by anthropologists and psychologists. These interdisciplinary projects became known as basic personality studies (Linton, Kardiner)[15] and, later, as modal personality studies (du Bois). Although data were now collected by a different procedure from that utilized by Freud, the interpretive model utilized in these projects was a variation of the psychoanalytical analysis model he proposed.

If, by means of the research Boas initially encouraged, anthropology ended up relating the universal truths seen as "natural" in all human societies, psychology began to displace the axis of its reflections, which until then had been the "I." Freudian theory includes the ego, the superego, and the id, but not the you (Laing, 1966: 3). The *other* and the meaning of this other began increasingly to be viewed as fundamental to our understanding not only of social life but also of the whole process of reorientation of the *I* in everyday life. Psychoanalytical theories were reviewed in terms of notions such as social context, experience, and adaptation, which allowed the interaction approach to begin to impose itself on the field of psychology. Numerous psychologists began to point to the preponderant role of the "other" in the construction of self-awareness. The "I" was elaborated in close contact with the environment in which it developed; thus, it was anchored in the collective environment from which it emerged.

Inspired by George Mead's *Mind, Self and Society* (1934), various psychologists attempted to understand how self-awareness developed in the individual. It was no longer a matter of investigating biological processes associated with sexuality, which, according to Freud, determined the individual's development, but of investigating the issue from the viewpoint of interpersonal relationships that individuals maintained throughout their lives and within a specific cultural context. This is the great contribution of George Mead's work: to address the *self* as a process, not as an object. According to Bock, in a retrospective investigation of the relationship between psychology and anthropology, "the self is constantly being modified by interaction with significant others as part of what we would today call a system of positive and negative feedback" (1988: 148).[16]

Every time people make themselves the objects of their consciousness, they are doing it for the purpose of self-assessment based on standards of adequacy, that is, a mental representation of behaviors, attitudes, and traits viewed as socially correct and adequate. For some psychologists, the *self* "is an object-like entity that exists from the moment that the person is conscious of internal and external stimuli and, as such, is present to any other's awareness" (Duval and Wicklund, 1972: 33). The *self* is an organism endowed with perception, thought, and action, properties that, according to Duval and Wicklund, do not originate in interaction or biological development. To these psychologists, these properties are innate: "Once the person has the knowledge of a distinct causal agent self, he has gained the ability to be objectively self-aware, and prior to this discrimination there was no specific self upon which to focus consciousness" (1972: 52). Only when an individual sees himself or herself through someone else's eyes and perceives the differences between them will he or she be able to develop self-awareness. Self-awareness therefore depends on the individual's discovering the objective nature of the self. It is this concept of self that later changed the course of the discourse among these three disciplines.

Wallon's work gives us a better understanding of the importance of the *other* for the formation of our notion of *self*. To understand the evolutionary conditions of the life of the mind and the formation of the *I*, Wallon used the comparative historical method. According to him, "This me is not a primal entity; it is the progressive individualization of a libido that is at first anonymous, to which the circumstances and the course of life demand specification and that enters into the framework of a personal existence and consciousness" (1946: 87). In this sense, during the developmental process, the child asserts itself more and more through his or her relationship with the various others, with whom it identifies or from whom it differentiates itself. "The members of the entourage are merely the occasions or motives for the subject to express and realize itself" (1946: 92). Thus, the formation and evolution of the "I" implies constant and constantly renewed relationships between the being and the environment, which modify one another. The environment or milieu to which Wallon refers is "the combination of psychic, human, and ideological circumstances in which individual lives are played out" (Nadel, 1979: 368). Therefore, the *milieu* is not something abstract or immutable, even though it is actually submitted to a historical process.

Wallon was interested in verifying how children's actions constituted a process of exchange with a defined milieu and how this process informed about or elucidated the child's adaptive capabilities at that moment, as well as his or her utilization of available means and functions. Thus the child was seen as supporting a consistent behavioral whole in which it participated. Wallon always regarded the individual's adaptation as a relationship between means and ends:

> Ends have their field of application in the environment; the environment delimits their conditions. It is thereby a regulator of behavior. The individual generates the means alone or by way of the group. It is thus that his future belongs to him—and new means preside over the appearance of new, more specific means . . . increasing the possibilities of evolution and individual differentiation. In reference to this, Wallon theorizes dialectical relations between the individual and the environment, which translates the notion of functional equilibrium. (1979: 369)

What interests us as anthropologists is not the preexistence or priority of the "I," a theme that animates and divides psychologists and psycho-analysts. From the anthropological perspective, it is important to deter-mine which are the categories of thought and the mental representations that induce individuals to perceive the world and the "others" that inhabit this world in a specific manner and to be moved to action by this unique perception.

I am also interested in studying what happens when individuals from different societies come into contact in a specific historical process. How is the other perceived, assimilated, imitated, or denied? How do we understand the new forms of behavior that spring from the confrontation between two worlds?

Since the mid-1950s these issues have been described by specialists in the three disciplines. According to D'Andrade, the human sciences changed radically between 1955 and 1960. This change resulted from the culture and personality studies' lack of credibility and from the confron-tation between behaviorism, as a prevailing paradigm of psychology, and research in the field of cognition and perception. A new conception of culture began to impose itself: "culture consists not of behaviours, or even patterns of behaviour, but rather of shared information or knowl-edge encoded in systems of symbols" (D'Andrade, 1984: 88).

This new conception of culture devised by scholars such as Goodenough incorporates the notion of representation and the necessity of investigat-ing how the world is built into different cultures to explain how the world is experienced by each of these cultures. This new approach has taken psychologists and anthropologists to demonstrate how cultural systems affect an individual's conception of himself or herself and the manner in which he or she interprets the world, that is, "how culturally transmitted symbol systems inform the content of selfhood" (Smith, 1985: 83).

Bateson (1982) wrote an extremely interesting (but not well known) article on the interactive range of the self. He utilized the terms "identity" and "self" indiscriminately to show how the individual acquired these notions. To him, *difference* was the most important element for communication, perception, and practically all human activity. He illustrated his argument with examples such as, "if some event is going on continuously, a clock ticking in the room, you will very soon cease to hear its ticks. But if it misses a tick, you may respond with a startle. You can perceive, that is, the *absence* of an event" (1982: 3).

Besides *difference*, Bateson mentions another factor, *double descrip-tion*, which led him to the concept of *boundary*. "In monocular vision the data are the materials on the basis of which [the] eye makes its report, while in depth perception of binocular vision the data are precisely the differences between the reports made by each eye" (1982: 3). He has questioned the limits or boundaries of the so-called *self*:

> Is there a line or a sort of bag delimiting "me"? . . . Insofar as we associate a self with a mind, the language to answer a question of that kind cannot be a language of space and time. The metaphor— the bag, the delimiting time—is spatial, but the mind does not contain things. It contains ideas, news of difference, information about "things" . . . the mind contains no time and no space, only ideas of time and space. (1982: 4)

This perception of difference, that is, of boundaries or lack of boundaries, allows us to understand not only the self but also the changes that take place within the limits of this notion, "that you and I are in fact part of a unity, or that there are artificial boundaries so that now at one moment we can think in terms of me here and you there, and at another moment we can think in terms of a unity composed of you-plus-me" (1982: 4). Certainly, this perception and the learning it implies are related to a *context* involving a relationship between two people.

Bateson's observations are important to an understanding of the possibility of analyzing the building up of self-image based on a play of mirrors: "An external relationship is always a product of what I am calling double description. That is, the relationship as seen by B and the relationship as seen by A. Or, to spell it out, there is what A does as seen by B, what B does as seen by A, and equally, what A does as seen by A and what B does as seen by B" (1982: 5).

Although Bateson employed the expressions *self* and *identity* indiscriminately, he related the concept of identity to more dynamic and multidimensional (individual, social, and cultural) aspects of the self. This notion is established only in Goodenough's anthropology (1969),[17] even though it appeared earlier in Erikson's work (1950).[18]

Psychoanalyst Renato Mezan views identity as the point of social impact on the individual. To him, the *feeling of identity* implies two conditions: "consistency and continuity of an existence inside a circumscribed body, and the necessary difference between this psychosoma and all others—a difference to be acknowledged not only by myself but also by those people around me" (1988: 255). According to Mezan, identity is not a mere subjective feeling. He recognizes in identity its cultural facet—ties such as class, occupation, sex, language, or ethnic community—which "makes it possible to situate an individual within the socius unit through each person's roles and functions in the various collective instances" (1988: 255). Mezan comes quite near an approach that, even if emphasizing the viewpoint of its discipline, provides a sound basis for the anthropological analysis of this theme. Mezan concludes: "Thus identity appears as an intersection of heterogeneous determinations, some of which are imposed on the individual; others, selected by the individual according to criteria admitted by the society in which he belongs; and others yet bound to his feeling of subjective continuity between successive psychic conditions or to his awareness of being limited and distinguished by his own body" (1988: 256).

Even though they come from psychology and psychoanalysis, these statements are very useful to an analysis of interethnic contact. From an emic perspective, such an analysis tries to capture the images that society draws of itself and of other population segments with which it makes contact in order to understand the manner in which it relates with these other segments. Here there is no strict opposition between "psychism" and "culture," since, according to Mezan, "the psyche functions in accordance with its own laws, though with representations that are partly supplied by social experience" (1988: 260).

Because I work from an anthropological approach, culture will not be viewed in this book as learned behavior and analyzed solely in terms of my direct observation. Nor is culture "in the mind"; thus, my analysis of cultural manifestations is not restricted to a survey of symbolic codes that, once decoded, could be understood. In this book, culture will be addressed from the semiotic viewpoint proposed by Geertz: "Believing, with Max Weber, that man is an animal suspended in webs of significance he himself has spun, I take culture to be those webs, and the analysis of it to be therefore not an experimental science in search of law but an interpretive one in search of meaning" (1973: 5). Provided that the articulations of cultural forms, which are not necessarily consistent, are inferred by the flow of social action and behavior, analysis must be based on a "dense description" of the narration. This description is not limited to that which is readily visible and observed; it must cover the manner in which the event was produced, perceived, and interpreted by the people who took part in it. According to Geertz, "the important thing about the anthropologist's findings is their complex specifics, their circumstantiality" (1973: 23). Precisely because of this perspective, this book includes descriptions of a series of events that I witnessed and the account of a time that obviously I did not directly observe, but reconstructed from a number of documents. Geertz suggests that the objective of these descriptions be "to support broad assertions about the role of culture in the construction of collective life by engaging them exactly with complex specifics" (1973: 28).

I do not dwell on concepts drawn from linguistics and semiotics, such as sign, symbol, signifier, signified, and simulacrum, although they will be discussed in the next chapter, where I intend to show, by analyzing a concrete event, exactly how identity is constructed in a broad sense.

2.
Identity in the Broad Sense: The Other as Model

It is never the simulacrum that disguises the truth; it is truth that hides its existence.
—Baudrillard, *La précession des simulacres*

The Fabrication of Identity

As we have seen, the relativization of "universal truths" and the criticism of the ethnocentric vision that, like evolutionism, claims a single historical process for all human societies, has been the job of anthropologists who, since the 1920s, have been conducting field research focused on the so-called primitive societies. These research projects by U.S. and European anthropologists revealed the internal coherence of societies that have since been viewed not as a mirror of earlier stages of society, but as totalities whose manifestations can be understood only in light of a systemic vision.

Nevertheless, this approach was limited to the realm of anthropological theory. Throughout the world, colonial domination causes tribal societies to be viewed as backward and halted in time. Colonizers take it on themselves to impose "progress" and the "benefits of civilization" on these societies, thus allowing them access to a historical trajectory.

This imposition of western standards, whether in terms of values—work as a virtue, Christian morality, monogamy, and so on—or in terms of eating habits, clothing, notions of time and space, and the like, begins at first contact. Although this imposition is more systematic and compulsory in some societies than in others, it occurs in all societies, whether the colonizers are members of the clergy or laypersons.

In chapter 5 I shall analyze in detail the Salesian missionaries' behavior, prompted by their ideas of "redemption," among the Bororo. Here I shall discuss one effect of the imposition of standards and values by describing an event that I witnessed. This event, which could be regarded as a "fabrication of reality" by means of the manipulation of signs and codes, included representatives from several of Brazil's Indian societies. My approach in describing this event is based on linguistics and semiotics. The Indians, however, have adopted Western signs and codes, which they have used strategically to claim their rights to a different code: the code of Indian societies.

In June 1982, the Primeiro Encontro dos Povos Indígenas no Brasil (First Meeting of Indigenous Peoples in Brazil) brought together in Brasília approximately three hundred Indian leaders representing various nations. The event, organized by UNI (União das Nações Indígenas— Union of Indian Nations), forwent, for the most part, the collaboration of entities that support Indians (the Conselho Indigenista Missionário— Native Missionary Council [CIMI]; the Centro de Trabalho Indigenista— Center for Native Work [CTI]; and the Comissão Pró Índio—Commission for Indians [CPI]). The Indians made a point of holding the meeting in Brasília, the locus of political decision-making. The closing ceremony took place in the Brazilian Senate building.

Representatives of the Indian nations discussed the invasion of Indian territories, and representatives of various Indian nations from northeastern Brazil and the Guarani from the state of São Paulo emphasized the need to acknowledge the existence of Indian populations in these areas. These representatives declared that they had come to Brasília to show (1) that they existed, that is, that there were indeed Indians in areas where they were thought to be extinct; and (2) that the recognition of their existence was a legitimate claim.

In a clear attempt to demonstrate publicly their individual identities, the Indians of the Northeast came to the meeting wearing headdresses, clubs, and other "typically Indian" ornaments—many of which are no longer worn on a daily basis.

The three-day event held at CONTAG (Confederação dos Trabalhadores Agrícolas—Confederation of Farm Workers) headquarters followed a strict protocol: all participants wore identity badges; the press was admitted only to certain areas determined ahead of time; non-Indian representatives of supporting agencies were not allowed to attend all sessions.

Meetings were scheduled around geographical region. Sessions began with the presentation of problems that affected the nations of a particular region, followed by discussion and proposals. Indians recorded the meetings, and a non-Indian representative of a support entity was chosen for his or her familiarity with the issue and asked to take minutes and type proposals.

The Brazilian national anthem was played at the opening of the last session. Representatives of all political parties, foreign ambassadors, a representative of the Associação Brasileira de Antropologia (Brazilian Anthropology Association), a CONTAG representative, and the Fundação

Nacional do Índio (National Indian Foundation—FUNAI) chairman were invited.

In their speeches at the closing session, Indian leaders emphasized the possibility of their nations' undergoing development compatible with that extolled by non-Indians. When referring to the amount of rice produced by the Xavante, the Terena cited and adapted biblical passages ("The Sabbath was made for man, and not man for the Sabbath; FUNAI was created for the Indian, and not the Indian for FUNAI"). They requested machinery to improve farming and the security and demarcation of their land. Some spoke in their own language, with consecutive interpretation.

The meeting was thus also a semiurgy, where the signifier was more "real" than the signified to which it referred.[1] That is to say, if we admit that, in addition to its meaning function (the mental image that results from the relationship between signifier and signified), sign has a referential function (denotation) between sign and referent (the real object) (Ducrot and Todorov, 1988: 103), what we conclude from the event in Brasília is the dereferentialization of reality, or a hyperreality that leads us to the notion of simulacrum.

The account of the meeting shows that these signs point to apparently opposing realities. If inhabitants of a region regard Indian identity (particularly in the Northeast) as evanescent, it is necessary to re-create and overvalue it. If, however, we wish to destroy the image of the Indian as incapable of controlling the modern world's various codes, we must overemphasize the meeting's protocol. Throughout the gathering—not only in their public utterances—the Indians seemed to be saying, "See, we can be just like you; we can master the rules of the non-Indian world, and we can claim our rights just as you claim yours. But please remember that we are different, that this difference is real and must be respected." Because our society has trouble coexisting with differences—which it always tries to eliminate—the Indians were required to show that they could be equal before they could claim their right to be different, with the social visibility difference creates. For this to happen, they had to appropriate this broad category created by westerners—*Indian*—as a way to unite and to face confrontation. This invented identity, that is, the "*We Indians*," was not meant to erase the differences between them, which, on the contrary, were emphasized. Each speaker presented his issue as the representative of a specific nation. But it was as "*Indians*" that they managed to organize themselves and present their claims to the government and to society in general.

Concerning how indigenous people incorporate, appropriate, or assimilate non-Indian discourse, Eni Orlandi writes, "This mode of incorporating the other's discourse, which takes the form of a precise reproduction (simulacrum or collage), becomes so similar that it ends up revealing itself as an index of difference" (1984: 6). Orlandi's first objective is to "reflect on the specificity of the colloquy between Indians and non-Indians in the last few years" (1984: 1). Her second objective is to contribute, by observing language, to the creation of a history of contact as well as to the study of ethnic identity (1984: 2). She concludes that, "if the non-Indians were absolutely determinant, the Indian would have to let go of his identity. He would reproduce in himself the non-Indian's identity. And this does not happen, because the game that establishes the Indian's identity is not completed in non-Indian action. Something slips through" (1984: 11–12).

Although they spring from an analysis based on discourse, these reflections may be generally applied to nonlinguistic aspects of the fabrication of Indian identity as a result of contact with the national society and, as we shall see, to the analysis of minority groups within a single society.

The Maintenance of Preestablished Differences

In *Signes, traces, pistes: racines d'un paradigme de l'indice* (1980), Carlo Ginzburg's extremely suggestive reflections help us understand how Indians present their identity to the outside world while taking for a model their image of non-Indians. He discusses the emergence of an epistemological model—the inditial paradigm—that is widely utilized in various scientific fields without ever having been explicitly conceptualized. For a better definition of this model, Ginzburg refers us to the most diverse facets of artistic and scientific practice in the nineteenth century: Morelli's criteria for distinguishing original from forged art; Sherlock Holmes's strategies invented by Conan Doyle; and Freud's methods of psychoanalytical interpretation. According to Ginzburg, "Toward the end of the nineteenth century—more precisely in the decade 1870–1880—a presumptive paradigm began to assert itself in the humanistic sciences that was based specifically on semiotics. Its roots, however, were much older" (1980: 102). From hunting society roots—which strove to reconstitute the shape and motion of animals from footprints, broken twigs, excrement, chunks of hair, smells, and so on—and from divinatory Mesopotamian texts written in the third millennium BC, Ginzburg looked for "the minute investigations of even trifling matters, to discover the traces of events that could not be directly experienced by the observer" (1980: 103). To Ginzburg, the knowledge of both "pseudo-awareness" (such as divination and physiognomy) and the medical and juridical sciences was based on the analysis of individual cases that could not be reestablished without the assistance of traits, symptoms, and clues.

Ginzburg showed how Morelli led the connoisseur to seek evidence of a piece of art's authenticity not in its most clearly explicit aspects— (such as the eyes looking up at the sky in Perugino's models, or the smile in Leonardo da Vinci's models)—which are, therefore, easier to imitate— but in its details, "the most trivial details, which would have been influenced least by the mannerisms of the artist's school: earlobes, fingernails, shapes of fingers and toes" (1980: 19). In all the cases Ginzburg analyzed, it was the sometimes infinitesimal traits that led to the understanding of a deeper reality that would be unreachable through other means. He tried to resolve the deadlock created by the opposition between "rationalism" and "irrationalism," which presents an unpleasant dilemma to the social scientist: whether to adopt a fragile scientific canon to arrive at important results, or to adopt a solid scientific canon to arrive at less important results (1980: 43). To Ginzburg, the scientific rigor based in quantitative and anthropocentric criteria that has permeated science since Galileo was not only impossible but also undesirable in those forms of knowledge more directly related to daily life—or, more precisely, "to all those situations in which the unique and indispensable nature of the data is decisive to the persons involved" (1980: 20).

As Orlandi reflects on the colloquy between Indians and non-Indians, "the game that establishes the Indian's identity is not completed in non-Indian action. Something slips through" (1984: 12). This is precisely where we may relate the considerations of an art critic such as Morelli (which Ginzburg revisited) and the work of an anthropologist who comes face to face with the issue of identity in contemporary Indian societies. In both instances we are dealing with imitation. The forger seeks to duplicate all details of a painting, though he cannot reproduce the artist's swiftest brushstrokes—his most unconscious motions, which do not depend on conscious effort. Likewise, while being forced to accept the non-Indian as an imposed model, the Indian does not lose his or her original identity. That is, the formal appropriation of formal aspects of discourse, clothing, greeting, and so on, does not ensure the appropriation of the identity that provides the model. Actually, it is a *simulation* (which is different from pretense, which involves *dissimulation*), that is, "the generation of models of what is real without origin or reality: hyperreal" (Baudrillard, 1978: 3).

This is the point at which "something slips through," and native peoples seem to be the first to acknowledge this fact. I would say that what slips through is the possibility of the existence of a "truth" or a "reality" (in this case, the appropriation of the non-Indian identity)

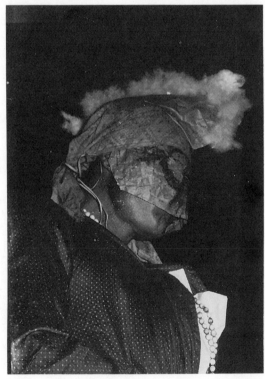

Baraedu ku kuri. Pantomime in which the Bororo imitate non-Indians. *Sylvia Caiuby Novaes, Tadarimana, 1975.*

based on its simulacrum. In the process of simulation (which alludes to the difference between true and false, or to imitation, as Ginzburg stated), the operation, as Baudrillard showed, is only a reflection in a mirror and discursive. "What is real is produced from miniaturized cells, matrices, and memories. . . . It is a hyperreality, the product of a radiating synthesis of combinatory models in a hyperspace without atmosphere" (1978: 4).

The irreversible character of the identities of the non-Indian and the Indian is clearly described by a Palikur: "It is the Indian who feels and holds knowledge, not the outsider. . . . Civilized man could enter the Indian's world, live there for up to fifty years, pierce his lips, pierce his ears, let his hair grow, everything; he could wear a loincloth but he could never become an Indian like us natives. And we cannot become civilized. We cannot" (Orlandi, 1984: 4).

Simulacrum as a Strategy

Simulacrum, the Indians' imitation of non-Indians or any minority group's imitation of the dominant model, seems to be an important step for entire societies or groups within a society that seek to assert their difference. Thus, we are faced with a paradox that seems typical of postmodern times (Ferreira dos Santos, 1986), that is, the dereferentialization imparted by simulacrum. When "dressing up like an Indian," the Indian of the Northeast "sells" an image that no longer corresponds to his or her reality. Likewise, although appropriating the clothing and conventions of non-Indians, "acculturated" Indians utter a false discourse: that they are like non-Indians. These diacritical signs (headdress or name badge) permit the manipulation of stereotypes of who "the Indians" actually are. These images should be seen as a form of rhetoric, in which type and stereotype manipulation as message to be decoded is much closer to the interlocutor—a "receiver" as abstract as "government" or "society"—than to the emitter.

The same thing happened in the 1960s and the 1970s to feminist women, who, in their quest for self-assertion, adopted the masculine societal model of insertion as the one that would ensure them space and social recognition. While Indians were being criticized for their cultural decharacterization (in Brazil they are referred to as, for example, "*caboclos*"—half-breeds—or "*bugres*"), these women were often labeled as "macho."[2] According to Laing (1971: 131), however, given that the body is "the core and center of my world," it is possible to dress it up and present it in any way one likes, and it will remain intact inside. In turn, given that the body is "an object in the world of others" (1971), it is necessary for it to dress up and act, in effect, in accordance with the attributes these others are accustomed to so that it may be recognized as a body.

While attending the meeting in Brasília, so carefully organized and based on a stereotypical model, complete with all details of the "non-Indian's" code, Indians paradoxically seemed to be saying, "We are not non-Indian," as if constantly paraphrasing the title of Magritte's famous painting *This Is Not a Pipe.*[3]

This game of signs covers up a reality that, as I mentioned in connection with my conception of *identity*, arises from the need to construct political subjects that organize themselves to claim visibility and social action. In this process, the differences within each of these groups are apparently "effaced," thus permitting the construction of this "collective us" as a macrosocial structure. Paradoxically, the simulacrum, that is, the representation of oneself based on the prevailing cultural model, is the possibility of these political subjects acting for the rupture of their historical submission.

3.
Literature as Mirror: Different Views of Social Change in Bororo Society

Well, because a point . . . the central point, I mean, the one right in the middle of all the points you see . . . it's a geometric point; you can't see it because it has no dimension, and if something has no dimension, it can't move, not right or left, not up or down. So it doesn't rotate with the earth. You understand? It can't even rotate around itself. There is no "itself."

—Umberto Eco, *Foucault's Pendulum*

Among native South American societies, the Bororo have attracted anthropologists most because of its complex social organization, its cosmos peopled with spirits and souls "embodied" in the living, the relationship between the animal world and the supernatural, and their sophisticated material culture. Beginning with Levy-Bruhl, various scholars have tried to understand the Bororo, which has resulted in a somewhat rigid and self-contained idealization of this society. This process is similar to the "Orientalization" of Asian societies, which Said discusses in *Orientalism* (1979). Paraphrasing Said, one could say that, to most scholars who have devoted themselves to the Bororo, the latter are much less important as individuals than are the writings about them in the anthropological literature. According to Said, modern Orientalists' analyses are deeply affected by a certain melancholic feeling toward the imaginary constructed about the Orient. "Memory of the modern Orient disputes imagination, sends one back to the imagination, as a place preferable, for the European sensibility, to the real Orient. . . . The mind learns to separate a general apprehension of the Orient from a specific experience of it" (Said, 1979: 101). For the Orientalist, the Orient is not the Orient as it exists, but as it has been Orientalized. And Orientalism "views the Orient as something whose existence is not only displayed but has remained fixed in time and place for the West" (1979: 108).

Therefore, there is a great similarity between the experience of those authors who have studied Bororo society and those who have turned to Asian societies: "to the Orientalist, who believes the Orient never changes, the new is simply the old betrayed by new, misunderstanding dis-Orientals" (1979: 104). Or, as Baudrillard writes, "those savages are posthumous: frozen, embalmed with creosote, sterilized, protected from death, they have become referential simulacrum and science itself has become pure simulation" (1978: 9).

Several authors have analyzed transformational processes in Bororo society and have incorporated the ideology of the "eternal return." Like some of their informers, they regret the impossibility of this return.

Herbert Baldus

In 1937, following the release of an essay collection by Herbert Baldus, anthropological studies in Brazil began to focus primarily on accultura-tion (Schaden, 1965: 17–22). Baldus's collection—*Ensaios de etnologia brasileira* (Essays on Brazilian Ethnology)—deserves discussion not because it introduced acculturation studies (to which I refer in chapter 1), but because of its intent. Baldus included two chapters entirely devoted to the Bororo: "A posição social da mulher entre os bororos orientais" (The Social Position of Women among the Eastern Bororo) (pp. 60–91), and "O Professor Thiago Marques e o caçador aipobureu" (Professor Thiago Marques and the Hunter Aipobureu) (pp. 92–107). His last chapter—"A mudança de cultura entre índios do Brasil" (Culture Change among Indians in Brazil) (pp. 160–186)—analyzes very interest-ing data, some of them about the Bororo.

In 1934 Baldus visited the Bororo at Meruri and Sangradouro and, in 1935, he visited the Bororo at the Tori-Paru village. Using data on the social organization of this society, Baldus showed that Bororo women's status was neither inferior nor superior to men's. He discussed the various facets of Bororo society more as a cluster of traits than as a structured society.

Baldus quoted census figures (fewer than one thousand), noted the Bororo's anatomical features, food, clothing, and body ornaments, and remarked on the extent to which these domains were affected by contact with the larger Brazilian society. He attributed to the Salesians the Bororo's behavioral changes with respect to family planning—contra-ception and abortion, infanticide, and the like—and, principally, the dominance of family life, which was strengthened by "clan dissolution" (1979: 171).

Interestingly, despite this interference in Bororo family life, Baldus believed that the Indians would at some point resist change. He attributed the strength to resist to the "individual's innate character." To him, this innate character "comprises willpower, sexuality, in other words, a unique combination of all their *natural endowments*, inborn rather than acquired—a combination that allows an individual to be and to remain an individual, that is to say, that distinguishes him or her from all other individuals" (1979: 83, my emphasis). To Baldus, it was this "natural endowment" that kept the Bororo from accepting European patterns of male/female relations in which the man was the master of the house and "a beat-up wife is preferred to a woman whose husband has left her" (1979: 83). This same natural endowment was not strong enough, however, to stop the character of an Indian tribe from decisively changing in relationships with the non-Indian (1979: 172).

Next, Baldus provided numerous examples that demonstrate the extent to which the character of different tribes had changed. Baldus trod the paths that demonstrated the "macho attitude" of western society. He was interested in finding out whether the male or the female was on top during sexual intercourse; he discovered that they faced each other during intercourse (1979: 80), which led him to conclude that women's social status was equal to men's. He then proceeded to assess the contribution of male and female to the family's support, and even their ability to carry weight (1979: 76–77). To Baldus, the parity between male and female was further demonstrated by the distribution of subsistence tasks.

Thus, by observing their sexual relations, work distribution, utilization of personal ornaments, roles in the organization of the nuclear family, and infanticide practices (in which the Bororo did not show any sexual bias), Baldus tried to determine women's status in this society. It is primarily in these aspects of social life that men's supremacy is manifested in Brazilian society; therefore, Baldus focused his inquiries on the corresponding aspects of Bororo daily life.

Baldus's bibliography includes not only Colbacchini's monograph *I Bororo Orientali*, but also Lévi-Strauss's article on Bororo social organization. Baldus's findings on the status of Bororo females, however, did not add anything new to the literature. He did not discuss in any detail matrilinearity, for example, nor the role assigned to women during funeral rites, nor even a more careful analysis of the feminine figures that people Bororo mythology. This type of data would likely have posed problems when discussing the "innate character of individuals."

Baldus also discussed the individual's natural endowment or innate character in "O Professor Thiago Marques e o caçador aipobureu." He began by endorsing Boas's claim that "when assessing an Indian's intellectual ability one must remember that he has the same capacity as a European to learn how to think, and he is educated since early childhood for this purpose" (1979: 92). Baldus used the life history of Thiago Marques, a Bororo reared by Salesian missionaries, to show that "the native environment is powerful enough that, soon after returning home, the Indian goes as far as disdaining nearly all the advantages of our civilization that he once enjoyed" (1979: 93). Behind this "native environment" there is a sort of magic power that lures the Indian and forces him to yield to his "natural endowment." Thiago Marques showed Baldus that culture changes constantly and thus cannot be viewed as a hermetically sealed set of traits stashed away in footlockers, as if each of these chests corresponded to a selected stage.

Upon learning that Marques has referred in a somewhat melancholic manner to the old days, Baldus asked him whether "it wouldn't be better to *return the Bororo* to their previous condition." Marques replied, "Nowadays we can no longer go around dressed up in feathers" (1979: 107, my emphasis). Baldus understood that one of the main tasks of ethnology was to study the continual change of cultural expression and the causes of this change (1979: 1). This task presented a problem even in the author's definition of culture: "Culture, in the sense attributed to it by ethnologists, is the all-encompassing, harmonious expression of feeling, thought, wish, capacity, action, and reaction of a social unit. It springs from the combination of hereditary, physical, psychic, and collective moral factors and that, together with civilizing equipment (instruments, weapons, etc.), impart to the social unit the necessary capacity and independence for the material and spiritual struggle for life" (1979: 1). This definition, which is not so different from Tylor's classic definition and which was, as we have seen, the most widely accepted when these essays were written, presents culture as a sealed phenomenon that lacks its own dynamic. Baldus's concept focused on a set of actions (feeling, thought, wish, etc.) and the products of these actions in relation to a set of given factors—such as psychism and civilizing equipment.

Cultural change, as the definition of culture predicts, alters these expressions, which are harmonious by nature. Baldus referred to both the partial and the total change of culture. As paradoxical as it may seem, his conception of cultural change was also an absolutely static conception wherein certain traits of the original culture were replaced by others of European origin in whole or in part. Thus to Baldus changes in the realm of material culture, for example, were more visible and took place within a shorter period of time than those in the spiritual realm. The advantages and disadvantages of elements of material culture are clearly visible, and the adoption of tools such as the iron ax, for instance, led to their quick incorporation. Adoption was not as quick when a new creed, a new social structure, or a new chant was offered to the Indian (1979: 180).

Baldus's observations of the relative changes in Bororo dwellings (form and interior layout), the organization of labor to provide a means of subsistence, the incorporation of elements such as tobacco, alcohol, and salt, and the changes in traditional handicrafts such as weaving and pottery were made by someone who had investigated a culture by looking at its exterior aspects and most evident traits. His analysis did not go beyond appearances to capture the true meaning of change. He did not, for example, question how the Bororo assessed these changes or what these changes meant to them. He stated only that certain "traditional" objects were no longer used or even made, and that some objects still coexisted with others that had been incorporated from the larger Brazilian society for the same purpose.

Baldus's most pertinent observations on the Bororo referred to the nuclearization of family life and the fact that, "among the Bororo of the missions, Christianity and the old tribal religion exist separately" (1979: 176). Although he did not dwell on the nuclear family and religious coexistence, his remarks are to a certain extent still valid, as I shall demonstrate in the next chapter. It was this "generation of civilized Christians" (1979: 180) created by the Salesian missionaries that led Baldus to ask himself how long it would take for their culture to change completely. He conducted his research after the Bororo had undergone thirty years of indoctrination. Even so, they had not yet lost the desire to devote themselves to their traditional way of life.

I can affirm that today, after ninety years of indoctrination, nothing indicates that the Bororo, even those who live in the missions, will surrender their culture completely. Indians and missionaries coexist and represent one another in ways that allow us to understand their mode of action. Certainly, Baldus was not concerned with the relationship between Indians and missionaries as they themselves saw it, although a few of his contemporaries, such as Malinowski and even Thurnwald, were interested in understanding the so-called native point of view. Baldus "did not let himself be constrained by concepts preached by the masterminds of functionalism," Schaden wrote in the prologue to the second edition of Baldus's *Ensaios da etnologia brasileira*. The same cannot be said about the researchers who succeeded him.

Guilherme Saake

Saake, a Jesuit priest, considered an issue that was addressed fairly frequently by researchers who studied acculturation: the possibility of Indians' transforming themselves into *efficient workers* and integrating themselves once and for all into the local mixed-blood population of Indian, white European, and African origin.

In 1952 Saake spent two weeks among the Bororo of the Córrego Grande village. After gathering data on depopulation, incorporation of elements such as money, language, clothing, and eating habits, that had led to social changes, Saake pointed out factors that, in his opinion, determined the Bororo's conservative way of life. To him, the most important "ramparts" of tribal cohesion were associated with the leadership of highly influential individuals, be it the *bari* (shaman) or the chief. This would explain why, among these Indians, "burial ceremonies maintain . . . every detail of their elaborate traditional forms" (1953: 46).

Saake went as far as to suggest that the integration of the Bororo was accomplished by training them for Western-type work, and he warned that, "as much as ethnologists may resent it, such integration will not be feasible as long as the influence of the chief and the bari prevails" (1953: 52).

If, on the one hand, Saake (and other authors) insisted on changes leading to the potential integration of a tribal group into the surrounding society, on the other hand, he incorporated into his approach the nostalgic discourse that satisfied elderly tribesmen. He often heard from the older Bororo (and certainly from members of other native societies) that the younger generation was different and not interested in learning the traditional culture; consequently, traditional culture would disappear following the elders' deaths. This type of observation, which incorporates as the sole and irreversible reality a nostalgic discourse and foretells the extinction of cultural standards in the short run, is no longer restricted to researchers such as Saake, who had but two weeks to collect data.

Esther Huestis

The vision of cultural decharacterization is also featured in Huestis's "Bororo Spiritism as Revitalization" (1963). According to Huestis, a Summer Institute of Linguistics missionary, changes in the Bororo religious domain could be understood as a revitalization process—a deliberate effort made by a society to establish a more satisfactory culture as result of the stress to which it had been subjected (Wallace in Huestis, 1963: 189). After listing the difficulties—scarce resources as result of territorial reduction, depopulation associated with a complex social organization, loss of chiefly status to a foster agency's authority, and so on—endured by Bororo society in its efforts to reproduce itself as a society, Huestis anticipated two possibilities for Bororo society, both of which implied cultural decharacterization: "All of these things seem to be driving the Bororo towards an emphasis on spirit worship, which needs fewer people to be workable, does not have the taboos connected with totemism, and is enough like the spiritism (Macumba) of Brazilians that it is not likely to be taken away by outside forces" (1963: 189). She concluded that the Bororo religion would not survive another generation and "in its place spiritism will function as the integrating principle in Bororo culture" (1963: 189). The second alternative seemed to be a warning that led to Huestis's wish: that the Bororo be persuaded that Christianity was the revitalizing force (1963: 189).

Given that Huestis did not reveal her data source and mentioned only the Colbacchini and Albisetti (1942) monograph in her bibliography, one could assume her knowledge of the Bororo to be extremely superficial. She did not, for example, mention the schemes devised by the Bororo to carry out funeral rites that had long been prohibited by the Salesian missionaries. She made no reference to the system under which a child was adopted by a different clan in an attempt to solve the depopulation problem. She did not discuss adequately the issue of double chieftaincy and the internal solutions that the Bororo had adopted.

Huestis's analysis seems to be part of a plan for and an alert to the clergy: either the missionaries take on the task of persuading the Bororo to become Christians, or the Bororo will soon become spiritualists or turn to African voodoo. In any event, Huestis's prognosis regarding the future of this society implied its total decharacterization.

Renate Viertler

The most recent research on the Bororo—particularly the works of Crocker and Viertler, who concentrate on various aspects of Bororo social organization—does not focus on these Indians' relationship with national society. Both Crocker and Viertler merely refer to the "current status" of this society and, in so doing, restrict themselves to the deleterious effects of contact—the main consequence of which has been territorial reduction and the ensuing restriction of subsistence activities, namely, hunting, fishing, and collecting.

Viertler has published numerous essays on Bororo society. In 1970 she researched the Bororo around Sangradouro and Córrego Grande; in 1977 and 1978, at the Tadarimana village; and, in 1986, at the Córrego Grande village. I shall discuss two of her works (1982 and 1987) that address the issue of social and cultural change.

Despite her original intention to analyze Bororo funeral rites while focusing on the adaptive implications of beliefs and practices related to this ritual, Viertler (1982) chose a theoretical perspective—cultural ecology—that impoverished her reflections whenever interethnic relations and the emergent reality arising from contact were under discussion. According to Viertler, "funerals involve the provision of minimal nourishment and moral conditions for the Bororo hired as cheap fishing or handicrafts labor to supply the regional market; at the same time, they represent integration mechanisms at the food and handicrafts markets for the Bororo settled in villages as a consequence of periodic decimation of belongings owned by the deceased" (1982: 593). Viertler's choice of theoretical perspective led to the belief that cultural practices were only a means of rationalization with a view to the solution of practical issues confronted by human groups. Thus, during a Bororo funeral, souls must be fed at collective meals that men prepared in the central hut, and this food "corresponds exactly to the high protein-content food whose distribution is maximized by the traditional criteria of quartering and allotment" (1982: 565). Viertler went on to state, "Our provisory hypothesis concerning the Bororo funeral practices is that, rather than representing an alternative, they represent a requisite for adaptation to the conditions generated through interethnic contact *mainly with respect to the distribution of the most valuable food*" (1982: 600, my emphasis).

Even if true, this conclusion diminishes to a great extent the importance of this ritual. It is difficult for me to accept that the burning of the deceased's possessions should be regarded as a mechanism of integration among the Bororo, who, once deprived of these assets, must turn to the regional market.[1] Viertler admitted that this distribution of personal effects precludes "the forms of social differentiation based on money and material wealth" (1982: 596). This apparent contradiction (the funeral as a phenomenon that maintains the Bororo as a differentiated society while driving them toward insertion in the regional market) resulted from the different historical movements, that is, the dialectics of the interethnic contact process. This process, if exacerbated, could "jeopardize the efficiency of this strategy" (1982: 597).

My reluctance to accept Viertler's conclusions as the most pertinent to the Bororo funeral (and its implications for interethnic relations) springs chiefly from her theoretical perspective and its implied meaning for cultural phenomenon. To admit that, "in terms of the solution of practical problems met by human groups, there is always some form of deep rationality underlying mystical associations" (1982: 564) is to restrict cultural practices not only to an instrumental and utilitarian dimension, but also to a rationality imbued with values typical of our contemporary, capitalist society. Furthermore, in Viertler's analysis of interethnic relations, the processual perspective is lost to the point that different viewpoints become indistinguishable.

Within Viertler's theoretical construct, only an analyst and observer has a global vision of the historical process. Using personal rationality, that observer interprets different "truths" held by different agents. These truths are not gathered from an exegesis of speeches and attitudes that considers the enormous diversity of cultures and the variety of meanings that may be attributed to the same experience. They are gathered from a supposed universality of solutions devised for the issues posed by the environment. Within this theoretical perspective, which dilutes the symbolic into the instrumental, cultural practices necessarily pass through the strainer of right and wrong, good and evil, integrator and dis-integrator.[2]

In 1987 Viertler published an article that expressed considerable resentment about the young Bororo's attitude concerning both her presence and her research in the village. She lamented the death of her favorite informer, an old man who knew everything about the Bororo tradition and who seemingly personified for Viertler all the ideal attributes of the Bororo male (the essence of which she unfortunately could no longer find). She felt insulted by the young Bororo engaged in the land struggle movement—all of them dressed in T-shirts, using tape recorders and VCRs, and demanding that researchers pay for their research.

Viertler was more careful than her peers and did not refer to the group's extinction, as did other researchers who studied a native society from an external and superficial standpoint. Her conclusion not only demonstrated the impossibility of her capturing the processes of cultural change of this society, but also invalidated the attitudes of the young Bororo, who, I believe, did not oppose their elders, who "retain traditional knowledge."

Viertler's conclusion (or perhaps catharsis) was that "currently the Bororo fight for places at non-Indian discothèques and video rental shops, thus clearly heading toward the folklorization of their cultural traditions" (1987: 140). The attitude of the young Bororo (which I discuss in detail in chapters 4 and 7) implied establishing alliances with a few groups among the large number of whites with whom they were forced to coexist (which, in fact has always constituted a strategy of resistance) and using elements such as T-shirts, tape recorders, and VCRs to help accomplish the community's political ends. To characterize this attitude as leading to the *folklorization* of cultural traditions and, consequently, to their petrifaction, is to become insensitive to culture as an extremely dynamic phenomenon that utilizes not only its own elements but also those elements that it seeks to incorporate for its own benefit. In so doing, culture attributes to all these elements a specific meaning that does not necessarily match the original meaning. In fact, this vision of culture as something petrified in the old people, and as something that dies with them, is consistent with Viertler's view of the anthropologist's work—which she tried to explain to those Indians who demanded a large sum to allow her to carry out her research: "My work consists of collecting the traditions that the elders take with them when they die and that the young are not willing to, or can no longer, learn" (1987: 128).

I do not mean to invalidate the discourse of the older informants. To the contrary, their words emphatically return us to the reality to which they are exposed—the constant memory of a past that does not fully coincide with the present. And this is precisely the elderly's function, that is, "to recall and advise—*memini, moneo*—to connect beginning and end, thus linking past to future; . . . they are the source that spawns the essence of culture—a point at which the past is preserved and the present is being prepared" (Chauí, 1983: xviii). Many anthropologists believe that they are the only ones who pay attention to this nostalgic discourse. It is critically important, however, to be aware of how this discourse is perceived and assimilated by subsequent generations, that is to say, how the words of the elderly impress the minds of the young.

Anyone who has the opportunity to watch Indians for more than a decade ultimately realizes what happens with "the younger generations." They may at first seem unaware of the cultural standards of their community. Hartmann says that "during our last stay, we found that many young people who had previously and in the name of 'modernism' assumed either a critical or a frankly scornful attitude toward traditional practice began to participate either actively or as noncritical observers" (1964: 7). I agree with her. The young Bororo I met in 1970—who spent most of their time playing soccer or cards, chatting at the Indian post, or attending parties organized at the post house—were totally ignorant of the traditional Bororo rituals. Sixteen years later their attitude was completely different in that they showed a keen interest in Bororo culture, took an active part in rituals, and readily fell back on mythology. Gradually, they began to adopt a nostalgic discourse that was also a criticism of the younger generations—*plus ça change* . . . Perhaps the change mode in these societies involves being the same, but in a different way.

Certainly, changes in a society's cultural expression are verifiable. One of the main characteristics of a cultural phenomenon is its dynamic scope. To Indians, the great paradox is the necessity of change as the only way of remaining the same. By "remain the same" I mean maintaining a broad-based social structure, a cosmic vision, and self-recognition in one's ancestors. Evidently, it is up to the younger Bororo to become familiar with and to appropriate elements from the world "out there." Should the *other* (the non- Indian) appear as a model to be imitated at a certain time of life or in specific circumstances, this model is not necessarily perennial in all contexts, and as a function of which the Bororo will relinquish their culture.

Furthermore, the insertion of the "seasoned" young person into the community will not occur exactly as it did for earlier generations. Even those societies that are unwilling to change and that adopt an "eternal return" model as the ideal defined in mythical times are changing continually. According to Eliade, "The existence of an exemplar model does not fetter creative innovation" (1963: 141); however, this change does not occur as a process that gradually and mechanically substitutes elements of the prevailing culture for elements of the original culture in such a way that the original culture is gradually extinguished or completely loses its original characteristics.

Jon Crocker

This catastrophic view also imbues the works of other researchers who more recently have studied Bororo society. Crocker began researching the Bororo in 1964, at the Pobojari village. Following the advice of a prestigious Bororo chief, in 1965 he moved to the Córrego Grande village, where he remained until February 1966. In June 1967, Crocker began his last research phase. The results of his extensive data collection and study were published in *Vital Souls: Bororo Cosmology, Natural Symbolism, and Shamanism* (1985).

Crocker believes that the extinction process affecting South American Indian societies—currently in a state of "putrefaction" or even "defunct"—is about to end, and that it is up to ethnologists—true undertakers—to embalm their remains: "Their [native societies'] remaining choice is to die or to acculturate" (1985: 265).[3]

While allowing himself to be influenced by the nostalgic memories of the elders without verifying their recollections within a broader context, to be impressed by the alcoholism rate,[4] and to regret the disappearance of the *aroe-etawara-are*, or master of the soul's way or path (which in my opinion is not extinct), Crocker seemed to anticipate not only a great collective funeral, held strictly in Bororo style, but also the tribe's complete extinction; only the name would remain in the memory of non-Indians.

The book ends by taking away from ethnologists even the possibility of embalming the remains of a once-living society: "in choosing to die as a people, the Bororo acknowledge their final helplessness against these *bope*-inspired forces: they assert against them the dominion of the transcendent dead. The aroe live in all our memories" (1985: 332).

I find it interesting that Crocker seems to consider the Bororo funeral the most important social ritual, the future that a wicked destiny has in store for the Bororo. This melancholic and apocalyptic tone prevails throughout the last chapter, which he bitterly entitles "The Stench of Death." Since 1970 I have attended more than twelve Bororo funerals. To me, the Bororo funeral is a ritual in which this community not only rearranges the society of the living, but also re-creates the meaning of life itself. For the Bororo, the funeral provides an opportunity for socialization in which the elders convey to the younger generations the sophisticated myths, chants, dances, handicrafts, and other aspects of Bororo society. By means of this ritual, the society of the living rearranges itself and creates new bonds among its members through their intricate ritual kinship system. During this period, subsistence activities introduced by outside contact (principally mechanized farming) are suspended and the Bororo resume group fishing, hunting, and other subsistence activities that, in this ritual context, are very important.

Through their funeral rituals the Bororo formally acknowledge new members: the male initiation rituals are always held during the long period (up to three months) of the funeral cycle. Paradoxically, without funerals the Bororo could not propagate as a society, nor enable their dead (recalled by their living representatives during rituals) to meet the society of the living. To the Bororo, death literally re-creates life and, consequently, all possibilities of social reproduction.

Literature as Mirror

What impression does a written work make on its readers? How should we assess an author's reflections on and analyses of a given society? How does an author position herself or himself in relation to predecessors who have tried to address themes that are, to a great extent, interrelated? Do we all discuss the same society at different times? If the society is the same, then what prompts the difference between writers? Certainly this difference is not restricted to mere approach.

We know that "anthropology exists in the book, the article, the lecture, the museum display, or, sometimes nowadays, the film" (Geertz, 1973: 16). Different books, however, may cover the same subject or, at times, the same society. This is why different authors who have studied the changes in Bororo society to some extent serve as mirrors for my own work.

Whenever we look at what most differentiates a written work from others, we consider when it was written, the theoretical and conceptual references available to the author, and the empirical data. The duration of field research and, principally in the analysis of Indian societies, whether the work was written by an anthropologist or by someone who, despite having some knowledge of anthropology, was motivated by religion to contact the Indian society also situate an author's work.

The authors I have discussed wrote about Bororo society at different times between the 1930s (Baldus) and the 1950s (Saake). Research projects initiated in the mid-1960s, such as Crocker's, were not published until the mid-1980s.[5] This approximately sixty-year period constitutes a considerable time span in terms of the possible formulation of new theories and new conceptual schemes. It represents an even greater amount of time if we take into consideration the process of change that was affecting Indians in Brazil and that seems to be accelerating, partly as a consequence of the nation's encroachment on the territories of these societies. But this span cannot explain the different views of Bororo society, nor why they all sing the Requiem in unison at the opening of the funeral ritual. None of the authors who wrote about the changes in Bororo society could see beyond this catastrophic perspective. All of them—Baldus, Saake, Huestis, Viertler, and Crocker—associated the Bororo's processes of change with imminent decadence or cultural decharacterization and disintegration. Catastrophism marks them all.

Implicit in all these studies (or even explicit, as in Baldus's work) is a conception of culture as a finished product or a stock of cultural traits that, like genetic stock, is passed down as social heritage. Since we are not dealing with traits that have the same guarantee of preservation as genetic traits, however, cultural traits could be irretrievably lost. Thus, they understood the effects of contact only as a substitution of the prevailing society for original cultural traits. This assumption enabled them immediately to affirm the decharacterization of the original culture—or to affirm a syncretic combination of these aspects (Huestis), which also enables them to view the culture as decaying.

Crocker and Viertler did not share this simplistic view of Bororo culture, although their analyses of the "ethnographic present" (see also Van Velsen, 1967) were more sophisticated than their attempts to understand interethnic relationships in the day-to-day life of the Bororo. Both devoted more time to their field research than did Baldus or Saake; Crocker spent eighteen months (from August 1964 to February 1967) studying the villages of Pobojari and Córrego Grande. In June 1967 he returned for more research (Crocker, 1985: 10–12). Viertler spent time in Sangradouro and Córrego Grande in 1970, Tadarimana in 1977 and 1978, and Córrego Grande in 1986. But even after having remained on site for a longer period, having visited different villages, and not having a religious perspective (as did Saake, a Jesuit priest, and Huestis, a missionary associated with the Summer Institute of Linguistics), neither Crocker nor Viertler demonstrated any sensibility toward the Bororo process of resistance and the possibility of analyzing social change from a nondisintegrative perspective.

The catastrophic perspective is not, however, exclusive to researchers who have studied Bororo society. With few exceptions, it is found in practically all literature focusing on the effect of contact on Indian societies in contemporary Brazil. One of these exceptions—Terence Turner's "From Cosmology to Ideology: Resistance, Adaptation and

Social Consciousness among the Kayapo" (1987)—is an extremely interesting analysis. Turner analyzed Kayapó society by using an ethnography of native and cultural standards that did not exclude the historical, political, and economic reality of the interethnic contact. He investigated the political and cultural resistance of the Kayapó as a process that, besides allowing them to conserve their ethnic, cultural, and social identity, did not keep them from assimilating certain standards of national culture, such as the Portuguese language, medicine, and telecommunications. According to Turner, "the pattern of dependency established at contact has been 're-colonized' from within by the Kayapo, leaving them in control of the apparatus [means of transportation, radio transmitters, education, etc.] originally established by the Brazilians to control the Kayapo" (1987: 21–22).

Turner returned to the principal aspects of Kayapó society and provided a brief historical background of Kayapó contact with the national society and the effect of that contact. According to Turner, despite all the threats posed by their historical relationship with "white men," the Kayapó had attained a high degree of political and social cohesion and the continuity of their culture (including the revitalization of shamanism). This cohesion resulted from a cosmology that should be regarded from two complementary levels. First, the Kayapó were deeply aware of how essential their culture was for their existence as a society. They have been able to assimilate the contact situation in terms of the traditional cultural structure, which had certainly prompted important changes in this structure. Turner described the structure as the process that leads "from cosmology to ideology."

Turner related the Kayapó's assimilation of Brazilian goods (such as clothing, weapons, trucks and airplanes, VCRs and camcorders) into the *nekretch* (traditional ritual items). According to him, the *nekretch* are generally "items (artifacts, songs, or names) taken from alien peoples or (supposedly) natural beings like fish or birds. These valuables function within the traditional ceremonial system as repositories of the social powers of integration and renewal associated with the value of beauty, *but their ability to do so depends in Kayapo eyes on their very alienness,* from whence the powers and values they embody are thought to derive" (1987: 41–42, my emphasis).

In the Kayapó language, *nekretch* designates both these traditional ritualistic goods and the incorporated Brazilian merchandise. As with the Bororo, these goods are not subject to inheritance. Traditional *nekretch*, such as ceremonial ornaments, weapons, and instruments, as well as the adopted non-Indian merchandise, are buried with the dead, preventing accumulation and internal differentiation in terms of material wealth.

In traditional Kayapó cosmology, society—represented by the village center—is synonymous with full humanity (in which neither other indigenous societies nor whites take part). A new view of the world begins to take shape from the developing relationship with Brazilian society, however. Brazilians are now also acknowledged as full human beings. Now that the Kayapó are no longer the paradigm of humanity, it is evident that they share with other Indian societies their status in relation to the national society (1987: 33–35). Rather than a substitution of one view for another, both coexist. While the traditional view is focused mainly on internal Kayapó social relationships and mechanisms, a new view—which is not expressed through myth or ritual or by differentiating between village structure and cosmology—is implicit in new social modes, attitudes, and even in the rhetoric used in relationships with Brazilian society. In an analysis that seeks to focus on "the cultural shape of the situation of 'inter-ethnic friction' as seen from the vantage point of native societies, and how . . . terms in which they see it relate to their general social and cosmological structure" (1987: 5), however, Turner, like other authors before him, takes up a unidirectional perspective. Without a doubt, the point of view now is that of native societies, but this is only one of the segments involved in the contact situation.

In my opinion, Turner's conclusions about the Kayapó's new reality are excessively optimistic, maybe to compensate for the catastrophism of researchers before him. His conclusions also seem to be imbued with the humanitarian and environmental values so much in vogue now. Militant intellectuals, personally engaged in the social movements they analyze, end up transforming themselves into spokespersons in a discourse that supposedly originates in the people they study. Turner concludes:

> These relations are the opposites of each other, and taken together repeat the pattern of contradictory, positive and negative transactions which articulate the internal structure of the social domain. That of the Indians is constructive, consisting in the traditional processes of transformation of natural energies and materials into social powers and forms, in ways that permit the continuing renewal of nature and its powers. That of the Brazilians, on the other hand, is destructive: the chopping down of forests and their conversion to grass-land, the pollution of rivers, the mining of the earth, or the damming of rivers and flooding of the surrounding land, all of which permanently despoil nature and render it unfit for habitation and agriculture, hunting or fishing. (1987: 37)

How do I position myself in relationship to these authors? In what way has their work contributed to my analysis? The answer requires outlining here—rather than in the Preface—my beliefs about the conditions under which this work was produced, as well as my motivations and perspectives.

Various sources have supplied data for my study. Since 1970, when I began to research the Bororo in the state of Mato Grosso, I have spent approximately seventeen months among them. During my trips—the shortest of which was one week and the longest, about three months— I came to know the existing Bororo villages (Córrego Grande, Piebaga, Perigara, Tadarimana, Meruri, Garças, and Jarudori, the last of which has been completely taken over by a town called Jarudori). In 1979 I cofounded with a group of anthropologists, indigenists, and educators, the Centro de Trabalho Indigenista, an organization that supports the Indians' right to self-determination. Through the CTI, I became familiar with other Indian societies and the contact to which they have been exposed.

Between 1982 and 1987, I spent eight months among the Bororo. In addition to the research I was conducting, at the CTI, I held ongoing discussions about the situation of Indians in Brazil and, above all, the political actions anthropologists were likely to undertake. "Scientific neutrality" and the search for "objectivity" had provided anthropologists with an external view of the societies they surveyed. The anthropological literature of the 1950s and the 1960s bears witness to observers who reported on a process they regarded as nearly natural and spontaneous. Those anthropologists viewed the assimilation process, explicitly contained in official Indian policy, as the irreversible future of these societies. If these societies were not extinguished, they would be reduced to a few remnants totally decharacterized in cultural terms.

A few more-engaged anthropologists such as Darcy Ribeiro and Eduardo Galvão, among others, tried to transform government action into an instrument to ensure the protection of native populations. The Serviço de Proteção aos Índios was transformed into FUNAI, but not even the conviction and devotion of various anthropologists could inspire the government to commit itself to the Indian issue without corruption and involving third-parties (see Azanha and Caiuby Novaes, 1981).

At the CTI, we worked to demystify this "neutrality" and to become more involved with the "subjective reasons" of the Indians. We believe that fieldwork requires a certain amount of complicity and the need to understand these societies' capacity to resist and to act. Researchers must remember that Indian societies have always coped with adversity.

Anthropologists such as Darcy Ribeiro analyzed the role of different agents and contact fronts. Then we debated the anthropologist's role in these societies. We knew that both our involvement and the Indians' appeal basically derived from the fact that we appreciated that which, in most cases, was not regarded highly by the region's inhabitants, government employees, and missionaries: indigenous language, stories, material culture, and the like. In this sense, we anthropologists also regarded ourselves as agents, because not only did we leave an impression on the native societies, but we somehow interfered with those societies we researched. For this reason, too, we became the Indians' "buddies," or we were adopted through a strategic kinship system that they made available to us. We became accountable to them. They no longer assist researchers who are interested in "neutral" and "objective" knowledge, or in research projects that aim at reconstructing their past without any commitment to their present and future.

The second phase of my research among the Bororo (beginning in 1980), therefore, resulted in the maturing of my reflections not only about anthropological knowledge, but also about the object that constitutes it. During my trips to the villages, the Bororo asked me to discuss several of their problems. The drawing of territorial boundaries was the main subject of meetings at which we discussed how to act, how to pressure FUNAI lawyers, and with whom to establish alliances. Some of these meetings were organized by the Salesians who were working with the Bororo and who today are extremely involved in the resolution of boundary issues. More informal meetings were called whenever necessary. I was also asked to apply for money from foreign organizations for the acquisition of boats, motors, rice-processing machinery, and other items that would allow the Bororo greater independence in their relationship to FUNAI and the local non-Indian population.

At the end of 1984, I was asked to form the team that was to assess the Bororo area of Vale do Rio São Lourenço, which was affected by the POLONOROESTE Project. As part of this survey, between 1984 and 1986 Paulo Serpa and I took several trips during which we discussed with the Bororo their problems and claims, verified whether the funds were received and properly applied, and tried to involve the Bororo in project design.

While performing these types of functions, anthropologists assume even greater commitment to the communities they are working with; however, they cannot guarantee that the government will accept their recommendations. I believe that the greatest benefit to the Indians of these types of surveys is the opportunity to discuss, with project advisers, each village's situation and, consequently, to acquire a broader and more systematic view of the problems that trouble these populations. (I hold the same opinion about the anthropological advisory service rendered as part of the Carajá and similar projects.) Such discussions allow a more critical view of each situation—a view that is no longer exclusive to community leaders.

Our achievements, however, were relatively small in relation to our goals. The result was a smokescreen behind which the mere existence of anthropologist consultants put those very consultants at risk of legitimizing the country's disastrous Indian policy. I therefore withdrew from the assessment of the POLONOROESTE Project in July 1986.

I was aware of the risks of political involvement in terms of knowledge. I did not intend to become an "observer participant" and leave aside my interest in learning about and interpreting (instead of merely intervening in and reporting on) the reality I was studying. Political involvement with Bororo society was not only one of the Indians' demands, but also a concrete possibility for learning about their behavior and their attempts to enrich their culture under new situations. How did the different villages relate to one other? How and why did they join or separate? What was the relationship between "young" and "old" in the context of interethnic relationships? Regardless of their antagonistic positions, in what way could missionaries, anthropologists, journalists, and other categories of the broad "non-Indian" world become "allies" to be conquered through the intricate strategies that were implied in their contact with these societies? As anthropologist, interlocutor, and, possibly, mediator, I was called to participate in the drawing up of several of their strategies to resist the advances of national society. My involvement might explain why I cannot share the catastrophic, petrifying, and folklorizing view of those who have written about the future of Bororo society.

Besides consulting several Salesian publications for this project, in 1988 I researched the archives of the Inspetoria Salesiana de São Paulo while trying to reconstruct the history of the relationship between the Bororo and the missionaries. My goal was to understand and assess the development of this relationship. I tried to restrict myself to the missionaries' accounts of the first years of this contact. These accounts show the daily building of this relationship, including discoveries and mistakes that were made. They are also important for assessing the relationship between the Salesians and the Bororo since the 1970s. I have analyzed that relationship using data that I collected and assessments of the Catholic Church's role during this time period. The Salesian missionaries, who in 1972 barred my entry to the mission, invited me to witness the cultural reinvigoration that the Bororo of Meruri had initiated with the support and encouragement of Master Mário Bordignon and Father Gonçalo Ochoa.

In 1984 and 1985, I taught a course on cultural identity to undergraduates in the Social Sciences Department of the University of São Paulo (USP). I tried to systematize the literature on the subject and several approaches to the identity issue in the anthropological literature. I asked students to conduct fieldwork on the identity issue within a specific portion of the population. Throughout the six-month course we discussed identity by using empirical data about the most diverse segments of Brazilian society: Afro-Brazilians, women, homosexuals, Jews, Gypsies, religious groups, individuals with physical and mental disabilities, and so on.

The basic empirical evidence utilized in the development of this book includes that which I was able to collect among the Bororo and the archival material I collected on the influence of Salesian missions. The data I collected at the CTI and from discussions with my student assistants (who helped me research the course at USP) are either discussed explicitly in this book or incorporated in my account of the theme.

4.
Self-Image as Formed in the Play of Mirrors: Structural Distance and Reference Values

> Human beings are constantly thinking about others and about what others are thinking about them, and what others think they are thinking about the others and so on. One may be wondering about what is going on inside the other. One desires or fears that other people will know what is going on inside oneself.
> —R. D. Laing, *Interpersonal Perception*

Images in the Play of Mirrors

In this chapter I will use Bororo society as an example to show how the self-image of a group or society can be analyzed using a metaphorical resource: the play of mirrors. Whenever a society focuses on another population segment, it simultaneously forms a self-image based on the way it perceives itself in the eyes of this other segment. It is as if the viewer (the original population) transforms the *other* (the other population) into a mirror in which it can see itself. Each *other* is a different mirror that reflects a different image of the original viewer.

Given that there are usually several population segments with which a society coexists and which it transforms into looking glasses, the original society ultimately forms several distinct self-images. These images are not static, immune to change; they change just as any image reflected in a mirror changes as the viewer moves. It is these images reflected by the *other* that allow alterations in self-image and in attitudes.[1]

To use the mirror as a metaphor to allow us to understand a society's self-image is to follow the course of *reflection* and *speculation* that a society sets up for itself, a metaphor that is introduced by the word *mirror* itself. The play of mirrors is, therefore, a metaphor that adequately illustrates the process through which an image of the self is both formed and transformed in a society that is in contact with social groups that are different from itself.[2]

I am not discussing the psychological processes that lead to the formation of the *self*. That is, I am not referring to the specular image, as proposed by Lacan (1966). His statements, however, show how, to a child seeing his or her image reflected for the first time, the mirror determines a very important moment, one that marks the passage from the imaginary self to the symbolic self. My objective is to use a society's historical and social determinants to understand its self-image rather than, as Lacan proposes, to undertake the investigation of a primordial *self*, which precedes its objectification by the dialectics of identification with others. I wish to suggest that to understand the issue of self-image as determined by the play of mirrors is to understand it in more complex terms than those proposed by Roberto Cardoso de Oliveira (1976).

This approach allows a more dynamic vision of identity, since it does not entail simply observing the manner in which a group establishes who its members are and draws the borders that determine the differences between various groups with which it finds itself in contact. In the play of mirrors, every reflected image corresponds to a possibility for action. The group's assessment of this action leads to the formation of a new image that, in turn, will allow for new action.

Once a society comes into contact with different groups, it creates different images of itself; these images engage in dynamic relationships with one another. Furthermore, the *other* that doubles as a mirror into which society looks to find an image of itself could be that same society, but in another time—perhaps the past—and another space. And, exactly as in a play of mirrors, these several images combine and reflect to form new patterns (as in a kaleidoscope) that are defined by the vantage point. In this sense, the play of mirrors that I propose closely resembles Laing's assumptions. Although I make my assumptions to analyze interpersonal relationships, they can be extremely helpful in dealing with the relationships between different social groups:

> My field of experience is, however, filled not only by my direct view of myself (ego) and of the other (alter), but of what we shall call *meta*perspectives—*my view* of the *other's* (your, his, her, their) *view* of me. I may not actually be able to see myself as others see me, but I am constantly supposing them to be seeing me in particular ways, and I am constantly acting in the light of the actual or supposed attitudes, opinions, needs and so on the other has in respect of me. (Laing, 1966: 5, original emphasis)

This metaperspective allows Laing to speak of a metaidentity, which is not dissociated from identity and which to anthropologists is also associated with the notion of person, as we shall see in the last chapter.[3]

On whom does a society focus its gaze? Certainly, on the groups with which historically it maintains contact, but also on groups about which it is so well informed that—despite the distance that separates them—it creates very clear images of these groups.

Besides turning their gaze constantly onto themselves, the Bororo take the neighboring Xavante, other Indians, and non-Indians as reference points. Within the large non-Indian segment they identify, first, those with whom they maintain closer contact: the Salesian missionaries, FUNAI agents, neighbors and farmers (many of whom have invaded Indian territory). Among the "non-Indian aliens," special mention should be made of those who constitute the entity the Bororo call "government," foreigners (principally German, Italian, and U.S. citizens), and those Brazilians or foreigners who fit the category of researchers, anthropologists, and journalists. These categories, which I call "population segments," are present in the contact that the Bororo maintain with national society and appear as characters in the Indians' everyday speech. The Bororo, whether they be in villages linked to the mission or to FUNAI, or in independent villages, have quite a clear and recurrent image of these population segments. These are the segments that double as mirrors from which Bororo society is reflected as trying to act in accordance with what the reflection calls for—be it validating the reflected image or attempting to correct it.

How do the Bororo see each one of these segments and how do they imagine themselves to be perceived by them? My objective is to show how these several images combine and self-reflect in a dynamic way. Thus, I will not speak of each population segment, but of the way I see them reflected in Bororo representation. Obviously, I am not referring to graphic images but to categories of representation whose very nature implies value judgments. Our discussion involves those *representations of the self* provoked by the play of mirrors, and thus we should remember Durkheim's assumption "that they are phenomena but endowed with reality, with specific properties which behave in different ways with each other according as they have, or have not, common properties . . . They form the network of social life and arise from the relations of the individuals thus combined or the secondary groups between the individuals and the total society" (Durkheim, 1965: 15, 24).

The behavior of individuals from different societies is ruled by different value systems. Therefore, the representation of the self, this reflection of oneself prompted by contact with an other, implies confrontation between these different value systems as a result of which one speculates about oneself and others. At present, when seen from the viewpoint of their contact relationships, the Bororo have an extremely negative image of themselves, one that fights other images formed from other vantage points. Going back to Durkheim (1970: 96), we could say that these images are positive or negative, depending on the *value* at stake—in other words, depending on the relationship between "something and the different aspects of the ideal." Let us see how these images are formed.

"Tame" Indians

The Bororo have built an image of themselves as "tame" Indians (Indians who neither impose themselves nor frighten enemies); this is especially true in their perception of the Xavante and of how they imagine the Xavante perceive them. According to the Bororo, one of the resources for imposing their will is in knowing how to speak; this does not mean correct grammar. "To talk tough" is to speak with conviction and authority, which the Bororo cannot do when they address an interlocutor outside their own group. If the Bororo have a better grasp of Portuguese grammar than the Xavante, they fall far behind the latter when it comes to "talking tough." "The Xavante came here to talk this land business. They get a little tongue-tied, they don't know how to speak too well. But they are the ones who know how to talk, because they talk tough. Bororo doesn't know to talk" (Meruri, 1982).

This self-image, which the Bororo have formed as a reflection of their image of the Xavante, is not exclusive to the Bororo who live in Meruri, under the direct influence of the Salesians. The same self-image is clearly visible in the following excerpts: "More Bororo land was invaded. With the Xavante, when they find someone occupying their piece of land, they take away everything from them. And they say: What are you doing here? But the Bororo don't. The Bororo are very calm. [Why? I ask.] Because the Bororo understand something so the Bororo are very calm. . . . Now, the Xavante are a people born to be really mean, so they are really mean" (Garças, December 1983).

In reference to two Bororo who didn't obtain permission from FUNAI to travel to Brasília and who didn't demonstrate against this rule in front of the government agency, one Bororo commented: "Xavante doesn't lower his head, no. When they want they are really tough. Bororo is the one that is very weak and exploited. What I think is wrong with FUNAI is that they stop Bororo from getting out. Bororo doesn't leave because Bororo is well exploited and slandered." Another Bororo, listening to the conversation, added, "Xavante is clever and Bororo is more humble, has a little more education, has learning. Xavante really demands, but we . . ." (Meruri, 1982).

The image that the Bororo have formed of the Xavante and their own self-image developed from the perception they have of how they appear to the Xavante is not in the least arbitrary. Aside from the fact that these two tribes were frequently at war, the Salesian missionaries witnessed, between 1907 and 1935, several Xavante assaults (see Albisetti and Venturelli, 1962a: 290–292). The Bororo word *Kaiámo*, a generic designation for any enemy tribe, is currently used to designate the Xavante specifically, "for being the last with whom the Bororo have fought up to the present day" (Albisetti and Venturelli, 1962a: 702). Although at present the two tribes are not formally at war, there is still plenty of friction.

The Bororo regard the Xavante as proud Indians who are capable of imposing their will, and they feel less competent than the Xavante. As the excerpts reveal, however, this is not the only image they have of themselves and the Xavante. The reflections generated by the play of mirrors become more complex as another image enters the picture: the image that the Bororo have of themselves based on their perception of how the Bororo and the Xavante appear to the Salesians and the non-Indians in general.[4]

Whenever a self-image is formed using these other parameters, the Bororo's "lack of pride" is concealed by those attributes that the Bororo believe to be appreciated by the *barae* (the "civilized"): more serenity, better manners, more education, and humility. Around 1957 two Xavante groups settled next to the Bororo living under the mission's tutelage.[5] A Bororo female's description of the Xavante's arrival is interestingly impregnated with Christian values such as modesty, helping one's neighbor, charity, and gratitude: "The Xavante arrived all naked, men, women, and children. [She mimics the way in which they speak Portuguese.] I felt sorry for those women with nothing to cover themselves. My daughter gave one of her dresses to a woman; she also handed her some soap. The old woman was happy. Then they went to the school, where the nun arranged for some clothing for them and only let them in after there was clothing for all of them" (Meruri, 1982).

But in the view of the Bororo (filtered by values instilled by the Salesians), the Xavante didn't deserve what they got. Besides never showing the gratitude the Bororo feel is due them, the Xavante do not behave morally (they steal from the Bororo), and, what is worse, they do not think rationally when carrying out the everyday tasks required to learn a living. The same woman continues:

They cut down all the coconut palms. During the dry season we also cut them down, but only a few small trees, and we use them. They cut them down just to get the coconut. They kept on begging and begging, until this guy called Pedrão (a civilized fellow) took them to the Kieria [Córrego Fundo]. And they came all the way from there to ask for things. They stole my daughter's dress, camisole, and sheets. And didn't give it back. They thought of moving them to Meriri Bai [Providência] but it didn't work. They put them in the Penori [São Marcos] and left them there until they found another place for them. And they are still there. The land they are on now isn't theirs at all; we gave it to them. And last month they almost ran us out of here. It's not that they steal the cattle, but we are a little suspicious.

The Bororo also feel outstripped by the Xavante in the relationship these two societies maintain with their neighbors. The constant presence of the Xavante in certain places that the Bororo view as strategic—for example, the banks of rivers that supply them with the highly sought after feathers used in handicrafts—poses an obstacle to the Bororo's access to these materials. By the time the Bororo arrive at these places, the farmers tell them that the Xavante have already been there and taken macaw chicks, which means the Bororo must ask the Xavante for feathers. "We ask for macaw and parakeet feathers, porcupine bristles, but we have to pay dearly for these things that they hunt right here where we live" (Meruri, 1982).

Although they occupy adjacent territories and fight over the same natural resources, these two neighboring societies have different demographic density, which is a factor that most certainly should be taken into account. According to the last poll I took, in 1986 the Bororo population comprised no more than 730 persons; the Xavante population, according to data supplied by Guilherme Carrano, was 6,123. A Bororo chief from the Garças village remarked that "the Xavante are like pigs: they reproduce a lot. Pigs give birth twice a year. It seems like the Xavante give birth three times a year" (Garças, 1982).

Making themselves visible to "the outside world" is hard for the Bororo, who regard this conspicuousness—even when attained simply through media disclosure—as highly strategic. But even here the Xavante are seen as an obstacle. In the following conversation with me, an old Bororo man got his feelings off his chest:

I like to be in a photo. Now I don't really like it anymore. I think it's because I'm getting old. But I only like to be in a picture when I have on all my ornaments, I'm all decorated, like in the old days. I really like it because I think it's good for me and for the Bororo also. It may be that someday it will be published. One time I asked a priest why the Xavante are published. He said it was because

there were many Xavante and there were few Bororo. But that is
exactly why they should publish. (Meruri, 1982)

The data on the Bororo/Xavante relationship show that, while still
retaining the mirror as metaphor, this relationship cannot be understood
only by placing two mirrors opposite one another so that one's image is
reflected infinitely. Interethnic relationships cannot be restricted to a
relationship of contrasting identities in which one ethnic group affirms
itself by the simple denial of the other, as Cardoso de Oliveira assumes.
The assessment of any group by another does not imply a univocal view,
but a set of reflecting and obstructing views and interpretations.

The univocal view entails a profile that is manifested only at a certain
level of discourse. *Boe*, the self-denomination of the Bororo, can be
translated as person, human being. In this sense, all of the non-*boe* are
left out of this category. Naturally, the Bororo appreciate their own
cultural standards more than those of any other group. This does not
keep them, however, from assessing the actions of other population
segments, their achievements, and their failures. And when the Bororo
see through the eyes of an other, assess the actions of this other, or have
to face situations in which they are not the only ones involved, images
and self-images are reflected as in a play of mirrors. This leads to constant
self-evaluation, which, in turn, leads to deliberation on the attitudes to
be assumed.

Because of the several value systems at play, there is room for the
ambiguity of the images formed from this confrontation. In this sense,
the play of mirrors is an apt image of the many concurrent values
reflecting off one another. As Marilena Chauí says, "cultural beings and
objects are never bestowed, they are introduced by fixed social and
historical practices, that is, modes of sociability involving intersubjective,
group, or class relationships, the relationship with that which is visible
and invisible, with time and space, with the possible and the impossible,
with the necessary and the circumstantial." She continues: "Ambiguity
is the form of existence of the objects of perception and of culture. These
are equally ambiguous, as they are constituted of simultaneous dimensions rather than of elements or detachable parts" (1986: 122–123).

At times the images formed are not immediately comprehensible. An
astonished Bororo woman told me that *"barae* [the civilized] likes the
Xavante more than the Bororo." She had left Meruri when she was eleven
years old and her mother had told her that the Xavante had killed a Bororo
at Providência. "The *padredogue* always please *Kaiamodogue*. The
Kaiamodogue killed priest, but even so. At first *Boedogue* wanted to kill
Kaiamodogue, but the priest didn't allow it, he said it was sin."[6] Thus,
the Bororo's view of the Xavante is constantly intercepted by another

view, be it the one that the Bororo suppose the Salesians have about these two societies, or the view that the Bororo suppose the "outside world" has of these two groups.

It would be interesting to conduct research into the Xavante's opinion of their Bororo neighbors. On a few occasions, I met the Xavante in towns near Bororo villages—Barra do Garças, Aragarças, Rondonópolis—and they never seemed to care about being in town or even encountering the Bororo. The Bororo, however, always behaved in a reserved manner in the presence of the Xavante, speaking little and constantly suggesting that we return to the village.

In July 1986, while I waited at FUNAI headquarters in Barra do Garças for a ride to the village, I held a long conversation with a Xavante who became interested in learning who I was. He said he disliked anthropologists because he believed we were "increasing the Indians. Indians are few, not a lot."[7] According to him, there are no Indians in the northeastern part of Brazil, nor in São Paulo, although the mestizos from these parts claim to be Indians. "Four hundred, five hundred years ago there were Indians. Now they are all mixed, emancipated. Anthropologists from FUNAI go there, take blood test and say it's Indian. But pure Indian, authentic, there are few: Xavante, Kayapó, those of the Xingu."

Interested in what sounded to me like an inversion of indigenous speech, I asked him to tell me what these pure Indians were like and he replied that "Indians don't have curly hair, beard, mustache, body hair. Indian is not dark skinned." At this point I spotted a Xavante standing near my informant, He had extremely curly hair, barely spoke Portuguese, and was wearing a curled cotton "tie" that they commonly wear around their neck. I asked my informant if he considered that Xavante to be a pure Indian and he answered in an irritated manner, "You didn't understand a thing!"

I asked him if he didn't think it would be better if the indigenous population were large. He said that anthropologists have increased the number of Indians, thus posing difficulties for FUNAI, and that it would be easier if it there were only a few Indians. At FUNAI facilities the Xavante do in fact behave as if they were the only Indians to qualify for assistance. For this reason, the Bororo refuse to stay at the Casa do Índio in Barra do Garças with the Xavante.

The relationship between the Bororo and the Xavante is very similar to the one described by Evans-Pritchard (1972) between the Dinka and the Nuer. It is marked by open hostility (including war), looting, and disputes for natural resources. Evans-Pritchard uses the concept of *structural distance*—a distance between groups of people in a social structure (which could involve distinct tribes, such as the Nuer and the Dinka). Since the political relationships are relative and dynamic, they must be seen "as tendencies to conform to certain values in certain situations, and the value is determined by the structural relationships of the persons who compose the situation" (1972: 137). It is the values, therefore, that limit and outline the distribution of groups in structural terms and rearrange the distance between them, depending on the situation in question. It is this *structural relativity* that allows enemy groups to become allies against another group. Just as the Nuer allied with the Dinka against the Egyptian government (1972: 130), the Xavante and the Bororo also became allies when farmers and squatters tried to invade Bororo territory.

In 1976, following the assassination of a Bororo, Simão, and a Salesian priest, Rodolfo Lunkenbein (which I will discuss in chapter 7), the Xavante were summoned and immediately joined the Bororo and the Salesians. Subsequently, they participated jointly in the boundary project of the Meruri Indian Reserve (for the Bororo's use), which was a target of threats and hostilities from farmers who had been driven off the land. This episode was handled by both societies in consonance with their historical relationship: as soon as the conflict with the outside enemy ended, the alliance unraveled, and the distance between the two tribes was reestablished in the form of hostilities and disputes over natural resources.

There was a time when the Xavante hunted in Bororo territory. Their hunting method—of which the Bororo disapproved—consisted of setting fire to the forest and then catching the fleeing animals. Warned that they should no longer hunt in Bororo territory, the Xavante went to Meruri to demand an explanation. One of the Xavante chiefs, known for his heated speech ("tough talk"), accused the Bororo of not keeping their pledge to allow the Xavante to hunt in the area in exchange for help with the reservation boundary project. He called the Bororo cowards and maintained that after Father Lunkenbein's assassination the Bororo had become afraid to conduct the boundary work on their own and had sought help from the Xavante. Finally, he accused the Bororo of having their minds set on booze—an accusation that ranks among the most frequent in relationships with the Bororo.

The Bororo chief of Meruri answered the accusations saying that the Bororo really do drink, but that drinking had nothing to do with the land issue. He refuted the accusation that the Bororo were cowardly by reminding the Xavante chief that a Bororo had died trying to defend Father Lunkenbein. He himself had been shot during the conflict, from which none of the Bororo had run. Finally, he argued that the Xavante had been highly paid for their help in the boundary work and consequently had nothing else to claim.

This episode is interesting in that it clearly shows the several images at play, and the way in which the Bororo are able to position themselves in relation to the Xavante. The Bororo in this instance were conscious of the Xavante's strength and also of the image the Xavante had of them. This image was reinforced by the Xavante chief's visit to Meruri. He began his speech by saying that in the old days the Xavante used clubs but that now they carried guns. But this speech did not intimidate the Bororo, whose reply was that guns were unnecessary, as their *bari* (shamans) were more powerful. While commenting on the episode, several Bororo assured me that the Xavante had been "amazed" at this statement.

This strategy is not new. The *bari* were feared by the Salesians in the early days and they are still respected by the missionaries. It should be noted that, if, on the one hand, the Bororo have adopted values that are not original to their society (e.g., modesty, the prohibition against stealing, mastery of Portuguese grammar, and gratitude), all of which they use to weaken the Xavante's image, on the other, it is through one of the most important institutions of their society—shamanism and the power of the *bari*—that they are able to stand up effectively to other groups, be they Xavante or Salesians.

"Poor Things"

Today many Bororo, especially in the villages connected to the Salesian mission, consider themselves "poor," in the sense of being people who have been deprived of the minimal conditions for living with dignity: their land, assistance to which they believe they are entitled (health care, education, and so on), the possibility of acquiring the goods they need, and, what is worse, their traditional culture (obliterated by more than eighty years of religious education). At Meruri and other settlements, this theme recurs every time the Bororo are visited by a "non-Indian." I heard the following complaint from a woman in Tadarimana: "We who are Indians, poor things, don't understand [the Bororo culture itself], only some of us. If the elders don't teach, we don't learn. That boy is the son of a great chief, but he doesn't understand. The son of this chief, in Tadarimana, also doesn't understand. This Kadagare is the only one; if he closes his eyes, it's over. João Caio, Zé Upe, Cirilo, Comari, Boigabe, Coqueiro, Joãozinho, Antonio, they know" (Tadarimana, 1985).

After speaking to me in Bororo, the chief rendered a Portuguese translation of what he meant to say: "I'm saying the Bororo are ending, right? Because there is no one to take care of the Bororo, there is no one to treat the Bororo, so the Bororo die, of disease, hardship, right? 'Cause there is no one to look out for us, Bororo Indians. With this also the whites make use of what belongs to the Bororo Indians" (Garças, December 1983).

The foregoing testimony shows that some Indians have an explanation for the poverty in which the Bororo find themselves—a situation that stands out whenever the questioner is a "white stranger." Because whites coming from afar, as the anthropologists do, do not belong in the category of the destitute, they throw into relief the marked differences between the state of being Indian (or "poor") and that of being white (or "rich").

In general, the Bororo blame FUNAI and government officials for this deplorable situation. Although the Bororo do not use the term "corruption," this subject often underlies their speech: "In two years, Nobre da Veiga [FUNAI's former president] ruined Meruri. Instead of sending money to the Bororo, he bought a building in Rio de Janeiro. Money was late, there was no oil, seeds, fertilizer. They were late because Veiga embezzled the money. Now it is a waste of money to plant so close to harvest time. He diverted $2,056,000 to other Indians. It wasn't lost, but it went to our brothers" (Meruri, 1982).

The Bororo's complaints are not focused on the "government" itself, but, rather, on government functionaries:[8] "The government sends stuff, merchandise, all stuff of interest for the Bororo to use. Sends full cars here in Brazil, in Mato Grosso, then when they get to the village, the merchandise disappears, cereal disappears, vegetables disappear. They arrive in the village, we get just a matchbox or a piece of candy, always a piece of candy. . . . The government thinks they have distributed . . . no, they haven't" (Garças, December 1983).

In this play of mirrors it is important to learn what image the Bororo have of their institutions and, based on this perception, what image they have of ours. The Bororo also have their own "government," their own political structure, which they consider more interesting than ours. Among the Bororo the chief is always the chief and the interlocutor is always someone known, who occupies this position after being validated by the group:

Our deal is different. The government dies, but the names of the government remain. You keep taking away the government, the government loses Antonio, today introduces a new one, tomorrow there is Chico. We don't disappear in the government. Name of the government is for all life, it doesn't end. That's how it is with us Indians, Bororo Indians. If this one is chief, he is going to die chief. When he dies, he puts his brother, a relative, that was good enough for him. Then he puts a chief in his place . . . the whites change chief every year, every month, but the name doesn't end with the man, the name of the government, name of the mayor, police deputy, it doesn't finish, it doesn't disappear. (Garças, December 1983).

For the Bororo it is really difficult to deal with an institution, be it a FUNAI agency (the closest "government" they deal with), or the federal government, where the top positions are filled by people who alternate in power. Certainly, this rotation of people hinders the possibility of establishing a serious commitment between Bororo society and Brazil's institutions.[9] Bororo chiefs always come from the same clan (the Baadojeba), and all have the same name (since each clan has a permanent stock of names). The chief holds the position for life and prepares a clan relative to take his place when he dies. The Bororo find it strange that in a clanless society, the "chiefs" come from different families (and bear different names) and can occupy the same position at different times.

If a mutual commitment were to be established between Brazil's institutions and Bororo society, the latter would in effect no longer be "poor" because the image of poverty, that is, the lack of material goods, has been incorporated into Bororo society since contact with outsiders. They know it is outsiders who establish the division between rich and poor. They do not need to be poor, since there is an institution—FUNAI—that, at least in theory, should provide what they need. But they know that if this doesn't happen, the people who hold the higher positions, not the institution itself, are to blame.

Dependency and Autonomy: Reality in the Play of Mirrors

Today the Bororo are known for their "dependency." One should understand, however, what this dependency entails, rather than simply stating it or attributing it to historical relationships of dominance.

The Bororo see themselves as dependent; they cannot picture themselves as a society without an institution interposed between themselves and national society. This does not mean, however, that they cannot criticize the agents—station masters, FUNAI deputies, and even the missionaries—who have assumed the role of guardians.

Nonetheless, from the Bororo viewpoint, outside intermediaries who represent a powerful entity and place themselves in a superior position are always present. Conscious of the power relations that are at play in local or national politics (which are hardly concerned with the interests of Indians), the Bororo (and, like them, numerous other of Brazil's indigenous societies) find themselves in the situation of having to seek legal and official protection. [10]

At any rate, the need for legal power that is exterior to Bororo society springs from a personal, collective, and territorial notion of security generated from within the relationships of contact starting in the eighteenth century. For example, though defense of territory is common to all societies, the Bororo could not defend their territory in the way

Otávio Kodo Kodo, a Bororo nurse's aide. *Sylvia Caiuby Novaes, Perigara, 1971.*

capitalist society would define this type of defense: land plotting with the aid of specific instruments, demarcation, ratification, notary registration, maps and land titles, and so on.[11]

Under Brazil's Constitution, the union owns the territory occupied by the Indians, who in turn hold tenure of said land. If, on the one hand, the law created by the whites has been designed to defend the land occupied by the Indians, on the other hand, it has introduced an ambiguous situation for the Indians, because the land is and yet isn't theirs. This situation is clearly described in the following excerpt: "The land belongs to the government, government gave it to Indian, so he has to hold it [defend it]" (Garças, 1982).[12]

If today defense of the land depends on the white world's intricate bureaucracy, which the Indians are unable to control, this defense, in Bororo opinion, should be entrusted to the government (the actual owner of the land) or to "educated" Indians (a point of view shared by the elder Bororo), who, as a result of time spent studying, should be able to understand the codes and procedures involved.

In the Meruri area there are those who know how to read, know how to study, to talk; so when someone asks how many meters

there are there, how much can be demarcated . . . they all gonna
talk like this: Oh! Like so and so! Like I know, oh! this hectare
business, like this and that. (Garças, 1982)

We, with us it's the following, because, like he said, it used to be
that we didn't have education, we didn't have the paper and this
and that, like the white man. What are we going to do, right? We
don't have any strength. That is why the white man does this to us.
We don't have support, any comfort at all. Because the white man
when he comes like this, right, he eats it whole, this I guarantee.
(Garças, 1982)

The Bororo once knew how to defend their land, and, on several
occasions in the eighteenth century, joined government troops to attack
enemy tribes. Between 1739 and 1751, Antonio Pires de Campos, a
young man also known as Pai-Pirá (chief of all), active in the region
of Camapuã, Mato Grosso, waved aside the whites' collaboration, took
it upon himself to lead a Bororo crew, and charged the Kayapó, the
Bilreiro, the Guaicuru, and the Paiaguá, taking them captive. With the
aid of his native warriors, for ten years or more Pai-Pirá committed
"awesome barbarities" among the hostile Indians (Mário Neme, in
Hartmann, n.d.: 2).

Hartmann quotes a document that demonstrates that it was possible
for the Bororo to defend their land and to serve the "civilized" in
exchange for food and strategic alliances:

In 1757 a royal order expressly designated the Bororo as escorts for
settlers heading for new areas "because since the Bororo are the
bravest Indians of these hinterlands it will be very useful to have
them on our side." They were not slaves, because the law guaran-
teed the Indians freedom and because settlers would eventually use
them to drive out other tribes. Nor were they free men, "because
they will not stop wherever necessary and they will cause endless
turmoil in this hinterlands." They should be reduced to the condition of the *sepoys* that serve in the troops of our East India, thus
gathering them into a Militia. (Hartmann, n.d.: 5)

Most certainly, the Bororo were not always victorious, nor were they
always on the non-Indian side. Hartmann's notes reveal the Bororo's
need to establish alliances with the whites:

In 1733 the Count of Sarzedas, governor of the Captaincy of São
Paulo, urged on by strong recommendations to annihilate the

Paiaguá, incited Lieutenant General Manuel Rodrigues de Carvalho to proceed "fighting the most ravaging savages of Cuiabá, particularly the Bororo." A systematic campaign is how the special magistrate, João Gonçalo Pereira, described it in his report to the general, adding that in the village of Cuiabá, in 1735, he came upon "Bororo who had been imprisoned unjustly, in the most treacherous manner, because at the time settlers invaded their land, they had surrendered peacefully, without ever making war on the civilized." (Taunay, 1949: 298, in Hartmann, n.d.: 1)

Thus, the need for "official" land protection emerged from conflicts that date from the first half of the eighteenth century. This need was strengthened in the late nineteenth century by the founding of the Teresa Cristina and Isabel colony (1886), which shortly after was turned over to the Salesians.

The Salesians capitalized on regional conflict to make their presence among the Bororo indispensable. They worked to establish themselves as the only protection against wars with and raids by enemy tribes as well as against rapidly spreading epidemics. The Salesians, as well as the people of the region and government troops, witnessed the courage shown by the Bororo in defense of their land. "The Bororo terrorized the region and rebuffed any friendly contact with civilization. In our encounters with them, we found only savages with a thirst for hate, revenge, and bloodshed, *defending inch by inch, with indomitable courage and fierceness, their land, which white men wished to conquer* (Colbacchini, 1939, my emphasis).

We know that, starting in the sixteenth century, the Jesuits used protection as a tactic to keep the Indians along the coast under their control. These Indians were essential in the initial phase of the settlement program, both as farm labor and as suppliers of food. Starting in the Duarte da Costa administration (1553), the so-called Just Wars were declared against the "pagan Indians" to intensify the program of religious instruction. The Jesuits tried to make the Indians see that, by adopting Roman Catholicism and remaining in the villages, they would be safe from the settlers' raids. Though the Jesuits were able to protect the Indians against attacks, their actions also successfully destroyed the foundations of tribal autonomy.

The Salesians worked no differently among the Bororo. The first missionary to direct the Teresa Cristina colony stated, "Those dear Bororo were convinced that, with the missionaries, they would be safe from raids and also protected by the government" (Balzola, 1932: 194). In my opinion, this statement and the Bororo testimony transcribed earlier are evidence that dependency, one of the most prominent traits of the

Bororo's self-image, derives not only from historical conditions but also from their having incorporated what was wanted of them: submission.[13]

It isn't only in these terms that the Bororo reveal their dependency, however. Since the establishment of the colonies in the late nineteenth century, the Bororo have had to assimilate *labor* as a virtue to be attained, but they have been regarded as indolent and lazy by both missionaries and government officials, as well as by non-Indians who live in the region. "The first and greatest enemy against which the missionaries had to struggle was the Indians' innate indolence and their disgust with respect to work, due to a great extent to the blazing heat and the prodigality of the land" (*Boletim Salesiano*, October 1902).

From this perspective, the Bororo started to depend on "outsiders" (missionaries or FUNAI staff) to undertake the work of subsistence— especially farming, considered by non-Indians to be vital to the community. The subjugation to labor, a concept that was absolutely alien to this society, led to a state of true dependence as a result of the intensified reductions in fishing and hunting areas. Farming thus became essential to survival. Furthermore, the subjugation to labor was established in accordance with a plan—the chit system—that further emphasized dependency. The following testimony illustrates the process in a dramatic way:

In 1955, 1956, 1957, we were subject to the white man's orders. We were the farmhands and the whites were the contractors, farmers. They received money, the national currency, and we received chits. As a result, we lost the spirit of self-reliance, the ability to fight for ourselves. Because of this, our community doesn't flourish. We couldn't buy anything in the shop inside the mission itself with the ticket [chit] we received, although it sold everything to everyone else. And the priest didn't sell anything to us. We got used to grabbing a cup and walking up to the priest's window to get coffee and green corn. The shop was full of rice the Bororo had harvested, but the Bororo didn't have the right to a single bag. An abundance of rice and corn to be exchanged for the chit. The rice mildewed and was burned; that was in the days of Father Bruno. These memories of the past haunt us and now we are completely dependent on the priests. We have remained like slaves and we've got used to this life of poverty. The rice, manioc, and cornfields have had it. Even with the Bororo working, even with them on the Bororo's backs to make them work. They began to eat manioc mush with beans. There wasn't even squash. That's God's punishment. (Meruri, January 1982)

As paradoxical as it may seem, in the Indian societies, *labor* (as conceived in the capitalist model) is frequently what generates *scarcity*. Although the Bororo no longer live under the chit system, the same situation of scarcity, hunger, and poverty is sometimes observed today. Despite the agricultural "projects" undertaken by both FUNAI and the missionaries, periods of famine succeed one another.

Scarcity results from several factors. First, intensive farming, without the necessary soil corrections, leaves the land exhausted and unusable. The crop, harvested all at once, is immediately sold, often without any provisions being made for that year's consumption. This does not happen with their own gardens, where the Bororo plant manioc, papayas, bananas, yams, and the like, which grow year round. But work on the large cash crop plantations draws most of the men away from work in their own smaller-scale gardens. This also prevents them from engaging in other subsistence activities, such as hunting and fishing. The money made from cash crops is mostly spent on items that have nothing to do with subsistence.

In analyzing the situation of the Kraho, which in many ways is similar to that of the Bororo, Azanha states,

> Limited—since 1943—to a territory too small for the demands of a society founded on hunting and gathering combined with rudimentary root crop plantations (which are, therefore, *culturally* adapted to the arid climate of the *cerrado* [savannah]), the Kraho have had to seek alternatives that allow them to deal with the limitations of their territory and the scarcity of game while allowing them to maintain their society *just as it was* . . . According to FUNAI staff, the "Kraho problem" was hunger. They did not realize that this "problem" was the *alternative they chose* in order to remain Kraho. As became evident, the Kraho went hungry because they refused to follow a policy of *"production intensification"* (Sahlins), which would force them to *increase the necessary time* to attain the subsistence level but with the cost of their lifestyle. (Azanha, 1985: 3, original emphasis)

I believe that, apart from the factors Azanha mentions, the failure of these projects is also associated with the alternative non-Indians visualized for the Bororo: the possibility of a labor organization based on a capitalist model, that is, an alternative that paradoxically seeks to match these people's image of Indians—the so-called primitive communism—in other words, a notion on the part of "civilized people" that the productive activities of native societies are conducted as collective projects.

In reality, every time the Bororo engage in subsistence activities, the work is done by domestic groups, that is, by individuals who share a house. The same applies to hunting, fishing, harvesting, and the so-called backwoods plantations. The collective effort occurs only when subsistence activities are associated with the ritual context (fishing and hunting on the occasion of a funeral, for example).

Although worked by families or domestic groups, household planting is determined by the village chief. Corn cultivation, for example, cannot be carried out without the chief's traditional guidance, which entails the fundamental task of having the crop cycle coincide with the ceremonial cycle associated with this specific type of planting. The chief's traditional role tends to lose its importance with the introduction of new farming techniques, especially in the large monoculture farming projects (see Serpa, 1988: 319).

Nowadays, many of the projects that Indian societies conduct with borrowed money are limited to large collective, mechanized plantations that require a collective effort for organizing work, a type of work to which the Bororo have never adapted. Furthermore, these projects require a field leader to represent the collective interests, skillfully "call the men to work," and afterward divide the crop between the various families (which is complicated).

This is a *job* that implies either the existence of a *boss* (and salary in exchange for work) or the existence of a "community," in the sense that the fruit of the collective labor will be divided among all in equal shares. This is far from the reality of Indian societies; thus, they are drawn into a second degree of dependency: when an outside element takes charge of collective farming activities.[14] This economic dependence on an outside agent that stimulates and organizes productive activities, like political dependence, sprang from the historical circumstances of contact, and the Bororo had to incorporate it into their society.

Economic dependence affects the daily lives of most Indians in Brazil today. While analyzing the "failure" of the Guarani trading activities in São Paulo, Maria Inês Ladeira writes,

> The Guarani sell the handicrafts they do not use, the hearts of
> palm they do not eat, and labor on jobs that, in general, they would
> not do for themselves (in construction and on farms) to obtain
> money. Their herds and fields are small because they *support*
> themselves with them and, to them, *life* is not a sellable commodity. That is why they do not sell their produce (occasionally, they
> undertake small-scale trade with immediate objectives—they sell a
> chicken, trade seeds for clothes, a radio, or an animal). In the same
> way, they are not "successful" businesspeople in issues relating to

their own land. Because they maintain a symbolic relationship with Life (land, food, work, etc., depend on transcendent strengths), they always do "business" on a small, marginal scale. (1981: 13)

Conformity, or compliance with practices imposed from outside, is often the only way to survive and, thus, can frequently be transformed into a resistance strategy. Conformity does not, however, imply the complete abandonment of original practices. The Bororo, for example, continue to hunt and fish for their own use, and numerous families tend backwoods plantations, from which they extract part of their sustenance. Work on collective and mechanized plantations is not equally accepted by all Indians, and often it is unfeasible (among the Bororo, for example, a simple ritual can render it impossible).

Today the Bororo face a twofold issue. The fields are necessary not only to provide nourishment, but also to provide the image of a group of people who work and use the land they occupy. The widely held view that there is "a lot of land for only a few Indians" who don't exploit it "properly" (i.e., according to capitalist models) must be corrected. Farming activities that demand intensive labor during certain time periods (the planting, cultivating, and harvesting seasons) must be coordinated with traditional ritual activities, which are essential to the group's ethnic survival. The Bororo know that, without farming, physical survival is extremely difficult. They also know that they will never be able to devote themselves to farming to the extent that their white neighbors do, since they do not intend to give up Bororo culture. Thus, the Bororo seem marked by the "tragic awareness" to which Marilena Chauí refers: "In its original sense, as revealed in Greek drama, tragic awareness does not struggle against an unavoidable destiny, but, on the contrary, discovers the difference between *that which is* and *that which could be* and, for this very reason, *violates* the established order. Even so, it does not reach the point of constituting another social existence, imprisoned in the instituted scheme" (1986: 1788).

Serpa shows that, "even in an environment of major changes, the material and ideological bases of traditional Bororo farming are in full operation in that indigenous area (Tadarimana)" (1988: 288). Even the distribution of produce from FUNAI project plantations is handled through traditional channels of distribution, which allows the Bororo of Tadarimana to proceed in a traditional economic order, despite plans to modify the tribal economic sphere, as provided for by FUNAI (1988: 302).

Within an integrationist and developmentalist conception, the Bororo can be seen only as *dependent*—an image they incorporate into their discourse about themselves in relation to non-Indians. This incorporated image in effect transforms itself into an *attitude*, as they begin to act in a dependent manner, be it in economic terms—to take on proposed/imposed plans—or be it in terms of defending their territory. This dependence is transformed into a resistance strategy, given that the conditions for Bororo survival have been completely altered. If, as I have suggested, through its various agents—SPI, FUNAI, missionaries—Brazilian society has worked to dominate and control the Bororo, leading them to a condition of submission, now they live within this situation as a condition of dependence that neither the missionaries nor the FUNAI staff can fight. And it is precisely in the spheres in which these agents have been most active—health, labor, housing—that this dependence has become most explicit.

Nowadays the Bororo's autonomy basically manifests itself through their traditional activities—such as funeral ceremonies, which halt all "productive activities."[15] Through these rituals the Bororo violate the order that is intended for them and stand resolutely against "harmonic integration into the national society." If, as Chauí suggests, autonomy involves having self-determination to think, want, act, and feel (1986: 36), then this autonomy is manifested in a way that deeply shocks our ethical and moral patterns. Even when the Bororo harvest an abundant rice crop, the main crop of these "projects"), which permits them to stockpile beyond their needs, the money received from the sale is rapidly "burned," be it on the purchase of "superfluous items" (watches, tape recorders, etc.), or on extraordinary group binges. My interpretation is that they acquire products that are foreign to their culture by means of an activity (tilling fields mechanically, which is foreign to them) that yields foreign produce (rice has been introduced in their culture). The *"burning"* of the money painstakingly earned with the "sweat of their brows" is essential to allow the Bororo to continue living as Bororo, a people who cannot be beguiled into "improving their lifestyle," much less into redeeming themselves through labor.

5.
The Salesian Missions in Mato Grosso

Notes on the Sources

The Salesians' publications provide most of the available data on the history of their missions in Brazil, particularly in the state of Mato Grosso. The anthropological literature mentions the Salesians' influence over the Indians, but does not delve into the specifics of their work. Even those researchers who have studied the Salesian missions in Brazil—for example, Claudia Menezes (1984)—have ignored the implications of missionary activity for the incorporation of attitudes and values resulting from the close contact between Indians and missionaries. Menezes analyzes the economic and social changes imposed on a segment of Xavante society by the Roman Catholic Church. The church forced the integration of the group into a new production mode within the framework of power relations created by interethnic contact while simultaneously recovering the ideological dimension of the process (1984: 2). As Menezes affirms, however, her study does not demonstrate the contamination of the relationship between the Xavante and the Bororo caused by missionary teachings (1984: 15). Furthermore, although she presents a comprehensive summary of the structure of the Salesian congregation in Italy, her treatment of the history of the Salesian missions in Mato Grosso is extremely superficial. She restricts herself to describing religion, education, health, and the political and economic organization of the São Marcos mission at the time of her fieldwork, between 1977 and 1981.

Since it was not Menezes's objective to "provide a cognitive portrait of the ethnic ideologies drawn by the Xavante about non-Indians, as well as those drawn by the Salesians and other agents" (1984: 522), we do not know how much the missionaries actually influenced Xavante thought. Nor can we know how much influence the Xavante exerted on Salesian thought, or how much resistance there was as a consequence of this coexistence. There is also no comparison with the Xavante villages that are not subordinate to the missions, which hinders comprehension of

Salesian actions and the reactions of these societies to the several agents with which they have been forced to coexist.

The Salesians have published the three-volume *Encyclopedia bororo*, by Albisetti and Venturelli (1962a, b; 1976); a book by Father Luis Marcigaglia (1955); and the letters of the Rev. Luis Lasagna (1985).

The diary of Father Giovanni Balzola (1932) is an extremely interesting work. In it he recorded nearly twenty years of work among the Bororo—from 1895, when he was appointed director of the Teresa Cristina colony, to the late 1930s, when he died in the missions of the Upper Negro River, where he had been transferred in 1914.

Other information about the missions can be found in periodicals published by the Salesians. The more interesting are the *Bollettino Salesiano*, published monthly in Turin since 1870, and since 1902 in Brazil as the *Boletim Salesiano*. These periodicals include a special section entitled "News from the Missions," featuring excerpts of letters written by missionaries working in different countries. They are extremely detailed accounts of the life of the Salesians in Brazil and are of special interest because, rather than sociological studies, they are records of the missionaries' perceptions of the culture of the societies with which they have established contact.

As we read these newsletters from a twentieth-century perspective, detaching them from the context of the time, they may seem merely anecdotal reports. Apart from the fact that we are learning about events that occurred almost a century ago, however, the confrontation between the two cultures undeniably involves events that, seen from the outside, seem absurd. In any case, these documents allow us a clearer understanding of the period when foreign priests coming from Europe (primarily from Italy) settled in the region near Cuiabá, then the frontier of nineteenth-century Brazil.

In the Kingdom of Satan: The Formation of an Image

> In '"objective" history, the "real" is never anything but an unformulated signified, sheltered behind the apparent omnipotence of the referent.
>
> —Barthes, *The Rustle of Language*

Before establishing themselves in Mato Grosso, the Salesian missionaries already had a very precise image of the societies in which they intended to be active. This representation was built on input from several sources: the prevailing ideas of the late nineteenth century, the "mission" that the Roman Catholic Church claimed for itself at the time, and the specific ideas spread by the work of the Reverend Bosco in Turin and, later, in other Italian cities.

The program designed by the Reverend Bosco, the founder of the Salesian congregation, drew on his work with street children in Turin, his hometown. His program (which nowadays would be oriented to needy children in large cities), worked to introduce these children into society by offering them professional training. For this purpose he and the Salesians founded "Oratories," where they educated youths to work in different trades and also, naturally, to become priests. Later, the Salesians founded schools and businesses.

Although they were reassigning their objectives and their "mission" to native societies located a great distance from Europe, the Salesians planned to use the same strategy designed for their work with Turin's street children. After all, were not the "savages" similar to children in that they were naïve and unprepared and needed someone to guide them along the true path?

Through dreams and premonitions, the Reverend Bosco formed a picture of the savage societies to which he would send his clergy. The "rescuing mission" of the Salesians was also based on data they had obtained from regional inhabitants and government troops, who, starting in 1880, had tried to halt Indian attacks. These reports confirmed for the missionaries the possibility of using the same strategy designed for the street children. According to the numerous accounts available to them, the Salesians would certainly have to deal with ferocious Indians ready to attack.[1] For all they knew, the Indians were little inclined to work, as indicated by the "intense poverty" in which they lived; were deprived of the true Christian values, such as brotherhood (as shown by the conflicts in which they got themselves involved); lacked modesty and true morality; were naïve to the point of believing in superstition and a great variety of creeds; and lacked a true civic spirit that would guide them to Brazilian citizenship.

This image of childlike Indians who disliked work and who were possessed by the devil allowed the Salesians to legitimate their power relationship with the Bororo. "To see the kingdom of Christ triumph over the kingdom of Satan" (as Father Balzola wrote in his diary, 1932: 196) meant precisely to exert a civilizing influence.

These are the more important elements that contributed to the Salesians' image of the societies where they intended to be active. It was a preconceived image that resulted from a "scrutiny" of which those under observation were unaware—an omnipotent image that the Salesians, whose self-image mirrored that of civilization intent on defeating barbarism, attributed to the Bororo as a concrete reality.

After living with the Indians, the missionaries slowly began to reformulate their preconceived image and to review their strategies. According to their own records, however, the Salesians maintained the image they brought from Europe in those first years in the mission. The following testimony by Father Colbacchini (1939) after thirty-four years of living among the Bororo demonstrates this point:

> In the beginning, this was the situation of the Salesian mission: completely isolated in the middle of overexcited savages engaged in barbaric and cruel fights in the heroic, painstaking defense of their rights, consumed with hate for the white man and full of desire to avenge an appalling past . . . far from every resource, exposed to all dangers, lacking quick means of communication, for although the telegraph line was only a few meters away, the closest telegraph station, near General Carneiro, was a whole day away on horse-back! It was then, as it still is, the most forward post of civiliza-tion, where pilgrims of Christ had settled their vanguard in the great and never-ending hinterland!

After half a century of religious education, other factors—the regional political context, which became more defined after the 1950s, and the Salesians' adoption of the church's new procedures almost a century after the arrival of the missions in Brazil—affected this image of reality. It is this preconceived image, however, that allows us to understand the early years of missionary activity. It was this image that allowed the Salesians to exert their true vocation. On landing in Brazil, they intended to engage in civilizing work, with the aid of all the modernity that was introduced in Europe in the late nineteenth century, except that in Brazil they clothed modernity in the Christian values that the priests were to disseminate. "The Lord is always admirable in his endeavors! Poor and humble missionaries put up their tent among barbarians in the immense and distant jungle, but that is the beginning of a great work of civilization and faith" (Albisetti, 1944: 7).

This craving for civilization and progress that characterized Europe and the New World in the late nineteenth century was revealed in numerous world expositions. There wondrous mechanical arts were exhibited next to the mystery of exotic lands, whose inhabitants had stagnated in the early days of the history of humankind. The opening of the Suez Canal in 1869 brought the Far East closer to Europe. To the Europeans, the canal offered a greater possibility of knowing the East and conquering it, through military force or by systematically acquiring knowledge that, while restoring forgotten languages and cultures, could situate itself well beyond the modern Orientals' mental perception of their own past.[2]

Certainly, the indigenous societies of South America were an important part of this exotic scenery that Europeans sought to monopolize. To the Salesians, the Bororo represented not only a possibility, but also a great motive for missionary action. The Salesians' daily contact with this society in its concrete reality rather than as an image forced them to reformulate the strategies that guided missionary work. This work, which is still under way, involves Bible instruction and the introduction of Christian morality, the incorporation of work as a value, and the awareness of true citizenship.

Missionary practice implied a systematic study of the Indian language, and several Salesians—Albisetti, Colbacchini, Venturelli, Ochoa, and Bordignon—wrote about Bororo culture. Many of them realized, from personal experience, that the Bororo lived in a different way, though in an organized world with its own values and organizational principles. It is not my intention to criticize the abundant ethnography produced by the Salesians. My purpose is to emphasize that, moved by their desire for knowledge of Bororo culture, several missionaries tried to learn the language and grasp the ideas and values that guide Bororo society. Many Salesians devoted themselves principally to writing about it. They thereby opened up the possibility of identifying themselves with Bororo culture.

Thus, beginning in the 1970s, many missionaries took upon themselves the task of *incorporating* (in the literal sense of embodying) this alien culture and making it understandable to the non-Indian. Knowledge brings people together and promotes union. It allows the recognition of oneself in the other and the possibility of identifying in another culture the traces of a religiosity that, if further developed, could better express the signs of God's will.

We have more data on the 1890–1945 period than on the 1945–1970 period. Beginning in the 1970s, the intensification of land conflicts in Mato Grosso placed the relationship between the Salesians and the Bororo back in the headlines of both large city newspapers and Salesian newsletters.

Beyond the World's End: The Salesian Saga in the Late Nineteenth Century

> At the end of the world there is a river; beyond the river there is a hill; behind the hill is Cuiabá.
> —Marechal Floriano Peixoto in Marcigaglia,
> *Os Salesianos no Brasil*

The Salesians, led by Father Lasagna, arrived in Brazil in 1883. The trip was sponsored by Pedro II, emperor of Brazil. The priests first established themselves in Niterói, a city located across Guanabara Bay from Rio de Janeiro. Two years later, they founded a school in São Paulo, which they named Liceu Coração de Jesus (Marcicaglia, 1955: 19, 37).

The government of the state of Mato Grosso had been trying since 1889 to move the Bororo of the São Lourenço Valley to the military colonies of Santa Isabel and Teresa Cristina. This problem-ridden initiative was led by Lieutenant Colonel Antônio José Duarte.

In 1894 the Salesians decided to set up missions in Mato Grosso. For this purpose they organized an expedition lead by the Reverend Lasagna, who had been installed as bishop by Pope Leo XIII. When Bishop Lasagna arrived in Cuiabá, the governor of Mato Grosso, the Reverend Manoel Murtinho, "transferred to him a colony of Bororo Indians, called Teresa Cristina, in which the governor kept a relatively useless garrison" (Marcicaglia, 1955: 52–53.) The cooperation between state government and missionaries was established as soon as the Salesians arrived in Mato Grosso. A government act on April 19, 1895, appointed Father Giovanni Balzola director of the colony. According to his diary, the colony housed around three hundred Bororo and twenty-five soldiers. In June 1895 he established himself at the colony. As director of the Teresa Cristina colony, Father Balzola relied on the support of Governor Murtinho, who offered him the services of his troops in the colony. "I have troops that serve me, but their commander cannot always leave them at my disposition" (Balzola, 1932: 34).

Before leaving Cuiabá, the Reverend Lasagna circulated throughout Brazil a letter in which he requested support for his program of assistance to the Indians. The following excerpt shows how this *mission*, in the literal sense of the word, was seen by the Salesians in those days: "For the love of God, who commands us to have pity on the poor and the abandoned, for the love of humanity so decayed and degraded in the form of these unfortunate Indians, lest it not be a heavy burden on you to protect the Salesian missionaries, who, with admirable self-denial, devote themselves to the salvation of the unfortunate" (Marcicaglia, 1955: 54).

One of Father Balzola's first acts in the colony was to introduce farming. The Bororo, however, who had never held a hoe, ran off to hunt whenever they saw an animal in the woods. In fact, Father Balzola claimed that they had "no inclination for work." By resorting to subterfuge, such as promising to take them to see their brothers far away, though, he got the Bororo to prepare the land for sowing corn, rice, beans, and sugarcane. According to the missionaries, this was accomplished only because of Father Balzola's perseverance.

It is hard to understand such obstinacy and perseverance in a young man (he was then thirty-four years old) newly arrived from Italy. But patience and perseverance are the main characteristics of missionary work. Obviously, Father Balzola was able to maintain these qualities only because of the rescue mission the Salesians had embarked upon. The following excerpt from his diary demonstrates the Salesians' belief in the possibility of introducing a future to the barren present: "Meanwhile, the nuns continued to work to start up the mission. We considered it a true apostolic field, where the destruction of Satan's kingdom should lead to the triumph of Jesus Christ. Then Jesus began to reign among us, and the Virgin covered us with her maternal mantle. In the midst of a life of privation and sacrifice, joy reigned because we considered ourselves the founders of a work of religion and civilization" (Balzola, 1932: 39).

The priests encountered many hardships while establishing the missions. The Indians, used as they were to hunting and fishing, customarily roamed from place to place in their traditional territory, never settling in one place. This wandering rendered the missionaries' work unfeasible. The Indians needed to settle in one place so that they could receive the education the priests intended to give them. Otherwise, how could the children be introduced to formal education? How could the adult Indians be kept from attacking farmers and other civilized people whom they saw as enemies? How could religious education be instilled in them? How could clothing be provided to cover their nakedness?

To keep them in one place, however, be it the mission or the colonies, implied supporting the entire population. It also implied agricultural production, to which the Indians contributed little, particularly when game and fish were still abundant. The Bororo would remain in the mission for a while, but soon leave for the woods to live as they had always lived. One of the priests' major tasks was literally to gather their flock. "Now I lack men and horses to prevent them from scattering and, when they run away to the forest, to gather them is a great deal of trouble. However, it is necessary to take on this task of providing work and food for these poor Indians" (Balzola, 1932: 33–34).

The first demarcation of the Teresa Cristina colony dates to this time. It comprised twenty-four thousand hectares measured by an engineer and granted by the government of Mato Grosso to the missionaries, with the right to use the fruits of the Indians' labor, and eighteen thousand hectares of land owned by the Salesians themselves (Balzola, 1932: 33–34). Also dating to this period is one of the first records of an activity that affected Bororo society in a very negative and painful way: the consumption of alcoholic beverages: "In the evening they lighted fires and shot their rifles. The men drank rum" (1932: 52).

Little by little the missionaries came into contact with Bororo society and recorded its traits, which they meant slowly to eradicate. They focused especially on the role of the *bari*, the Bororo shaman who hastened the death of terminally ill tribesmen. When faced with an incurable illness, the *bari* hid the head of the dying person with a fan and, behind the fan, placed wads of cotton into the ill person's mouth and nose, thus suffocating him or her.

How could the word of God be spread and given credence among the Indians? What type of strategy should be adopted to allow the Indians not only to accept the presence of the Salesians among them but also to see them as examples of true values indispensable to their own style?

Father Balzola relates that he once heard screaming in the Teresa Cristina colony and knew that an Indian was about to die. He ran to the dying man's house and saw that he was still breathing. Father Balzola asked everyone to leave and to stop screaming. He bathed the dying man and gave him a drink of water. "He lived another five days. I used this fact to reveal to everyone the *bari*'s shrewdness. From then on they always viewed me as superior to him, and they always came to me to find out whether the sick person was to die or to get well" (1932: 38).

The disputes between the missionaries and the *bari* continued for years. They did not interest the Bororo particularly. They were willing to let the priest keep all his beliefs, but they wanted the *bari* to keep his as well. During the 1904 flu epidemic, the *bari* was away hunting. In his absence, the priests dispensed medication to the Bororo and assured them that in two days they would be healed, which in fact they were (Balzola, 1932: 146). This episode increased the Bororo's confidence in the missionaries, although it did not diminish their appreciation for the *bari* and for the beliefs with which he was associated. For example, when the Bororo hunted an animal that the *bari* had to exorcise before it could be eaten, they hauled the game fifty kilometers to the *bari*'s place. On one occasion, Father Balzola offered to bite the meat and do whatever the *bari* would do. The Bororo replied, "When we are baptized, we will eat everything with you" (1932: 146).

In 1905, malaria killed many in the Sagrado Coração mission. One night, Father Balzola found all the Indians seated around the *bari* Totó, who, in an alleged communication with the souls of the dead, asked for an end to the epidemic. At the end of the session, the *bari* blew heavily over the head of each Indian to "rid him of the disease." Father Balzola spoke immediately, "I will not commend you to Our Lord (God) nor I will give you medicine, because the *aroettowarari* Totó has sent away the disease" (Balzola, 1932: 54). But the Indians asked the priest to remain, and he heard the explanation for the epidemic from Totó himself: before giving birth, a mother had had a premonitory dream, according to which the birth of her son would bring the death of many Indians; she should therefore sacrifice her son, which she had not done.

Father Balzola seemed to recognize that he was assimilating some of the *bari*'s behavior: "During that epidemic, I found myself embarrassed many times. They consulted me, they asked me a thousand questions, and *I had to use terms as ambiguous as those of their bari to keep my authority*" (Balzola, 1932: 155, my emphasis).

Father Balzola was not the only one to argue with the Bororo *bari*. In 1907, Father Antonio Colbacchini, who replaced Father Balzola in one of the missions in Mato Grosso, wrote a letter to the Reverend Rua in which he described a win against a *bari*. Father Colbacchini had been called to help an Indian boy who had been bitten by a snake and was very ill. The women stood around the youth screaming and pulling their hair, as is their custom. Father Colbacchini made a small incision in the wound and gave the boy potassium permanganate. Later he wrote, "Rev. Dom Rua, you may believe that I prayed and I made him pray a lot, because we were really concerned that the poor savage be healed so that everybody would be persuaded that our remedies were more efficient than their sorcerers' superstitious treatment: the more so as everyone was saying that the sorcerer had no power against snake venom" (Colbacchini in *Boletim Salesiano*, April 4, 1908: 67).

In a village on the Mortes River three Indians died within a short time. Father Balzola was told that because of these deaths some families were planning to move into the mission. He said, "The Captain Father has medicines and keeps us from dying. Although I made them see the advantages of medicine, which experience would confirm, nevertheless, I tried to correct their exaggerated concept, *referring all power to Our Almighty Lord, that is, God: the Lord of life and death*" (1932: 149, my emphasis).

If, however, the Indians came to the missions looking for shelter from enemy attack and for better help during epidemics, this increasing concentration of people spread disease. In 1913, for example, after arriving at the Sangradouro mission, eighty-eight Indians came down with flu and scarlet fever.

An increasing number of Indians flocked to the missions, seeking the medical care dispensed by the Salesians. At the turn of the twentieth century, the Bororo were hit by epidemics of flu, scarlet fever, German measles, malaria, and yellow fever. Death and life, health and sickness— between these extremes the missionaries obstinately struggled to carry out their mission. In so doing they tried not only to guarantee their presence among the Bororo but also to instill in them, little by little, a belief in new values and the incorporation of new habits. As time passed, they became more and more convinced of the "reality" of the image of Bororo society they had created, as well as of the legitimacy of their mission.

Michel de Certeau shows that belief is made possible through the recognition of an otherness and the establishment of a contract. He refers to Benveniste, who sees in the word *creed* the typical function of certain economic obligations—a sequence that relates donation to remuneration (De Certeau, 1985b: 192). He who believes, that is, the believer, acquires a *right*; thus, in this sense, his creed has the value of a receipt. But belief does not necessarily lead to action. It is more closely related to the possibility of salvation, of efficient reciprocity and therefore a successful undertaking. From this comes the need of an immediate coincidence between that which is given—for example, medical assistance or the need to have faith in God—and that which is received—that is, the possibility of cure and salvation (and the priests seemed aware of this fact, as the reports show).

When disseminating creeds, however, primordial values are not replaced, nor can a past be erased that is meant to be abolished in the present. "In many ways, a credibility network upholds the conventions that regulate social communication. Between partners, it also makes for all kinds of games, manipulations, and surprise effects with these conventions (making believe that one believes, or that one does not, etc.)" (De Certeau, 1985b: 195). This game of simultaneous alternatives coupled with the possibility of manipulating different belief systems has been a constant in the Bororo-Salesian relationship.

Europeans took Indians to Europe to work as slaves and to exhibit them as curiosities (a practice that started with Columbus), but they also wanted to expose them to "true" civilization so that on returning to their homeland, they could share what they had seen and learned. In 1898, Father Balzola traveled to Italy with three Bororo men. His travel plans included a religious art show for which he had the Indians prepare several artifacts. They remained in Italy for five months. To Father Balzola, this was also a way of recruiting new missionaries, raising funds for missionary work, and demonstrating, by means of the Indians' behavior, the Salesians' difficulties in civilizing "that terrible tribe" (1932: 64). The Indians' interest in the trip would probably would have lain in getting to know the land from which the priests had come so as to better understand them and manipulate them.

Father Balzola brought several young priests back from Italy, including Antonio Colbacchini, who later published a monograph on Bororo society. On arriving in Rio de Janeiro, however, Father Balzola learned that the Salesians had been removed from the Teresa Cristina colony, allegedly for not having accomplished anything in three years of missionary work (1932: 64, 70). The Salesians may have been withdrawn because, in 1898, following the election of a new president, who "needed to tend to relatives and political friends who coveted the colonial administration for themselves, he went as far as dismissing the Salesians" (Marcicaglia, 1955: 103).

For the first time the Salesians saw themselves in a situation where they had to face the hardships not only of dealing with the Indians, but also of having as sole motivation their mission, whose objectives did not always coincide with those of the government.

Images and Reality: The Establishment of the Missions

In December 1901, fourteen missionaries chose a new location for the colony, in a place called Barreiro, near Ribeirão dos Tachos, eighty leagues from Cuiabá. Under Father Balzola's direction, this colony, which was renamed Sagrado Coração de Jesus (Sacred Heart of Jesus), was located in a place called Meruri, where it remains today (Marcicaglia, 1955).

The Salesians waited for eight months until the first Indians came. In August 1902 (Balzola, 1932: 106), the Bororo, led by Chief Joaquim, approached the mission camps, where Father Balzola greeted them in Bororo: "We have established ourselves in this place with the sole objective of doing you good and defending you against persecution by the civilized—if you behave properly" (1932: 109).

The mission as protector from both enemy tribes and the "civilized" and as provider of health care was the Salesians' most effective instrument. This role involved a concrete reality manipulated from the start.

Eight years later, from Father Colbacchini, Father Balzola learned about the Bororo's interpretation of this encounter. During the eight months before they came to the mission, the Bororo closely watched the priests and nuns from a distance, until finally deciding to go to the mission and decide whether to allow the missionaries' to remain or to kill them. According to the *bari*'s prediction, the missionaries were good people, different from other civilized people with whom the Bororo were having numerous conflicts. Three months after the first contact with the missionaries, the Bororo returned to settle at the mission.

A new village was built comprising twenty houses erected on the four sides of a square; in the center the men's house (*baito*) was constructed. About 140 Indians came to live in the village, which could not house more because of "the lack of means" (Balzola, 1932: 129, 139).

The happy missionaries summoned all their patience to coexist with those "slaves of the devil" over whose territory the kingdom of God was yet to rule (Balzola, 1932: 110, 196). This image of "slaves of the devil"

Bororo village next to Salesian mission, early 1900s. *Courtesy Inspetoria Salesiana de São Paulo.*

recurs often in the testimonies of all Salesians from that period and certainly encouraged them to continue their work.

Little by little, the priests were able to get clothes and to have the Indians wear them. Whenever relatives of the Bororo living in the missions came to visit, however, the inhabitants of the mission followed the Bororo tradition and gave their clothes away as gifts to the newly arrived. The displeased missionaries once more found themselves having to deal with naked Indians.

Although Father Balzola knew about the distribution of goods in Bororo culture—a system linked to the *mori* (reciprocity, in the broad sense)—he stated that he would not interfere because it "in one way pleased me because it would train them *to practice charity*, but in others, it was unpleasant to me because thus I saw them in the same miserable condition" (1932: 140, my emphasis). This passage is interesting because it clearly translates a view of the world and interpersonal relationships— the *mori* system among the Bororo—into a category that is typical of the Christian world: charity. Certainly, it becomes much easier to accept the other's world after it is translated.

The newsletters of the time publicized Salesian missionary work and showed the advances of and the obstacles to its early implementation. The reports were also a faithful portrait of European ideas about the world's tropical regions and the tropical climate's influence on people. In October 1902, the year in which the Portuguese edition of the Salesian newsletter was first published, an issue of the *Boletim Salesiano* featured the following considerations: "The first and greatest enemy against which the missionaries had to fight was the Indians' habitual idleness and their aversion to work, due mostly to the blazing hot climate and the lush exuberance of the land" (p. 21).

In 1906, the Salesians founded a new colony, which they called São José, on a farm on the Sangradouro River. This property was purchased from a farmer named Joaquim Manoel dos Santos shortly before his death, and on it the Salesians continued their work under the Reverend Malan's guidance. The new colony attracted "several Bororo from São Lourenço and the Vermelho River, as well as civilized folk seeking further development."[3] The colony comprised twenty thousand hectares, five hundred head of cattle, one hundred mules, fifty sheep, and a brick house. Several families transferred from Tachos (Sagrado Coração colony) to Sangradouro, so by 1908 the number of Indians had grown to 67; in 1910 the number reached about 300, and in 1911, 374 (Marcicaglia, 1955: 36).

These figures are quite high for Bororo villages and result from the initiatives of missionaries who tried to attract the largest possible number of Indians to the missions—as many as could be supported by agricultural production, which they continued to increase. In 1904, in a letter to Father Balzola, the Salesian superior in Turin, the Reverend Rua suggested that the missionaries start planting cotton as well, so as to provide clothing for the Indians who flocked to the missions. It was so difficult to obtain clothing that a special outfit was reserved for mass: "We would make them wash themselves well, we would give each one a shirt that they would wear for the mass; then they would give it back to us" (Balzola, 1932: 139).

When he realized that the Indians were going to increase the population of the missions, the Reverend Rua wrote, "Consider the possibility of bringing them together, a few at a time, until a village (*paese*) of five hundred to six hundred people has been formed" (Balzola, 1932: 121).The image of the *paese*, which the Salesians intended to establish, came directly from the Piedmont villages (in a spatial representation that had no counterpart in Indian territory nor in the Brazilian territory of Mato Grosso). The missionaries were obviously interested in increasing their flock. The numerous attacks of "civilized" men against the Bororo further hardened their resolve. To rid themselves of the Bororo, the invaders resorted to all sorts of measures, including adding strychnine to spring water, thus poisoning several Indians (Balzola, 1932: 90).

In 1900, the Bororo attacked a few families and slaughtered those of Manuel Inácio and Clarismundo Gonçalves for having invaded their land. Gonçalves pursued the Bororo to avenge the deaths of his family, but the Bororo managed to escape. Upon being informed of the attack on the Gonçalves family, Father Balzola told Captain Joaquim, "Captain Joaquim, you should not have done that. Had you been with us no one would have dared touch you: away from us something might happen to you. Call them back" (Balzola1932: 131).

To protect the Bororo from attacks by the "civilized" settlers as well as by other tribes such as the Kayapó, the Salesians relied on official support. This support consisted of money to buy gifts for the Indians, and troops sent upon request. Several times the government summoned the Salesians to intervene in conflicts between whites and Indians, for example, in 1907, when the Reverend Malan led an expedition to terminate the struggles in São Lourenço. Protection was offered in exchange for the "good behavior" of Indians, who were expected to act like "good Christians."

Security and goods distribution were always important elements in the missionaries' approach to the Bororo, regardless of the time or the religious order. The Jesuits had adopted the same strategy for dealing with the coastal Indians, as shown in this excerpt from a letter from Brother Pero Correia to the Jesuit Provincial in Lisbon, written from São Vicente in 1553: "The easiest way to reduce the Indians to the civil and religious cause involves not giving them anything they need, unless they have converted to Christianity; they all say they want to be Christians but they should be able to distinguish some material advantage in this process" (Azevedo, 1976: 381–382).

When they arrived at a village, the Salesians gathered the Bororo and distributed the gifts provided by the government, assuring them that peace would be established. At one of these meetings, usually held after mass, the priest told the Indians he was there "to invite them in the name of His Excellency, who holds you in high regard, to live in harmony with the white people, who will no longer do you any harm if you behave like gentlemen" (Balzola, 1932: 240). In another village, after the distribution of gifts such as knives, fabric, and fishing line, the same admonition was repeated, followed by a request from the government: "to leave the nomadic life they had until now and live like Christians and, most of all, not to attack the whites" (1932: 241).

The security offered by the missions was constantly evaluated by the Bororo. In 1907, a village on the Araguaia River with a population of some eighty Indians was completely wiped out by whites. The episode benefited the missionaries, as noted by Father Balzola: "But many times

God brings forth good from evil. On learning this news, our Indians in fact were more and more persuaded that staying close to the missionaries would free them of misfortune" (1932: 183).

Also in 1907, the Kayapó murdered two Bororo women who had left the village to pick fruit. While some of the Bororo pursued their enemies, others found it more prudent to head south, where their stronger tribesmen were located (Balzola, 1932: 193). The missionaries decided that the best way to protect the mission, which was about to be emptied of its Indian population, would be to request official support in the form of troops to protect the Indians and the colony.

By coming to the defense of the Bororo, the Salesians undermined their initiative and placed them in a position of total dependence. It was easier for the Salesians to defend Bororo society (especially with the support of government troops) than to have the Bororo beyond their control, arming themselves to fight their enemies or retreating to ever more remote places. From Turin, the Reverend Rua wrote Father Balzola the following words of advice: "But be alert not to let them have firearms" (Balzola, 1932: 119).

Father Balzola identified a bonus for the missionaries in the dependency relationship: "Those dear Bororo were persuaded that, being with the missionaries, they not only would not be persecuted by the civilized people, but they would also be looked well upon and protected by the government" (1932: 140).

Salesian Catechism

The discussion thus far clearly demonstrates that the Salesians' religious education of the Bororo had three basic objectives: (1) to introduce Christian morality; (2) to introduce work as a virtue; and (3) to teach civic principles that would entitle the Bororo to claim Brazilian citizenship. The strategies adopted by the missionaries to accomplish these objectives involved, as we have seen, providing the Bororo with proper health care and, with the help of government troops, protection against attacks from other Indians and non-Indians.

In a publication on the Salesian missionary presence in Brazil (*Missões salesianas em Matto Grosso*, 1912: 17), the order's missionary work was assessed in the following manner:

Religious education without morality cannot subsist in practice. The missionaries work with families and individuals slowly to eradicate the numerous, erroneous, and immoral superstitions of their tribe. Some superstitions threaten the extinction of the race. For example, a Bororo woman kills a newborn who does not match the dream she dreamed the night before giving birth. Another example is the religious ceremony called *bacururu*, during which relatives perform the repugnant task of boning their dead. This ceremony ends in a saturnalia at which several attendants commonly die.

Concerning work as a virtue to be attained, the priests were equally emphatic: "The notion of work and its due compensation is instilled little by little. This notion offers them a vigorous stimulus to overcome the hereditary traditions of indolence and to conquer the noble and productive work habit" (*Missões salesianas em Matto Grosso*, 1912: 21).

Why, then, did the Salesians commit themselves to an undertaking that involved cultures so unlike any in Europe and that required so much sacrifice on the part of the missionaries? They answered this question themselves:

> The church needs these cultures, even though it may not identify with any of them. It needs them to express its own faith, to deepen the message of salvation it delivers, and to reach concrete decisions concerning Christianization.
>
> It strives to understand them, incorporate them, assume them, and promote their enhancement and transformation, to the point of collating them in accordance with and, at the same time, in opposition to the present situation, in its constant endeavor to obtain an answer in its openness to God and the Gift of itself to its brothers. It tries to build a civilization of love among men. ("A formação dos Salesianos de Rev. Bosco—Princípios e normas," n.d.: 37–38)

Thus the introduction of Christian morality implied performing work that aimed at gradually replacing certain practices that were considered erroneous or superstitious with more "civilized" customs. Action was necessary that would adapt the Bororo reality to the Salesians' and the Roman Catholic Church's image of human society as taking as model the image of Jesus Christ.

The church's view of native culture as "incorrect," and therefore as subject to correction and completion, was first expressed in Pope Gregory I's instructions to Saint Augustine in 601. To convert pagans in England, the Benedictine missionaries were to "make the best of the elements of the pagan culture that could be incorporated into Christian life." It would be impossible to eradicate at once all of the horrors of those uncouth spirits (Azevedo, 1976: 367). This is the model of human society that propelled Salesian action and that, at the same time, created the greatest obstacles to their missionary work.

**The Salesians have educated Bororo youth from the beginning of their
missionary work.**

One of the customs the Salesians most tried to change was the Bororo
funeral rite. Anthropologists who know Bororo culture and read Father
Balzola's diary are deeply impressed by his description of the Bororo
funeral (1932: 36–37). What is most impressive is precisely the fact that
this ritual, which Father Balzola described almost a century ago, is still
carried out in the same exuberant manner that has such an impact on
those who see it for the first time.

Clearly realizing the importance of this ritual in Bororo society,
missionaries have always tried to act with caution. From Turin, the
Reverend Rua wrote to Father Balzola advising him on these matters:
"As to some customs that these savages have, particularly in relation to
their dead, try not to disdain them, but (taking as an example what the

church would do in the old days, among the pagans) try to sanctify them if the customs do not harm soul and body" (Balzola, 1932: 120).

In the old days, the washing of the dead person's bones, which preceded their ornamentation, was done twenty days after death. In the same letter, the Reverend Rua suggested that they wait a little longer to avoid the risk of infection. Of all of the changes that the missionaries tried to introduce into the funeral ceremonies, this seems to be the only one that was definitely adopted by the Bororo. Today they wait about two months before decorating the bones of the dead. But they claim that this longer wait is due to their taking medications, which delays decomposition.

I suspect that, because the Bororo engage in numerous rituals involving the entire village population between the burial, decomposition, and bone ornamentation, they accepted this longer interval between the two phases because it allowed them to devote themselves more extensively to their rituals. A longer mourning period allows them to justify their absence from activities introduced by missionaries and FUNAI agents, such as farming and school attendance, all of which are suspended during this period.

The New Generations and the Expectation of an Image Turned into Reality

At first the Salesians viewed the Bororo funeral as a truly diabolical ceremony, a cult of horror. Epidemics killed many Indians; consequently, funeral ceremonies appeared to be unending. In 1905, immediately following an epidemic, Father Balzola wrote, "I thought I might succeed in hindering them from performing those horrible mortuary ceremonies that are their custom and my hopes lay in the fact that, since there were about thirty dead, although they might want to resume their custom, they would tire: but it was not so" (1932: 157).

Modifying Bororo funeral practices required not only putting a stop to all those rituals, but also having the Indians bury their dead in Christian cemeteries. The priests decided to build a small cemetery for their own dead on one side of the main road and another cemetery for the Indians on the opposite side. At first, the Indians conducted their traditional rituals and then buried their dead in the cemetery. Father Balzola's diary shows a photograph of the first cemetery built at the Sagrado Coração de Jesus mission, "where the Bororo abandoned their barbarous rites and rest in the shade of the Cross" (1932: 192).

Father Balzola tried to convince them to no longer touch the bones in order to avoid contamination (1932: 153). The missionaries hoped that, following the example of the Salesians, the next generations would end their macabre rituals. "Those were horrifying things but by now we could not stop them; so the best hope was the new generations" (1932: 149). The missionaries felt that other phases of an individual's life cycle, like death, should be commemorated with the proper Christian ceremonies. Thus, in the early twentieth century, the missionaries started to celebrate baptisms, weddings, and, later, first communion.

The Bororo's early adoption of Christian names exemplifies how they accepted some elements introduced by the missionaries without necessarily letting go of their original culture. It was usual among the missionaries to baptize children with names that honored Salesian or Roman Catholic personalities. Following the death of Pope Leo, for example, one child was named Leone Pecci; after the death of Pope Pius another child was named Pius (Balzola, 1932: 132), a name that is still very commonly found among the Bororo in Meruri. In 1908, one boy was named Michelle Rua (the name of the Reverend Bosco's successor) and another, Giovanni Bosco (Balzola, 1932: 232). These names, which were added to those assigned to Bororo children at traditional naming rituals, were employed mainly by the Salesians in their relations with the Indians.

Gradually, mass became part of the daily life of the mission and was attended by the Indians who had been baptized. Father Balzola tried to convince the Bororo to substitute their chants and rituals traditionally held before certain hunting trips with regular mass attendance. "Instead of trusting your *aroe, bope,* etc., and singing your songs all night to secure the protection of the souls and of the devil, come to the holy mass, which I will celebrate very early tomorrow morning" (1932: 125).[4] One evening, after the Indians returned to the village carrying fruits picked by the women and thirty-eight wild hogs and one hundred tapirs killed by the men, Father Balzola took advantage of the situation to assure them that "all that abundance had come because in the morning they had gone to mass" (1932: 127).

The Bororo in fact started to attend mass, not as an activity that substituted for their rituals, but, as they had done with respect to medical care, because they considered it strategically important. This model is present in several aspects of the relationship between the Bororo and the missionaries since the late nineteenth century. Instead of substituting one culture for the other, the model calls for the gradual incorporation into routine practice of those aspects that the Bororo consider strategic. And what was strategic from the Bororo's point of view? Why did they accept certain customs or alien elements into their culture? Looking at this model solely from the perspective of the domination that the Salesians certainly exerted over them does not seem to answer the question.

It is impossible to contemplate the incorporation of these alien elements without looking at them as trade elements in the relationship between the Bororo and the Salesians. The Salesians propose a belief in Christian values, in an all-powerful entity who dictates everything that happens to people, provided there is *faith*. This is not only the Salesians' proposal, but basically their *mission*. The viability of this mission depends on how the missionaries position themselves in relation to the Bororo and to what extent they are accepted by the Bororo.

As de Certeau demonstrates, creed is differentiated from contract "by the role of the partners and their inequality. . . . We have to presume a guarantee from the other, in other words postulate an other (a person, a fact, etc.) endowed with power, will and knowledge that can mete out 'retribution'"(1985b: 199). Azevedo made a very similar statement about the religious education undertaken by the Jesuits in the sixteenth and seventeenth centuries: "cultures have maintained their autonomy, that is, their own identity and mutually exclusive institutional support, although one may exert over the other a certain degree of supremacy; but the subordinate, or the receiver, remains sufficiently independent to select the cultural material that is presented to it and incorporate it in a creative manner" (1976: 381).

If we think of the relationship between the Salesians and the Bororo as one of mutual dependence, in which each one of the segments appears to the other as a looking glass, perhaps the notion of *strategy* to which I have been referring (and which, incidentally, applies to both segments) becomes clearer. For the belief in God and religious education to become a reality among the Bororo, it is not enough that the Salesians proclaim the existence of God. Missionaries of all orders who have worked with different Indian societies are well aware of this fact. They have to devise certain strategies to assure the accomplishment of their mission. From the point of view of the Indian societies, certain "advantages" (or "strategies," from the point of view of the missionaries), such as health care and protection from enemies, are assured only if they somehow correspond to what the missionaries expect of them. In their relationships with the missionaries, the Indians constantly evaluate the extent to which this correspondence jeopardizes their own culture and its most characteristic values. Strategies imply, calculating the cost-benefit ratio, an analysis that is not exclusive to western capitalist civilization:

> The guarantor is seen as the reflection of the characteristic features of the believer. He functions as his mirror . . . in order to presume its object (the expected thing) believable, belief must also presume that the other, in a certain sense, also "believes" and that he considers himself obligated by the gift given to him. It is *a belief in the belief of the other* or in what he/one makes believe that he

believes etc. A belief of the other is the postulate *of* a belief *in* the other. (De Certeau, 1985b: 199–200, original emphasis)

The Salesians' relationship with the Bororo was thoroughly governed by punishment and reward—exactly like the parent/child relationship. Once when he had to leave the mission for a while, Father Balzola "admonished the Indians to behave and promised gifts to the best behaved" (1932: 185). As long as obedience did not challenge their own convictions, the Bororo agreed, for example, to attend mass, but did not eliminate their own chants and rituals; they accepted the medicine dispensed by the priests, but did not forgo the *bari* or their beliefs in the *bope*; they took Christian names, but did not stop using their Indian ones.

In some ways, the incorporation of cultural traits that did not replace the original ones was restricted to the adult members of Bororo society. Thus, the missionaries placed great hope in the younger generations, which, at boarding school, became socialized in a culture different from that of their parents. Baptized Indians and pagan Indians, Indians who had received their first communion, children of couples joined in the sacrament of matrimony, all of these were categories invoked by the Salesians to demand "Christian behavior" from the Bororo. If these categories were not incorporated by all the Bororo in the same way, they were certainly used to justify their attachment to "old customs." "After we are baptized we will eat everything," they said, to justify the need for the *bari* to bless certain foods.

The missionaries themselves recognized that, although the adult Bororo were not opposed to Christian education, they continued with their "diabolical and savage" customs (as Balzola and Colbacchini would so often write), which, the priests knew well, had to be tolerated with only minor reproach. There was one thing, however, on which the missionaries would not relent: the fruit they believed they would reap in the new generations brought up under their influence and according to their own example. To the missionaries, these new generations were true mirrors of their endeavor and proof not only of the feasibility but also of the legitimacy of their mission. The Salesians assumed that, having abandoned the stupidity of their parents' customs, these generations no longer fit preconceived images of the future: they were the concrete reality of a society, the result of systematic disciplinary influences, for which the Salesians spared no effort.

A typical case involved a youth named Romano, educated in the Salesian boarding school, and who had received his first communion and was very religious. The youth's father wanted him initiated, according to the Bororo custom, in the *aije* ceremony (the male initiation ceremony). Father Balzola denied the father this right: "I told him no, that his son had no more need of that foolishness." Unresigned, the father took his son to the village, where Father Balzola spotted him and four other boys, all of them naked and painted with annatto dye, ready for the ceremony. "I showed my dissatisfaction with the fact that they were painting those youths who had already been baptized." In response, the *bari* and the captain apologized and told the priest that that ceremony was absolutely necessary. They also told him it was the last time they would hold an *aije*. Father Balzola could do nothing but hand a piece of soap to each youth so that, at the end of the ceremony, he could wash himself (1932: 169).

The missionaries refused to be discouraged and continued actively to prepare new generations. Before giving first communion to a group of young men, Father Balzola asked them to promise "to remain always with Him and to swear that they would not go back to their barbarous customs, which displeased their Lord Jesus and their Holy Mother Mary" (1932: 175). Although first communion was solemnly celebrated to the sound of Gregorian chants and religious marches performed by an Indian band, before long the priests heard the chants of Bororo getting ready for hunting the following day, and once again the Salesians had to surrender to the imperative of the two coexisting cultures.

Introducing a new culture implied having the Indians incorporate all of those representations of western culture seen as "natural" by those who were born into it. The one that seemed most gratifying to the priests was the incorporation of *modesty*: "but as soon as they advanced into civilized life, and had for some time that with which to cover themselves, they felt very strongly the natural force of shame, and they suffered when they had to appear without a rag on them" (Balzola, 1932: 180).

The success of missionary activities among the Bororo was announced in the major urban centers in the early twentieth century, when, after displaying their results, the Salesians raised money to continue and expand their activities in other native societies. In 1908, the federal government organized a great exhibition in Rio de Janeiro to celebrate the centennial of Dom João VI's initiative to open Brazilian ports to international trade. The Reverend Malan, an enterprising missionary and the main disseminator in the great urban centers of information about missionary work, saw in this exhibition an opportunity to both raise funds for the ongoing work with the Indians and publicize missionary work. For some time the Salesians had noticed the Bororo's interest in music. They realized that this could be a promising area of investment, one that could be more easily contraposed to the unending rituals that the Bororo insisted on holding.

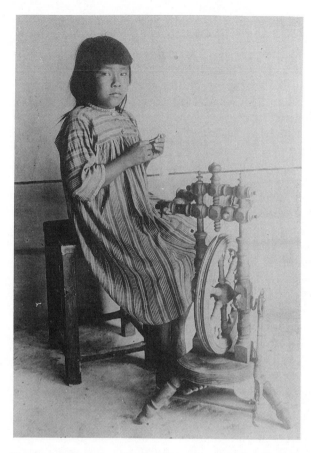

Bororo girl with spinning wheel. *Courtesy Inspetoria Salesiana de São Paulo.*

Toward the end of 1907, the Reverend Malan, the Salesian inspector, had the idea of sending the Bororo boys who played in a band at the Sagrado Coração de Jesus colony to perform in Rio de Janeiro. The band rehearsed with the master tailor of the school in Cuiabá, who was also a proficient music teacher. The youths were dressed in uniforms and excused from farming. The trip was financed by the government. Of the twenty-one Bororo musicians who left with the Reverend Malan for the exhibition in Rio de Janeiro, three died along the way, confirming the *bari*'s predictions. Despite the missionaries' concern with the Bororo's reaction to these mishaps, however, they sighed with relief when they realized that the Indians did not hold them responsible for the epidemic that raged through Rio de Janeiro (*Missioni Salesiane*, 1925: 76–80).

In the hall of the Rio de Janeiro Geographical Society, the Reverend Malan held a conference in which he told about Bororo society and the work conducted by the missionaries. He tried to demonstrate to Rio society that missionary work was an initiative shared with the government and prompted by its interest in ending the numerous conflicts involving whites and Indians in Mato Grosso, which had worsened since the late nineteenth century.

He emphasized those Bororo qualities that were similar to Christian morality, such as the propensity to chastity, the lack of rapes of female prisoners, and the lack of cannibalism. He also told his audience, however, that the Bororo lacked a basic tradition, on which the missionaries focused: work. Hunting, fishing, and harvesting were not seen as activities that deserved to be called work; thus, the Reverend Malan emphasized the need to introduce the Indians to farming and discussed the difficulties related to this activity. He mentioned the need to educate youths capable of mastering skills, workshop crafts such as carpentry, mechanics, leather tanning, sewing, and the like. He demonstrated the need and opportunity for missionary action among them: "They are highly superstitious, eternally childish individuals with regard to most of their customs. They would be fortunate if their lives were touched by the notion of a true God and knew how to love the Brazilian nation, whose destinies, limits, and enchantments they do not know."[5] By illustrating the efficiency of missionary action, he also illustrated the dissipation of a culture and its replacement by another, viewed as superior:

> In three distinct centers, if you should visit them, you would see hundreds of former Indians gathered around priests, lay brothers, craftsmen. They spontaneously devoted themselves to the cultivation of the friendly land, they tended the cattle, and little by little became aware of notions such as property, goodness, the Christian and social constitution of the family, care of their offspring, whom we educate nearby, right there in the backlands, in unique schools. They form a pleiad of new Christians and new citizens.[6]

The Reverend Malan also seemed conscious of the misconduct of the colonization effort and the pacifying role that the mission should assume:

> It is a just crusade, a holy crusade undertaken to restore a peace that we were the first to disrupt; to restore a liberty that we, the civilized, first violated; to restore a homeland that was stolen from them in the name of a false conquering, libertarian civilization. A

homeland, Sirs, of which they are the true owners, and which they
will know how to love, defend, and elucidate, if only we teach
them this, through our effort and example.[7]

The conference with all its inherent contradictions ended with an
animated and passionate speech that was frequently interrupted by the
applause of a "select" audience. In this national exposition of 1908, at
which "the brand new Republic superseded similar events of the old
Empire in terms of grandeur, neoclassicism, and flaring lights" (Foot
Hardman, 1988: 95), savages were turned into talented musicians. The
high point of the conference was the performance of the Bororo band on
the final day.

The Bororo's presence at the national exposition in Rio de Janeiro and
Reverend Malan's speeches clearly show the missionaries' image of
these societies. Furthermore, they demonstrate the potential, perceived
by the Salesians, for restructuring "savage" society using new points of
reference that in some way annihilated previous ones. This was a vision
of a new society emerging as a result of Salesian activity.

How could the Salesians create credibility for the new society they
introduced in 1908? How could they produce a "multiplying effect" so
that, by collecting funds, missionary work in other societies could be
made reality? According to de Certeau, two traditional sources ordinarily yield the elements that lend credibility to any apparatus: politics
and religion.[8] The success of the Salesians derived precisely from the use
of elements from both sources. It was through religion, Bible instruction,
and the introduction of faith that the missionaries, with government
support, intended to transform the Bororo into true citizens. As the
Reverend Malan remarked at the end of the conference, these new
citizens had incorporated the true values of citizenship even more than
had the "civilized" themselves, who, moved by anti-Christian principles of greed and violence, introduced not only unrest, but also raging
bloodshed that killed Indians and non-Indians alike. This new "reality"
of Bororo society was revealed through the young musicians who
performed in Rio de Janeiro and proclaimed, by means of their presence,
a society that abided by those values that supposedly distinguished a true
citizen: work, Christian morality, love, and honor for the homeland.

From Image to Simulacrum

In analyzing the difference between *simulation* and *representation*,
Baudrillard states that the latter rests on the principle of equivalence
between sign and reality. Furthermore, he proposes that, even when the
equivalence is entirely Utopian in nature, it still constitutes a fundamental axiom. Simulation, however, is based on the radical denial of the

sign as a value rather than on the principle of equivalence: "As representation tries to absorb simulation, interpreting it as false representation, simulation envelops the whole building of representation as simulacrum." Images are constituted through successive phases that he enunciates in the following manner:

> it is the reflection of a deep reality
> it masks and denaturalizes a deep reality
> it masks the absence of a deep reality
> it has no relation to any reality at all: it is its own simulacrum.
> (Baudrillard, 1978: 6–7)

It is important that we understand these concepts in the history of relations between the Bororo and the Salesians, that we understand how *representation* and *simulacrum* appear in the constitution of the images that each of these population segments has of itself and of the other. At certain times in the history of this relationship, that which is representation to one is experienced as simulacrum by the other, and vice-versa.

Father Colbacchini, who replaced Father Balzola as head of the Sagrado Coração de Jesus colony, had a keen interest in Bororo culture

Father Giovanni Balzola, first director of the Salesian mission to the Bororo. *Courtesy Inspetoria Salesiana de São Paulo.*

and wrote the first monograph on this society. He was also extremely conscious of his *mission*, that is, the need to convey true Christian values to the Indians. He often wrote to his superiors to tell them how the Bororo had finally transformed themselves into a tame flock. The following excerpt is from a letter to the Reverend Rua, dated November 1907: "It is beautiful and pleasing to see them disciplined and quiet, obeying the sound of the bell that calls them to mass or to work, and sometimes in the middle of a game see them suddenly break and run with smiling and uninhibited faces to hear the voice of the missionary who is calling them.[9]

Anyone who reads Colbacchini's monograph immediately realizes the distance between the ethnography he draws and the content of the letters he wrote to his superiors. How do we explain this lack of coincidence in Colbacchini's perception about Bororo society as expressed through such different images? Which one of them is illusory? Which is the perception that more closely mirrors reality? Certainly both, since they are not mutually exclusive. While one describes reality as it is perceived, the other inscribes into reality the sense intended for it.

In his monograph, Colbacchini tried to trace an "objective" portrait of this society in the form of notes taken by one who observed and reported data, without necessarily interpreting them. In his letters to his superiors, Colbacchini tried to show not Bororo society as it was, but the "reality" to which this society had arrived as a result of missionary action, that is, a society portrayed in terms of a future that already presented itself as if inscribed in a present from which the "past" (i.e., tradition, the "original" Bororo culture described in his monograph) had certainly been banned.

There is a great difference in content between the letters written by the Salesians in the early twentieth century in which they describe their missionary work among the Indians and, principally, among the new generations they were creating, and the letters of José de Anchieta, a Jesuit missionary who dealt with the same subject in the mid-sixteenth century. Anchieta seemed more aware of the difficulties of substituting one culture for another and more conscious of the resistance posed by indigenous culture. After reporting to his superior the method employed for the boys' religious education, he comments, "Nonetheless, we fear that when they reach adulthood, as a result of the will of their parents or the turmoil of war—which they say frequently occurs and breaks the peace between them and the Christians—they will go back to their old customs" (Anchieta, 1900: 51).

Anchieta and Colbacchini also held different opinions about how to treat the Indians, not with respect to the treatment itself, but with respect to the relationship. Colbacchini wrote to the Reverend Rua, "it is not force, nor violence, nor fear that will convert them, my dear father; they rebel against all this. What conquers them is the charity of Dom Bosco. . . . They are still barbarous and savage but they have delicate hearts."[10] Anchieta, however, states, "They will be converted out of fear, much more than through love" (1900: 51).

This does not mean that the methods employed by the Jesuits and the Salesians were essentially different, or that the three centuries that separate their missionary work explain any differences between them. On the contrary, there were great similarities in the guidelines adopted by the different orders of the Roman Catholic Church at different times and in relation to the several Indian societies with which its missionaries came into contact. Jesuit missionaries abided by systematic discipline in their work with the Indians. Although they did not forgo disciplinary methods (such as boarding school, punishment, and rewards), Salesian missionaries adopted the life of the Reverend Bosco and his dedication to street children as a model for action. Through his charitable attempt to provide professional training, the Reverend Bosco tried to create the possibility of a new life for those children.

A very significant episode was the tearing down of the men's house—the *bai-mana-gejewu*, or *baito*—one of the mainstays of Bororo society. This is where the male council congregates and holds most of its traditional rituals. Father Colbacchini described the tearing down of the *baito* in a letter that was later reproduced in the *Boletim Salesiano*.[11] Located in the center of the village, this house was viewed by the missionaries as a "temple of the devil." "It caused us great pain to realize how popular the house was, and we ceaselessly prayed to God that He please take it from our mission soon."[12] In a paper presented at the Congress of Scholars on Latin America held in Hungary in 1988, Chiara Vangelista stated quite appropriately that "in the missionaries' view, the circular shape of the Indian village, at the center of which the meeting house is located, symbolizes a culture closed in on itself—a horizontal culture lacking a hierarchy of social and spiritual values through which man could relate with heaven" (1988: 4).

The missionaries had to wait about twenty years—from 1895, when they started the mission, until 1914, when this episode took place—to be free from this important community center, which was replaced by those run by the mission, such as a school or church.

Two days before the feast day of Our Lady of Conceição, "the inspiration came upon me to propose that the Indians tear down that shack." In his letter, Father Colbacchini says he does not remember the reasons he gave the Indians (we know excerpts of several of the letters were published in newsletters in Italy and later in Brazil, which were

censored at the authors' request). But Father Colbacchini saw indica-
tions of the Indians' approval of his initiative and, when asked directly
about the request, the Indians replied, "'Yes, yes, we do. Down with the
house of the demon!' Deeply touched by their enthusiastic reply, I called
out strongly: 'If you really want to deliver yourselves definitely from the
demon, take machetes and pickaxes, knock down that center of all evil
and set it on fire.'" Where the men's house had stood a heavy cross was
raised as a "permanent symbol of Christ's triumph over Satan."[13]

The tearing down of the men's house was a milestone in the accomplishment of the Salesians' objectives. It symbolized the victory of the
sacred not simply over the profane, but also over the truly diabolical. The
erection of the cross in the village center by the Bororo was symbolically
important as well, because in 1914, the twenty families still considered
pagan were baptized. Finally, the division between Christian Indians,
who gathered at the church, and pagan Indians, who met in the men's
house or "the realm of the *bari* who consulted his *bope* every day" was
eliminated. Transformed into a heap of debris, the *bai-mana-gejewu* no
longer appeared to the Salesians as a counterpoint to the house of God
and a place where "mournful" pagan chants were sung simultaneously
with the sacred chants that came from the holy church.[14]

This episode, which took place twenty years after the missionaries'
arrival, can be analyzed from two perspectives. From the point of view
of the Salesians, the destruction of the men's house and the subsequent
erection of a cross in its place effectively *represented* the accomplishment of a goal for which they had fought so tenaciously. It represented
the victory of Christ over Satan, and the accomplishment of the Salesians'
mission. To the missionaries, there was an equivalence between the
"cross" (the sign) and its referent, that is, the reality to which it was
directed (Christ's overwhelming truth).

From the point of view of the Bororo, there was not necessarily an
immediate equivalence between sign and reality. To them, the cross as
a sign did not have the *value* that the Salesians attributed to it. In a
certain sense, the cross was its own simulacrum, a dereferentialized reference. Or, as de Certeau writes, "The simulacrum is what the relationship of the visible to the real becomes when the postulate of an invisible
immensity of Being (or beings) hidden behind appearances crumbles"
(1985a: 153). The cross stands where it is erected; its presence is visible
and in some way the values it stands for are gradually incorporated, not
to the extent or in the way the missionaries intended nor in detriment
to an earlier reality. The Bororo rebuilt the men's house far from the view
of the priests and continued to hold their rituals—principally the funeral
ceremonies that so horrified the Salesians—there.

The Salesians Assess the Fruits of Their Labor

Beginning in 1915, the news of missionary activity among the Bororo published in the Brazilian and Italian editions of the Salesian newsletter grew sporadic. Studies on Bororo culture conducted by some priests have deserved special mention, as for example the several steps taken in the production of the *Bororo Encyclopedia* by Albisetti and Venturelli, the publishing of Father Colbacchini's *I Bororo Orientali*, and the creation of a research center in Campo Grande. In the eyes of the missionaries, the Bororo seemed to have been "pacified," as shown by Father Colbacchini's letters. The darkness in which those savages had been enveloped was illuminated by the lights of civilization and progress. Other clearly visible symbols attested to these transformations: "Nowadays one is pleasantly surprised to see electric lamps shining like friendly light-houses in the dark of the night, as if heralding the proximity of an advanced post of civilization and progress" (Albisetti, 1944: 11).

Beginning in 1915, the Salesian mission in Brazil started to invest in other regions, and this new phase made the pages of the congregation's newsletters. In 1915, Father Balzola was transferred to the Negro River region, under the pope's instructions to work among Indians who, between the sixteenth and the seventeenth centuries, had lived under the Carmelites' supervision.

The expansion of missionary work depended on money. It was precisely with the objective of raising money for the missions that the Reverend Malan traveled to Rio de Janeiro, São Paulo, and Minas Gerais in 1917. To raise money and publicize missionary work, he either conducted private conferences on religious education or visited educational institutions and parishes. In the cities through which he passed he received cash donations, sacks of coffee beans, blankets, and complete outfits of clothing for the Indians. These outfits were sewn by students in exclusive Catholic schools in São Paulo, such as Sion, Des Oiseaux, and Santa Inês. In addition, the *Correio Paullistano* and the São Paulo aristocracy held the Pro-Bororo Festival, in the luxurious Trianon salons, which yielded 6,107,800 reals. In Juiz de Fora, evangelical workers created the Pro-Bororo Vestiary—an association of aristocratic ladies who gathered once a month to finish sewing yards of material "almost always generously donated by shop owners, nonsellable leftover fabrics that in this case were very useful, or yet obtained in some other way."[15] In this "Way of the Cross" undertaken by the Reverend Malan, the Bororo were invoked as calling cards of missionary work, that is, as an illustration of that which the Salesians could achieve among other indigenous tribes through adequate sponsoring.

In the 1930s, moved by the conversion to Christianity of the Bororo in the Barreiro River region, the Salesians decided to start working among the Xavante on the Mortes River. The slaughter of two Salesian priests, Father Fuchs and Father Sacilotti, by the Xavante in 1934, postwar hardships, and the difficult access to the Xavante area caused the Salesians to settle in Xavantina, close to the Mortes River in 1948, when they started their work with the Xavante (*Bollettino Salesiano*, 88 [November 1964]).

What fruits were the missionaries actually harvesting? What kind of criteria did they adopt to assess their work among the Bororo? The following description of the Bororo was featured in a Salesian publication: "So it was that, as of the second half of last year, any wayfarer landing in the Barreiro River colony was met by the spectacle of 245 Bororo divided by family into distinct ranches. They are obedient, submissive, hard-working, and industrious persons, already halfway down the road to civilization, running small carpentry, blacksmith, soap, and leather-tanning businesses, etc."[16]

This result, which sprang from the Salesian model of action proposed by the Reverend Bosco in Turin, could have been achieved only through regular education, a task to which the missionaries devoted themselves with great zeal: "Once the smaller children were distributed in two big sections, we began to teach, as regularly as possible, elementary reading and writing, followed by the teaching of Brazilian history, arithmetic, etc., to male students; the girls, besides attending these classes, took up sewing and other chores suitable to their sex."[17]

This kind of education, so alien to the Bororo, could be carried out only through a boarding school system, for which the Salesians received a fair amount of criticism at that time. In the eyes of the Salesians, to interfere in the Indian family by separating children from their parents was unavoidable: "How, in fact, to civilize a child who lives in a barbarian home?" The missionaries didn't think it possible to civilize the Indians without modifying their habits. They answered criticism not only with irony, but also in the "scientific" language of the time: "We confess candidly that it doesn't strike our minds, and we understand both the possibility of educating and humanizing barbarians without extirpating their barbarism, and the need to polish coarse gemstones without taking away their coarseness, to straighten out shrubbery without depriving them of their twistedness, or to correct a limb without healing its distortion. And if this is not the squaring of the circle, then we don't know what it is."[18]

The irony of the Salesian reply is interesting because it permits an explicit rendering of the missionaries' exclusive representation of the Indian culture. Certainly, they didn't see it as "culture," but as behavioral distortions that could be corrected only through the use of very specific methods. These methods implied, for adults, an "orthopedic"

Soccer team of Bororo
boys. *Courtesy In-
spetoria Salesiana de
São Paulo.*

Father Balzola and the Reverend Malan surrounded by Bororo youths.
Courtesy Inspetoria Salesiana de São Paulo.

treatment designed to correct a culture seen as a "distorted body." For children, it implied exposure to a whole new set of values that should necessarily replace those of their parents, from whose presence these children should remain as distant as possible.

In addition to limiting the children's contact with their parents' culture, the boarding school provided exposure to a new set of values by means of closer proximity with the children of the "civilized" people of the region who were sent to the missionaries for education. Boarding school enrollment included young Bororo and approximately eighty non-Indian youths, the children of local small farmers, livestock breeders, and placer miners who had flocked to the region to prospect for diamonds. The last group were the paying students, who, to a certain extent contributed toward the expenses of the school. "It's nice to realize the camaraderie established at school between the young Bororo and the civilized children with whom they compete for good grades and behavior" (Albisetti, 1944: 15.)

Both the all-girls boarding school run by the nuns and the all-boys school run by the priests adopted a similar schedule:

Morning	Afternoon
05:15—Classes	03:00—Snack
05:30—Mass	03:30—Work
06:15—Hygiene and breakfast	05:30—Singing, recreation
08:30—Work	06:15—Dinner, recreation
10:30—Bath	07:30—Prayers, bed
11:00—Lunch, recreation	
11:30—Classes	

This schedule allegedly led the Bororo to drop their "nomadic, savage life," which was highly feared by the local Mato Grosso population. Even the adult males "head peacefully and actively for work on the manioc, bean, corn, and sugarcane plantations, fruit orchards, vineyards, coffee plantations, etc., following the director's example."[19]

The transformations produced by the Salesians were also evidenced in the new spatial layout of the colonies. Vangelista (1986) shows the evolution of spatial organization in the Salesian colonies—the layout of the buildings and village at the mission, which changed from a circular to a square format and subsequently to the shape of a church nave, as a signifier of a new society re-created after a Christian model: "The new organization of space will serve as an ideological instrument to the extent that it can stand as a model of moral and civil order" (Vangelista, 1986: 195).

I found photos in the registers of the Salesian headquarters in São Paulo that date from that time. These nearly one hundred photos feature recurrent themes, with the objective of showing the results of the missionary endeavor. Several of these pictures show Bororo women wearing frocks and standing next to a nun in front of large looms. Other pictures show men wearing western clothes and handling hoes and wheelbarrows for farm work and always accompanied by a Salesian priest.

Of the various Salesian missions set up among the Bororo, the one in Sangradouro was apparently the most successful after twenty years under Father César Albisetti's leadership (1926–1934 and 1935–1947). Father Albisetti was extremely devoted to the Bororo, whose culture he knew in great depth. As early as the 1930s he became aware of the difficulties of missionary work conducted in a single nucleus. At that time, a large number of Bororo were employed as hired hands by neighboring farmers, which prompted many families to leave the mission. More than thirty years after setting up the first mission, the region had undergone a complete transformation. Survey data published in *Missioni Salesiane* (1925: 122–123) show that, in 1902, the region was

The Salesians boosted male and female labor. *Courtesy Inspetoria Salesiana de São Paulo.*

Sangradouro   Oficina dos Indios Bororós

inhabited by approximately 409 whites, most of whom had settled along the telegraph lines or in the vicinity of the colony of São José. In 1923, 11,247 "civilized" people lived in the area under the jurisdiction of the three colonies. According to Father Albisetti,[20] many of these families did not adapt to their new lifestyle, whether on the farms or in the neighboring towns. Eventually, they resumed their old habits and settled in villages far from the missions.

In view of these difficulties, Father Albisetti decided to make official something that had been common practice among the Salesians since the days of Father Balzola, and which the Salesians still maintain: so-called mobile Christian instruction. For this purpose, in 1935 he took a two-month trip to the various Bororo villages, where he conducted a census of the local population and dispensed the sacraments. Father Albisetti's census counted the following numbers in the Bororo villages (table 1). The total population included seventy people under age twelve; seventy-three between twelve and twenty; twenty-eight between twenty and fifty-five; and thirty over age fifty-five.

Although the missionaries believed they had achieved many of their objectives, the Bororo still faced considerable hardship. Their conflicts with the Xavante continued until around 1935 and resulted in many deaths. The situation was also difficult for those Bororo who did not live under the missions' protection. The 1940s saw the start of a period characterized by "a high mortality rate and the disappearance of various villages, by the loss of the largest part of the territory the Bororo had traditionally had use of, and the group's complete subordination to the dominating agents (SPI and FUNAI)" (Serpa, 1988: 336).

The cattle ranching business and the intensification of mining gradually imposed closer contact with the regional population. Many of the families who had lived in the missions began to settle elsewhere in the region. Furthermore, as I have mentioned, the contact between the Bororo and the "civilized" population was intensified at boarding schools.

Beginning in the 1950s, the struggles between Indians and farmers throughout the state of Mato Grosso became increasingly frequent and more aggressive. As shown by Davis (1978) and Martins (1986), these conflicts were not restricted to this state. Instead, they spread to the Midwest and the North as well as to some areas in the South and the Northeast, particularly after the installation of the military dictatorship. Policies concerning land occupation were completely changed, thus affecting not only small farmers but also, and more directly, numerous Indian societies: "Throughout the country, the rupture of personal dependency as a result of proletarianization, temporary work, expropriation, violence, etc., revealed the absurdity of land ownership. It revealed

Table 1. Father Albisetti's 1935 Census

Village	Population
Toriparu	68
Aijeri	23
Jarudori	108
Pobori	140
Porogi	124
Rondonópolis	5
Total	**468**

Source: Bollettino Salesiano 59, no. 1: 25.

the political mystery involving ownership. The struggle for land is propped on this discovery. For this same reason, the struggle for land is potent and the struggle for agrarian reform is ineffective" (Martins, 1986: 96).

The Roman Catholic Church assumed a new posture in relation to the national situation, which led its clergy to redirect their activities. These are the issues I shall address in the next chapter.

6.

The Salesians and the Progressive Church: The Reshaping of an Image

Conflicts in the 1970s

The 1970s represent a milestone in recent Brazilian history, and as such they have been thoroughly investigated by numerous scholars. Of most interest to anthropologists researching Indian societies in Brazil are the works of Shelton Davis (1978) and José de Souza Martins (1986).

Davis draws a picture of Brazilian economic policy and the settlement movement into the Amazon beginning in the 1940s. He focuses mainly on the indigenist policy of contemporary Brazil, particularly during the period of military rule, and on the status of the country's Indian populations—the main victims of the so-called Brazilian miracle.

The economic development programs designed by military rulers directly affected Brazil's Indians. These large-scale projects were aimed at the occupation of the nation's "empty spaces," and the presence of Indians there was ignored. The opening of important roads such as the Perimetral Norte and the Manaus–Boa Vista Highway, massive support for agribusiness and the cattle raising industry, and huge investments in mining and nuclear energy—particularly following the aerial photogrammetry surveys conducted as part of the Radar na Amazônia (RADAM) program to detect deposits of gold, diamonds, uranium, cassiterite, and other minerals in Indian territory—all these measures served to confront innumerable Indian societies with a scenario in which territorial conflicts became part of daily routine.

Development was based on plans masterminded by cabinet members who were also responsible for securing funding for their projects. Brazil became known increasingly for availing itself of the resources made available through so-called tax incentives, or tax breaks. The main objective of the National Integration Program announced by President Médici in 1970 was the relocation to the Amazon of throngs of jobless farmhands from the drought-plagued Northeast. In the second half of the 1970s, this project, which included provision for the settlement of farmhands along the Trans-Amazonian Highway, was replaced by the Polamazônia Program. The latter comprised major agribusiness set up for systematic extraction of wood and support of large ranches already established in Central Brazil. Once again the relocated farmhands ended up as surplus labor.[1]

Using as his main reference a report by Roman Catholic bishop the Reverend Pedro Casaldáliga entitled "Uma igreja da Amazônia em conflito com o latifúndio e a marginalizão social" (A Church in the Amazon in Conflict with Large Landed Estates and Social Marginalization), Davis shows how the large cattle raising projects designed for the state of Mato Grosso further deepened the conflicts between Indians, squatters, and landowners. Martins's commentaries are no different: "Large agribusinesses began to drive out peasants and Indians, or to play peasants against Indians, as a way of getting rid of both. . . . In other instances, counterfeit deeds were issued for unoccupied or Indian land by corrupt government officials or the occupants were simply violently expelled" (1986: 19).[2]

Barra do Garças and Luciara, two municipalities in the state of Mato Grosso, drew large-scale investors and an enormous number of laborers from other regions attracted by the promise of work and easy money. Squatters were driven off the land as new ranches and farms were established.

FUNAI, headed by General Bandeira de Mello, opted for an indigenist policy designed to integrate Indians so that they no longer presented an obstacle to development. In this context, the Xavante Indians of Sangradouro, São Marcos (both of them reservations run by Salesian missionaries), and Couto Magalhães became involved in several conflicts (Davis, 1978: 148–151; Menezes, 1984: 367–379). Similar struggles culminated in the killing of Simão, a Bororo Indian, and Father Rodolfo Lunkenbein, a Salesian priest, at the Meruri reservation in July 1976.

Small and large farmers and ranchers who possessed deeds issued by the state had been invading the Indian reservation for some time. The Bororo, supported by the missionaries, demanded that FUNAI proceed with the land demarcation that had begun in 1976. Squatters, however, decided to disrupt the surveying and refused all proposals for indemnification. According to reports published in several newspapers, seventy-two non-Indians under the command of Barra do Garças farm owners invaded the Meruri reservation, where surveying was being conducted by the Plantel Company.[3] While trying to establish a dialogue with the invaders, the mission head, Father Lunkenbein, was shot dead by the group's leader, João Mineiro. The five Indians who came to the priest's defense were wounded. One of them died aboard a rescue plane.

Fearing international repercussions following the German priest's assassination and wishing "to avoid international political exploration of the incident," Brazilian officials tried to convince the priest's family that his funeral should be in the mission. They claimed that the Bororo themselves had asked to conduct burial ceremonies in accordance with "their traditional tribal ritual."[4]

Brazilian newspapers featured articles announcing another impending threat: the Xavante's intention to join the Bororo to avenge the missionary's death. In the nearby town of General Carneiro, "many women [fearing the Indians' threats to take matters into their own hands] quickly gathered their few belongings and took refuge in the forest with their daughters."[5]

The conflicts in Meruri made news throughout Brazil. After surveying eight of the country's principal newspapers circulating in Brasília, São Paulo, and Rio de Janeiro, FUNAI media relations staff verified the publication of eighty-eight articles on this subject between 16 July and 30 July 1976, which corresponded to "13.3% of all articles featuring Indian issues published in the first half of 1976" (FUNAI, 1976).

This episode had a significant impact not only on the media and public opinion in general, but also on the Salesians' conception of their own mission. Furthermore, it affected the Bororo's self-image and their relations with non-Indians as well as with the Salesian missionaries.

The Roman Catholic Church's Preferential Option for the Poor

To understand the changes introduced in the relations between the Salesians and the Bororo, one should be aware not only of the relations between the Roman Catholic Church, Brazilian society, and the Brazilian nation-state, but also of those values supported by Rome that, ultimately, are interpreted in Third World countries and guide local church policy.

Beginning in the 1950s, the Roman Catholic Church in Brazil began to devote itself to teaching and spreading the Word of God among different segments of society—workers, students, professionals, farm workers, and so on. Consequently, distinct Roman Catholic youth movements were formed in contraposition to the exclusively parochial role that the church had played until then. These movements involved a significant number of laypersons in apostolic work, which resulted in the church's privileged insertion in these sectors of society.

In 1962, the Second Vatican Council engaged in a process of self-criticism of the Roman Catholic Church, which hitherto had referred to itself as "God's People." As a result, Vatican II discussed and redefined the segments of the population that fit into this category. In 1968, the bishops attending the Second General Conference of the Latin American Episcopate, in Medellín, Colombia, interpreted Vatican II's definition, from the viewpoint of the Third World, as the option the church should take, that is, as a preferential option for the "oppressed poor." Although the bishops in Medellín did not specifically address the Indian issue, "this 'preferential option' for the oppressed poor led to the draft of a nonconservative indigenist pastoral in defense of Indians' rights" (Ricardo, 1980: 1).

Brazil's economic and political model had produced an enormous mass of poor and oppressed people by rapidly accumulating capital and squeezing salaries. The military government's model "led the church to a virtual rupture with the regime" (Ricardo, 1980: 1). Ação Católica (Catholic Action), which had supported the church throughout the previous period, was practically eradicated "by the combined actions of the government, conservative church members, and the disaggregation and disarticulation of the movement itself" (Beozzo, 1979: 9).

The document signed by the bishops in Medellín did not affect all sectors of the Brazilian church with the same intensity. "At first the church in the Northeast, the country's poorest region, seemed to have been left alone." Even when, in the late 1960s and the early 1970s, the church in the South joined its northeastern brethren (by, for example, supporting the 1968 strike in Osasco), "the clergy's conservative hierarchy held out olive branches to the enemies of the church and the people" (Della Cava, 1986: 16–17).

In January 1971, anthropologists and intellectuals (including Darcy Ribeiro, Georg Grunberg, and Stefano Varese) gathered in Barbados and issued a document in which they criticized the missions for their intimacy with colonialism and appealed to the churches to discontinue all missionary work. In their opinion, native Indians should be masters of their own destiny. The Barbados statement had a profound effect on the missionary church. In March 1972, the Ecumenical Meeting in Asunción, Paraguay, produced a document with the purpose of resuscitating the church's mission in the world.

> The Mission is the church's reason for being . . . to uncover the presence of God the Savior in all peoples and cultures . . . Our churches have gathered efforts against ideologies and practices utilized to oppress man . . . The mission requires an ecumenical dialogue, the Indians' active participation in its organization, the expert contribution of human scientists, the assessment of church activities, and the disclosure, to the public, of the true image of indigenous peoples and their inalienable rights. (Ricardo, 1980: 3)

In April 1972, at the Third Meeting on the Native Pastoral organized by the Conferência Nacional dos Bispos do Brasil (National Conference of Brazilian Bishops—CNBB), the religious groups engaged in missionary work with Indians created the Conselho Indigenista Missionário (CIMI) to provide assistance to missionaries working in Indian communities in Brazil. A Salesian priest, Father Angelo Jayme Venturelli, was appointed its first chairman and treasurer.[6]

CIMI enjoyed a high degree of independence from CNBB. Together with the Comunidades Eclesiais de Base (Basic Christian Communities—CEBs, grassroots Christian community groups) and the Comissão Pastoral de Terra (Pastoral Land Commission—CPT), created in 1975, CIMI recorded accusations of atrocities committed by the military regime against various segments of Brazilian society, thus mobilizing church members in the struggle against the regime.

These three entities resulted from the adoption of new policies introduced by the Roman Catholic Church in Brazil. In accordance with these new directives, the church sought in-depth knowledge of the current status of oppressed social groups. Furthermore, this new role presented the missionary church (and, I believe, the church not directly involved with the Indians) a chance to rise above the criticism to which the institution had been subjected. In addition, "it was among the less-favored classes that the church's 'presence' had been strongly challenged by competitive faiths and ideologies" (Della Cava, 1986: 20).

It should be noted that said competition did not take place exclusively in the urban centers, as the native populations were also exposed to the influence of other religious missions, particularly those organized by Protestant religious movements. In this sense, a change in the church's modus operandi—which also led it to engage fiercely in a human rights campaign—was essential if it was to remain a pillar of Brazilian society.

Della Cava remarks that for the church to be effective in its new role, first it had to revise the symbolic meaning of Christ. "In other words, it had to change the institutionalized notion of the world's poverty as something prescribed by God into a symbol through which Christ was to transform the world." Hitherto regarded as the sufferer of Passion, Christ was to be seen from the opposite standpoint, as "Jesus Christ, the Redeemer" (Della Cava, 1986: 47).

In her commentary on the role of the CEBs, Carmem Cinira de Macedo shows how the Brazilian Roman Catholic Church introduced the process of recovering moral practice. In this process, the issue of sin switches from the field of ethics to the field of politics. The more progressive wings of the church denounce the unfair social structure, while "the notion of liberation is gradually installed in the bosom of history itself and outlined as a proposal for creating a new life for all in this world" (1986: 57).

Eventually the CEBs' position was adopted by CPT as well as by CIMI. The assumption was that oppressed groups, whether Indians, squatters, or slum dwellers, should choose their own destinies. In other words, they were expected to stop being passive individuals and to band together to articulate solutions for the problems that afflicted them. Solutions necessarily required the awareness, union, confrontation, and mutual assistance that defined the new way of "being Christian."

The Salesians and the Contemporary Church

Earlier I mentioned that at the turn of the century the Salesians became aware of the need to work among the Bororo to correct their "primitive" and "savage" behavior. Their viewpoint was, of course, consistent with the evolutionist theories of the time. As we have seen, the missionaries tried to focus their efforts on the teaching of new moral principles, the introduction of modesty as a virtue, and, subsequently, the conception of a new family structure to replace the traditional clan organization and constitute the so-called modern Christian family.

One of the Salesians' first actions was to introduce clothing to cover the nudity of those savage bodies. The missionaries maintained that virtues such as chastity (circumspection and embarrassment in the face of offenses against decency), honesty, and modesty (which is also associated with attitudes toward sexuality, which, though associated with specific parts of the body, is a universal human quality) were unknown to the Bororo.[7]

Particularly noteworthy is the fact that the Salesians not only disregarded the existence of this feeling among the Bororo, but also tried to instill in this society a Christian moral code by working consistently with the women. The typically ambiguous representation of the female—seen as having a "natural" inclination toward ambition (to date, Eve's original sin remains as an important attribute in the representation of the female) while simultaneously being endowed with a pure, dignified, and virtuous essence—led the Salesians to strive to awaken in those savage women these purportedly dormant feelings.

The Salesians' introduction of modern Christian family values was based on their perception of Bororo family organization. If, on the one hand, many missionaries could describe this family organization objectively, on the other, their description was interpreted in the light of western concepts. These concepts were unconditionally validated not only by the church but also by ordinary citizens, as shown in the following excerpt from an essay written by Father Albisetti:

> Bororo totemism gathered the families of a group in a single hut;
> three, four families that had no identity or existence of their own,
> but only that of the group to which they belonged. How many
> disastrous consequences resulted from this! Worst was the family's
> inconsistency. Under the roof of the hut reigned the superstitions
> and needs of the race, not those of the family. Besides, each man
> spent most of his time hunting or in the men's house (Bahyto) and
> he had a life almost apart from that of his wife. (In *Bollettino
> Salesiano*, 1925: 122)

In Father Albisetti's description of the Bororo family, the elements are
not articulated in the same way they are articulated in the conception
that both the Salesians and the ordinary citizens had of these same
elements. The common conception of that time (which, in fact, is still
held by the church as well as by society in general) necessarily involved
a relationship between family and Christian morals (which define the
roles of a man and his wife within this institution) and, consequently,
between work and citizenship. It is precisely these articulated conceptions—of family, Christian morals, labor, and citizenship—that still
guide the Salesians' work among the Bororo.

To the missionaries, the establishment of this new type of family
involved eliminating false beliefs and superstitions associated with the
totemic clan system—the base of Bororo social organization. The Salesians
considered this system responsible for the secondary role of the nuclear
family and the fragile bond between husband and wife.

In their attempt to strengthen the marriage bond, the Salesians made
an effort to offer the young couple not only the wedding attire but also
a trousseau, tools, seeds, draft animals, and livestock. Because their
objective was to detach the nuclear family from the totemic group and
to grant it the privacy required for a Christian family, the Salesians also
had to eradicate the custom of having families of the same clan share the
same house.

The Salesians' efforts to introduce a moral code among the Bororo
were accomplished with the tearing down of the central (or men's)
house, the *bai-mana-gejewu*. Until then, the missionaries saw their
flock divided into Christian families and pagan families, the latter of
which insisted on gathering in that profane place.

The central house posed a constant threat to the moral code that
should guide the Christian family. It was where young adults underwent
their sexual initiation and where women behaved in a manner that was
absolutely incompatible with the morality expected of a Christian
woman.[8]

Young Bororo newlyweds received their trousseau from the missionaries. *Courtesy Inspetoria Salesiana de São Paulo.*

In addition to introducing a new moral code that affected family organization, residential patterns, behavior in relation to one's body, and so on, the Salesians tried to instill values that were very dear to western society: the importance of labor and property. They tried to stop the gift giving they offered to attract the Bororo when they were first contacted: "Gifts don't teach religion."[9]

Beginning in the 1920s or the 1930s, a system was instituted at the missions whereby the Indians received coupons or chits in exchange for work. "With these coupons, highly treasured in the mission, the adult male and female Bororo acquired clothes, flour, meat, salt, sugar, tools, etc." According to the Salesians, the coupon system "gradually instills in them the notion of work and its corresponding worth. Therefore, it provides them with a powerful motive to overcome the inherited tradition of idleness and to acquire ennobling and fruitful work habits."[10]

The priests' main objective was to introduce habits and customs seen as more "noble and civilized"; these, from the Salesians' point of view, should replace those behavior patterns seen as immoral and primitive. This perspective prevailed until the mid-1970s. In January 1977, that is to say, six months after the struggles described earlier in this chapter, the Salesians published the "Diretório da missão salesiana de Mato Grosso para a atividade missionária junto às populações indígenas" (The Mato Grosso Salesian Mission Directory of Missionary Work with Native Populations). This publication drew up a pastoral plan for "the integration of Indians into a particular church, without losing their identity amid the diversity of the groups involved" (p. 3). This directory presents the Salesians' commitment to the Indians: "*Human development focuses* on the Indian's health, self-sufficiency, and literacy. *Christian instruction shall avoid* all conditioning" (p. 4, original emphasis).

The issue no longer involves substituting one culture for another or even correcting "deviant" behavior patterns. The focus is now on human development and Christian instruction. If at one time, however, missionary work revealed a certain consistency between objectives and modes of action, currently the missionaries seem to be facing an insoluble contradiction. Now the teaching of Christian values is carried out along with an appreciation of the traditional native culture. The Salesians are now trying to retrieve many of the cultural traits and values that for many years they tried to eradicate. According to a Salesian teacher extremely devoted to Bororo society, with which he has been working since the mid-1970s, "After Vatican II in 1965, the missionaries began to support the Indians' legitimate claims and to appreciate their cultural values" (Bordignon, 1987: 38). This stance is in full agreement with the new directives. "Christian instructors should be transplanting rather than chopping down; they should be adding something new rather than replacing; therefore, Christian instruction will be efficient only if it does not interfere with basic tribal beliefs and if it bases itself on tribal traditions" ("Diretório da missão salesiana": 4–6).

But how to overcome the contradiction between the appreciation of traditional tribal culture and a Christian instruction that "grafts" something onto a culture so that it does not remain "incomplete"? A brief analysis of the "Diretório da missão salesiana" reveals that, despite missionary work's being redirected, the church remains an institution that claims to know the Truth. As such, it takes upon itself the legitimization of existing cultures and the demonstration of God's presence in these cultures. The following excerpt from the directory clearly states this aspect: "missionary work frees from evil contagion all truthful and merciful values held by a people, as if secretly standing in for God, and returns them to Christ, their author, who annihilates the devil's empire and wards off the multiform viciousness of sin. All good things sowed inside men or in the rites and cultures of peoples not only last but are also healed, elevated, and consummated" ("Diretório da missão salesiana": 6).

If at the turn of the century native culture was regarded as the expression of a decayed lifestyle that included distorted habits and behavior patterns that were to be eradicated or corrected, the church's posture now implies a new conception of culture. Nowadays it views culture as a particular expression of human creativity rendered in the various contexts of the social and psychological life of groups, *though without being endowed with their own autonomous truth.* Essentially, every culture results from divine creation and delivers Christ's words to the people.[11]

This new conception of culture requires that missionaries methodically study the customs and rites of the peoples with whom they relate. Furthermore, persons engaged in missionary work are now encouraged to learn the language and the myths of each group. This is nothing new for missionaries who have worked among the Indians, from the Jesuits in the sixteenth century to the Salesians, who have kept in close contact with the Bororo and even the Xavante. Actually, many Salesian priests have not only devoted themselves to learning about native culture, but have also written about it. What is different about this new posture is that its objective does not involve the mere acquisition of knowledge or the acquisition of a type of knowledge that will permit the missionaries to intervene and correct distortions. Now, as they break into the culture of these societies, their objective is to identify the different expressions of divine creation. They wish to investigate the riches of a humankind that, despite being extraordinarily and immensely diverse, comes from a single origin: the truth that emanates from God's will.

These new directives adopted by the Salesian missionaries working among the Bororo are closely related to the direction taken in Brazil by the Roman Catholic Church in the 1970s. It should be noted, for example, that the "Diretório da missão salesiana" clearly reflects the posture that CIMI had been recommending since 1973, when it began asking the missionaries to report on their experiences among tribal societies: "If you have not yet risked undergoing a new liturgical experience, do it now. Engage yourself in a liturgy embodied in the native liturgy. To do missionary work is to proceed toward the riches that God sowed among the peoples and to cultivate them with all respect."[12]

This attitude has also been adopted in the large urban centers and even in the rural areas, where the more progressive priests and nuns have tried to approach the low-income population with the objective of understanding, accepting, and even incorporating religious manifestations that had been viewed as false beliefs and superstitions. The church no longer intervenes to eradicate these pagan practices; instead, it incorporates them as manifestations of "true faith," thereby purifying them.

The new attitude toward ecclesiastical ceremonies has played a very important role in the church's new posture. In a way, it simply recalls

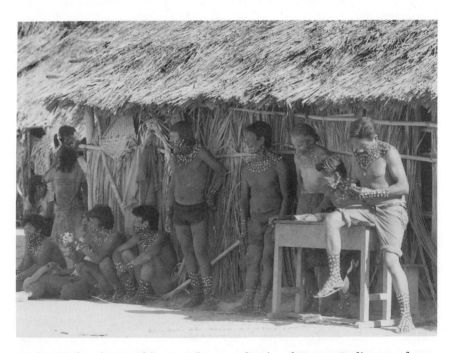

Father Ochoa (*second from right, standing*) and Bororo Indians performing the funeral ritual. *Sylvia Caiuby Novaes, Garças, 1986.*

(although for different purposes) the methodology of religious education announced by Pope Gregory I in 601, whereby he instructed the clergy to make the most of those aspects of pagan culture that could be integrated into Christian life.[13] By adopting a similar attitude, in the 1970s and 1980s the Salesian priests introduced to the Bororo a "nativized" liturgy that, as we will see in chapter 7, became important to the missionaries for identifying with the Bororo culture. The Salesians clearly assumed and explicitly disseminated this new position, as shown in the following excerpt from a text written by a Salesian missionary, Father Zavattaro: "The announcement of the Christian message should fit as much as possible the existing mental categories and cultural manifestations. The Word should be embodied in these categories, so that it can purify them and help them become authentic expressions of faith." As to the new mode of ecclesiastical ceremonies, Father Zavattaro writes:

It is not the church's desire to impose on liturgy a rigid and single form for those things that do not concern faith or the good of the entire community. On the contrary, the church propagates and develops values and spiritual qualities of various nations and peoples. With goodwill the church examines whatever aspect of a people's customs is in fact not indissolubly associated with superstitions and mistakes and tries to conserve it untouched. At times, it goes as far as admitting this aspect into its own liturgy, provided that it matches the criteria of the true liturgical spirit. (n.d.: 34–35)

In the Kingdom of God: The Salesians and the Bororo Today

What are the actual changes in the relationship between the Salesians and the Bororo in more than eighty years of religious education? I do not refer to the Salesian mission from the institutional viewpoint; I refer to the daily contact that promotes the relationship between clergy and Indians. How have these new directives actually affected the missionary-Indian relationship?[14]

Although today they have a greater knowledge of both the basic units of Bororo social organization and the importance of the clan structure, the Salesians spare no effort to guarantee the ascendancy of moral rules to guide the so-called modern Christian family: faithfulness, the indissoluble bond of marriage, man as the family head, assistance from and solidarity among members of the same nuclear family.

Everyone who has ever written about the Bororo, including the Salesians, emphasizes the fragility of the marriage bond, the high separation rate among couples, and the lesser importance of the nuclear family compared with the bonds that united clan members. Today, rather than having church weddings forced on them, the Bororo request them. Couples joined by the sacrament of marriage constitute "solidly structured families" and seldom opt for separation as a solution to serious conflicts, as I had the opportunity to witness in Meruri. Most of these couples get involved in the same everyday lifestyle non-Indians know. Conflicts between husband and wife may drag on for years and adultery eventually goes public and becomes a major topic for gossip, but the couple remains together "'til death do us part."

These couples bear children who in general (but not always) are baptized after the Bororo traditional naming ritual. In 1985 I attended a baptism ceremony held in Meruri on the same day of the naming ritual. Afterward, the priest who celebrated the baptism told me he did not understand the meaning of the Bororo naming or the various ritual procedures; however, he remarked that in all cultures children born to a father and a mother must have their birth formally announced to the community. Therefore, the baptism he had just celebrated was meant to complement the native ritual rather than replace it. According to the priest, by saying baptism *complemented* the Indian ritual, he did not mean to suggest that Bororo culture was incomplete. The baptism should be understood within a religious context: "Baptism is necessary as a complement to our flesh-and-blood existence."

The major changes in the relationship between the Salesians and the Bororo are the result of missionaries' having adopted a new conception of culture. If from the late nineteenth century to the 1920s they sought to see the triumph of Christ's kingdom over Satan's domain (at which task they believe they fully succeeded), today the Salesians' mission is to place at God's service those oppressed individuals who constitute God's true kingdom. The initiatives currently undertaken in their various spheres of action result from their new approach, not only to the Bororo but also to native societies in general. If the culture of native peoples today is seen as "a particular expression of human creativity that results from divine creation and is vehicle to Christ's words," the attitude of the missionaries as the earthly representatives of this superior entity should be one of safeguarding, conserving, and even striving to rescue traditional cultural standards. For this to happen, indoctrination and religious education must be relinquished.

The boarding school system had to be abolished. It is no longer a matter of keeping children away from evil examples to which they are exposed while living with their parents in the Indian village; nor is it a matter of exposing these children to the models of politeness and manners presented at boarding schools by local non-Indian children. The boarding system was discontinued in the mid-1970s, although Salesian priests and nuns still offer formal education. The student body, however, no longer includes non-Indian children. According to a Salesian nun, following Father Lunkenbein's assassination, all the non-Indian families whose children attended the boarding school moved away, and "it was they who attracted the Bororo students to the school. The Bororo no longer want to be boarding students. The Bororo want to be free" (Meruri, 1982).

The Salesians' teaching is now supported by textbooks written by the Salesians specifically for the Bororo. These books include heavily illustrated texts on the history of contact, the elders' knowledge of zoology, first readers in Bororo, Bororo stories and legends, and so on.

Today the missionaries say mass in Bororo, which is also used for hymns. During the homily at daily mass, the priest promotes the Indians' awareness of the importance of defending their territory, talks to them about that day's saint, announces the liturgical calendar, and indicates, through examples, how the Bororo could "improve their lives." Work as a virtue is still emphasized not only during the homily but also in daily conversations with the Indians. The Indians are told that, without work—in particular, without farming—their society probably could not survive. And how to conserve this culture, this testimony of God's will, without individuals to keep it alive?

Today the main concern of the Salesian missionaries working in Meruri is the rescue and reinvigoration of traditional culture. For a long time, the missionaries have used photography and tape recordings to record native rituals. Techniques such as VHS recording are now being utilized "not for commercial use, but for cultural purposes and exchange programs with other Bororo villages, including Meruri, which is trying to recover part of the lost culture, since its full recovery is impossible and too complex."[15]

At present in Meruri, the village that has been most directly affected by missionary influence, this attempt to recover traditional Indian culture is vigorously stimulated by the Salesians. They have asked for the help of a few of the older Bororo, who still maintain the cultural traditions, in engaging children and young adults in ritual ceremonies. These rituals are held whenever there is an opportunity; should such opportunities not arise naturally, these rituals are held on western religious or other commemorative dates, such as Indian's Day, Mother's Day, Christmas, Easter, or the anniversary of the death of Father Lunkenbein and Simão.

In the Salesian chronicles, 1914 is the date that symbolically designates the consecration of the mission undertaken by the Salesians. The tearing down of the central house following Father Colbacchini's suggestion and the erecting of a cross on the site previously ruled by Satan represent the triumph of Redemption and the conversion to Catholicism of those families still seen as pagan.

Seventy years later the Salesians organized a similar event that, however, followed a reversed agenda. In the mid-1980s, the crossroads along which the Bororo have built their brick homes in Meruri became the site of a straw central house constructed in the same style as those found in other Bororo villages. "But here's the detail: following the construction of the *bai-mana-gejewu*, eighteen *kioguaros* were produced for utilization at Bororo baptism ceremonies," Master Bordignon writes in a letter dated 3 June 1987.[16] Viewed as the main prop of Bororo society and culture and the expression of divine volition, the men's house can no longer be seen as a space from which all evil emanates. In a sense, this house is now a distinctive space in God's kingdom.

This current process of cultural reinvigoration, whereby the missionaries working in Meruri encourage the Indians to participate in their rituals, involves an attitude that is radically contrary to the characteristic posture of the Salesians at the turn of the century. The same ideology, however, still underlies this new posture; the only difference lies in the terms in which this ideology is stated.

As earthly representatives of this superior entity, the priests claim for themselves the role of bearers of Truth. Almost ninety years after the establishment of religious education among the Bororo, however, this truth is expressed through both Christ's words and those words Christ conveyed to different peoples on Earth. In this sense, the missionaries now stand as guardians of traditional Bororo culture—a culture that, like everything else created by God, is immune to the actions of time and history; the sacred is eternal, perennial, and unchangeable. In a way, the missionaries seem to have appropriated the mythical vision of native societies in which there is always the possibility of an eternal return.

The missionaries perform their role as guardians of traditional Bororo culture in different ways. Besides using various means for recording rituals (photography, film, video, etc.), they now encourage the young Bororo to speak their own language and to learn traditional handicrafts, chants, ritual canons, and so on from their elders.[17]

Despite the many difficulties involved in the production of certain feather artifacts, the Bororo have manufactured a number of objects, such as headdresses and sunshades, stimulated by the Salesian missionaries. The latter have taken it upon themselves to safeguard objects that the Bororo use in ritual ceremonies to avoid the risk of their being ruined, lost, or even sold.[18]

The difficulties and contradictions met by the Salesians have not gone unnoticed by the Bororo, as evinced by the following conversation (recorded in 1983 in Meruri while a man dressed pork for sale). The dialogue demonstrates the Bororo's loyalty to the missionaries and the Indians' feelings of indebtedness. It also shows the crossroads at which the Bororo of Meruri currently stand:

WOMAN   We are no longer Indians nor are we civilized.

MAN 1   At this point we are becoming quite an assorted mixture.

MAN 2   But it is no use trying to go back; it's easier for a camel to go through the eye of a needle.

MAN 1   This business of going away to study is quite destructive, because one leaves the tribe and goes out to become someone out there. We already had plenty of disagreement within the community; now with people going away to study it gets worse. If only they came back to teach the ones who remained in the village it would be better.

WOMAN   It's these more learned people who cause the greatest disturbance here.

MAN 1   I don't question priests, because our community owes a lot to them.

MAN 2   But priests didn't let us speak Bororo; now it's too late to go back.

MAN 1   They came to give religious instruction. They had to forbid. They were right. They forbade language use. Later we got better understanding through development.

WOMAN   I'm on their side; I'm in the wrong for not knowing all the good they do us.

MAN 1   The solution now is for the older people to teach children within their culture. But they don't want to teach everybody, only close relatives. Now I think it should be like my father, who taught everybody, no matter who. But this doesn't work, because not everyone wants their children to learn.

MAN 2   I was born in the backlands near Coxipó, far from the Christians. I've played the rattle since my childhood, but here . . .

MAN 1   I wish this generation would learn. The priest has ideas like me. For the Bororo to obey, it has to be a non-Indian, because we don't obey one another. They say "You're not a priest, you're not a sister, you're not my father." We need money to cultivate; we don't have enough tools to work. We lack unity. We were more united before we

	were civilized, and he who has more looks askance at those who have less. We can all get loans, but no one does because it'll be spent on booze.
MAN 2	The Garças folks are more united. They are more uncivilized, though more united.
WOMAN	The money someone requests for the community goes to his house and his family only.
MAN 1	FUNAI works against the Indians; they are the first ones to be against the Indians. This Andreazza character, a former Brazilian interior secretary, is like that.

The conversation continued along these lines while the man cut up and sold his pork. Buyers paid with money, necklaces, or even the simple pledge to share meat with the supplier the next time they slaughtered a hog.

After ninety years of religious education, it is clear that the relationship between the Salesians and the Bororo has not resulted in substituting one culture for another, nor in merely adding to the Bororo culture. A few values and behavior patterns have certainly been assimilated through the proper channels in each of the cultures in question (given that their influence is mutual, though not symmetrical). As I have mentioned, however, the words and attitudes of the Bororo as well as those of the Salesians have not come together as result of their attunement. Instead, they have been rephrased and reinterpreted during close contact that has lasted several generations. During this contact, each group has become more self-aware and has re-created its own images and attitudes in relation to the other.

From the Salesians' viewpoint, the ideology of incarnation, that is, the incorporation of the specific forms of a people's cultural expression, should be regarded as part of the church's strategy to reestablish unity among the peoples and to turn the church into an expression of this unity—"unity in Christ." According to Viveiros de Castro, in this movement, which seeks to attain "a mystical fusion between subject and object, where the subject transmigrates to the object and incarnates it . . ., *the existence of the other as a reality different from the self* is annulled and becomes *effectively dispensable*" (1980: 3–4, original emphasis). Macedo, who presents as empirical evidence the activities of the Roman Catholic Church in urban contexts, is also emphatic about this point of view: "It is impossible to ignore the fact that the Roman Catholic imaginary incorporated a prevailing precedence of the whole in relation to the parts, in which the individual becomes 'lost' and 'atomized' unless he finds himself and fulfills himself in the collective entity, which is 'superior' to each single individual" (1986: 62).

When reviewing Roman Catholicism, one should bear in mind that the issue of the church's universality constitutes a myth—unity. This myth of the church's fundamental unity overflows into the understanding of human collectivity and functions as if it were an element naturally "granted." The church's unity is "natural" in that it is sacramental, granted with the divine Gift of grace (Macedo, 1986: 62). Its need to assert a fundamental unity implies, in the case we have been discussing, a visible union between missionaries and Indians. This model of action necessarily presupposes the Salesians' identification with Bororo society. For the Salesians, this identification is rendered visible in Father Rodolfo Lunkenbein's funeral, as I shall show in chapter 7.

7.

Missionaries and Indians:
Identification Created
through Martyrdom

Tribute to an Assassinated Salesian

July 1986 marked the tenth anniversary of the death of Father Rodolfo Lunkenbein, a Salesian missionary murdered by João Mineiro during the struggle for land. In Meruri, missionaries and laypeople devoted to the Indian issue gathered to commemorate the assassination and for CIMI's annual assembly.

The Bororo in Garças (a traditional Bororo village, located 12.5 miles from Meruri) exhumed Father Lunkenbein's remains and gave him a traditional Bororo funeral, decorating his bones, as they do with the bones of members of their own society. Before this second funeral, the Salesians wrote to request permission from Father Lunkenbein's family in Germany. The priest's brother and nephew attended the burial ceremony in Garças.[1]

In the Bororo funeral rites, women of the deceased's clan dig a shallow grave in the center of the village. The body is buried by men of the opposite moiety. "When someone dies, his clan relatives gather to appoint the *aroe-maiwu* (literally, the deceased's 'new soul'). A prestigious male from the deceased's opposite moiety should be chosen" (Caiuby Novaes, 1983: 307). Between the time the corpse is buried, decomposes, is exhumed, and the bones decorated, numerous rituals are held. These are attended not only by local inhabitants but also by specially invited inhabitants of other Bororo villages. "The funeral ceremonies serve to gather the entire Bororo society. They are attended by the living and the dead (evoked through their relatives)—that is to say, by persons as well as by heroes into which the dead are transformed" (Caiuby Novaes, 1983: 304).

One of the most important rituals is the young men's initiation, during which young adult males are formally introduced to society. Following the initiation rituals, which are held during the three last days of the funeral ceremony, young men are given certain adult rights and obligations. The ritual marks when the boy is likely to begin his sex life and names the partners from whom he may choose. This is the transition from boyhood to young adulthood, and is ritually dramatized by the presentation of an *aije* (a mythical animal symbolized by a bull-roarer; during the ritual, the *aije* is personified by members of a given clan).

Like all other "civilized" people, Father Lunkenbein belonged to the clan of the Bokodori Ecerae, the Ecerae moiety. Therefore, his bones were removed from the grave by an Iwagudu man, from the opposite moiety (Tugarege) and washed by a Paiwoe man (also Tugaregedu) who, as I discovered later, had been chosen *aroe-maiwu*. A Bokodori Ecerae male presided over all of the funerary ceremonies. The bones were washed and dried, wrapped in a starched white towel—the kind used in church—and placed in a straw basket until the next day.

The next day, the master of ceremonies' wife, from the Paiwoe clan, started to make a *kodo,* or straw basket to hold the bones of the deceased permanently. Upon finishing the basket, she wailed ritually at her home (in Meruri), as is the tradition.

Late on the morning of July 12, Herman, Father Lunkenbein's brother, and Konrad, his nephew, arrived at the Salesian mission. Priests, nuns,

At the Meruri outpatient ward, Father Rodolfo Lunkenbein watches the vaccination of adults and children. *Sylvia Caiuby Novaes, Meruri, 1972.*

mission staff, and a large number of Bororo from Garças and Meruri were gathered in the courtyard, and the Meruri band had been summoned to play several marches to welcome foreign visitors.

Seated in two chairs on a straw mat in the central part of the mission's verandah, the new arrivals were greeted with a ritual wailing by a woman who then started to scarify herself, letting her blood drip around the two men as part of the traditional reception of a relative who has been absent for a long time. The master of ceremonies also paid homage to the newcomers by chanting a Bororo song accompanied by two gourd rattles. After that the Bororo and the priest's brother made speeches, which were interpreted by a missionary.

In his speech, Father Ochoa, who had lived among the Bororo for over twenty years, stressed that Father Rodolfo Lunkenbein's mother had accepted the sacrifice of her son. She also said that she forgave his enemies. "Were she to have a younger son who should want to come here and give his life to the Bororo, she would not refuse the opportunity to offer this second son in sacrifice."

A Bororo Funeral for a Salesian

On the morning of July 13, the basket containing Father Lunkenbein's bones was taken to Garças for the last three days of the Bororo funeral and the decoration of the bones. Many of the clergy gathered for the CIMI assembly attended the last three days, and a team of filmmakers taped the entire ceremony. Most of the Meruri Bororo village also went to Garças to attend the funeral. They had been emphatically warned—over the mission's loudspeakers—about the need to respect such occasions and not to laugh or play "childish games."[2]

Eight young Bororo from Meruri were initiated during the funeral ceremony and introduced to the *aije*. A chief from Garças spoke to them in Bororo about the importance of following the *boe* traditions. Several Meruri Bororo, many of them called *barae* ("civilized," but in an extremely offensive way) by the Garças Bororo, actively participated in the funeral ceremonies and were frequently taught by "learned" chiefs.

A French tourist couple, both psychoanalysts visiting Cuiabá, heard about the funeral from a Meruri Bororo and went to the Garças village to attend it. I was asked to serve as their interpreter. The Bororo wanted to be paid to let the couple watch the funeral. The French visitors claimed that they had already set everything with the Meruri leaders, but the Garças chiefs claimed that, since they were the ones holding the funeral, they, too, were entitled to payment. The couple agreed and remained in the village during the last two days of the funeral. They were anxious to understand the meaning of the ceremony and were concerned by the "terrible poverty," which they considered deeply shocking. They asked over and over again where the Bororo got protein, as they believed the Indians were all undernourished.

For the funeral ceremonies, two *aroe-maiwu* were chosen from the men of the Tugarege moiety. The choreography of the Bororo funeral was performed in minute detail. Because I have watched several Bororo funerals, in different villages, I can state that there were only a few differences between the ceremonies. In this one, more traditional ornaments were used because a missionary from Meruri stores several *pariko* (feather headdresses and other ornaments) at the mission post, which he brings out for these occasions. During this funeral, the Indians engaged very little in ritual scarification, which kept the tension that ordinarily builds on such occasions quite low.

On the last day, when the bones were ornamented at the *bai-mana-gejewu*, one could hardly breathe in the central house. The building was packed with several of the CIMI assembly attendees, missionaries from Meruri, Salesians who worked in other villages, filmmakers carrying their paraphernalia, and the Meruri Bororo.

In the traditional ceremony, the ornamented skull is placed on a covered tray (*baku*) and passed around to all the deceased's relatives. Holding the tray as if it were an infant, these relatives must cry over it and scarify themselves to let their blood drip over the skull. In Father Lunkenbein's ceremony, the *baku* was passed to the Bokori men and women (who belonged to the clan of the deceased) and to the priests and nuns in attendance.

Mass at the Meruri Village

At the end of the ceremony, the ornamented bones were placed in a basket (*kodo*) and taken to the Meruri village, where mass was to be celebrated. In Meruri, Herman and Konrad, both dressed in white—who had not attended the decoration of the bones—awaited the arrival of the funerary basket. They took the basket and placed it on a large altar set up in the mission courtyard. In the middle of the altar sat a Bororo tray. The words "I came to serve and give life," in Portuguese, German, and Bororo, were inscribed on the priest's gravestone.

A funeral mass was celebrated by thirteen priests and three bishops on the spot where the murder was committed. Many priests and nuns, Indians, and CIMI assembly members attended. Everyone sang "Unidos Venceremos" (United, We Shall Overcome) as a prelude to the speeches delivered during the Epistle. In the Introit, Father Ochoa mentioned the "care, art, devotion, and mercy" with which the Bororo performed their celebrations. He recalled the image of Christ Our Lord, "a model that gave strength to our brothers and whose sacrifice will be validated during mass." Father Ochoa referred to Christ as a martyr and noted that Father Lunkenbein and Simão were also martyrs. He mentioned that while mass was being celebrated the mother of Christ "looked down from heaven," Father Lunkenbein's mother "looked over from Germany," and Simão's mother, who had witnessed her son's sacrifice, was attending mass and "possibly representing the two mothers." "She also suffered the sore wound of her flesh, by scarification, as she mixed her blood with the blood of her son who had been immolated in this scenario."

The mass, celebrated in Bororo and followed by the congregation in a book prepared and published by the missionaries, was punctuated by statements in German and in Portuguese, as well as by hymns and chants. Lourenço, one of the Bororo wounded in the incident, reminded everyone of the "confusion and martyrdom" that took place in 1976. He reread a letter that he had mailed all over the world at the time: "Is it possible that we must take to arms and attack the white men as they did us? No, true Christians do not act this way. Weapons are the argument of cowards. We wish to join our strengths. We no longer accept the dominance and the manipulation. We demand to be treated as people, human beings, and, above all, as Christians."

Father Lunkenbein's brother Herman delivered a brief biography of the Salesian missionary:

Rodolfo was born on 1 April 1939, and studied in Göringstadt. At the end of fourth grade he told his brother he would like to enter the seminary and study to be a priest. However, financial hardships forced him to postpone his plans until seventh grade.

Despite his teacher's advice not to enroll in seminary studies because of the seriousness with which they were conducted, Rodolfo undertook the challenge and succeeded.

Upon arriving in Brazil he began his novitiate, in Pindamon-hangaba, and after that spent three years as an intern in the Meruri village.

Rodolfo celebrated his first mass in Göringstadt for the entire town. During the following week, everyone attended an affair that resembled the celebration that is being held here today.

In Germany, Rodolfo underwent aircraft pilot training and other preparatory courses, until his return to Meruri on Christmas Day, 1969.

Finally, I thank all of you for coming. Believe in Father Lunkenbein. Believe that he helps—this is certain.

Genoveva, Simão's sister, spoke next. She recalled the day when everything happened and mentioned that her brother spent all his time with the missionaries, working as a bricklayer or doing odd jobs.

The Reverend Pedro Casaldáliga spoke about the martyrdom at Meruri as a "blood bond." He recalled that, two years before the murder, the First Assembly of Indian Chiefs was held in Meruri and that, during the mass, Father Lunkenbein had anointed the Reverend Thomas and the Reverend Pedro with annatto dye. The Reverend Thomas had said, "Pedro, this is the blood."

Well aware of the prevailing unrest, the Reverend Pedro warned the congregation that the "confusion" had not ended, for there were still many enemies of the Indian cause, many people who coveted native land, many who were disrespectful of the identity and self-determination of the native peoples. He delivered an optimistic forecast, however, based on his faith in God and in life, "in the God of all cultures and in the God of all peoples." To him, "the native cause shall survive and overcome." Finally, he asked that we all sing "Unidos Venceremos" one more time: "United the native peoples among themselves, united the missionaries among themselves, united the missionaries and the Indians, if necessary until death, united in blood, united in the resurrection of Jesus."

Next a priest spoke of the love of work. He also mentioned Father Lunkenbein's sensitive, subtle manner, despite his size (the priest was a strong man, nearly six feet tall). He said that the deaths of Father Lunkenbein and Simão represented the seeds of a new life; that their blood had been spilled so that the land would become fertile and produce food; that those who worship death could give birth to life, as an answer to death and to hatred of life.

After mass, the missionaries were invited to dinner at the mission. To the Bororo who had come from Garças, the nuns offered sandwiches and oranges. That night I showed two films on the Bororo, made by Dina and Claude Lévi-Strauss in 1935.

The following day the funerary basket was placed in an urn and taken in procession to the mission's cemetery. At the graveside, Father Ochoa read an explanation of the events that had occurred during the last few days. He noted that Father Lunkenbein had been sacrificed because of the demarcation of the Indian reserve and that, for this reason, the Bororo community had decided to hold the same ceremonies for the priest that they ordinarily conducted for their own deceased. He reminded us that both the priest's family and the Salesian missionaries had agreed to participate in the rituals. He added that, in addition to the funerary basket containing the ornamented bones, the burial urn contained "gifts of clothing, found almost intact with the priest's remains." Among those people who attended mass he cited the bishop of the local diocese, the Reverend Antônio Sarco; the bishop of Guiratinga, the Reverend Camilo Parecim; the bishop of São Félix, the Reverend Pedro Casaldáliga; the inspector of the Salesians, Father José Marinoni; the director of Brasília's Anthropos, Father César; the inspector nun of the Salesians, Sister Barreto; and priests, nuns, and lay missionaries. Father Ochoa also mentioned that the mass, celebrated in Bororo, had been organized by the priests and nuns of Meruri: Father José Moschin, Master Mário Bordignon, Sister Elza Ribeiro, Sister Elza Zanetti, Sister Divina Bento, and the priests and nuns he had just named.

This speech, dated 15 July 1986, was signed by bishops, provincial authorities, mission directors, and the chief representatives of the Bororo families, and was placed in the urn containing the funerary basket.

To close the funeral ceremony, two Bororo songs were sung, then a woman performed the ritual wailing and began the scarification ritual, which Father Ochoa interrupted. At the end of the ceremony, everyone left the cemetery.

The Bororo give Salesian nuns the ornamented bones of Father Lunkenbein. *Sylvia Caiuby Novaes, Garças, 1986.*

Before offering my comments about the ceremonies themselves, however, I would like to describe discussions that included the Bororo, the missionaries, the filmmakers, and me. I believe that, when described, these data speak for themselves; second, description of the events allows interpretations different from the ones that I will present next; third, the account renders a good picture of the reality of an Indian village at century's end, including of the outsiders with whom the Indians have been forced to coexist: missionaries, anthropologists, journalists, tourists, filmmakers, and the like.

The Discussion

On several occasions during the filming of the funeral, I noticed the Bororo asking the filmmakers for payment. The filmmakers told them to discuss the issue with Father Thomas, who had asked them to be present. The filmmakers were accompanied throughout by Ivo, a Meruri Bororo.

After the funeral, mass, and burial of the urn, a meeting was held to discuss payment. Father Thomas invited the Bororo of the Meruri and Garças villages, the three-person film crew, a couple linked to the CIMI who had recorded the events on videotape, the photographers, and me.[3] Frederico, a "captain" of the Meruri village who had lived a long time among the "civilized" people, began to speak. He said that, despite having been exhaustively researched, filmed, and photographed, the Bororo continued to suffer and live in dire poverty; that no one, especially the anthropologists, cared about them—except for the missionaries who devoted their lives to the Bororo cause; that the movie had been shot; that filmmakers would make money off it; and that the Bororo should be paid for it. He said it was up to Father Thomas to figure out what to do, because this was a firm demand.

Father Thomas spoke next. He praised the Bororo for their courage in claiming their rights on their own initiative instead of bowing in submission. He argued that, in this case, however, he was only a go-between and that, for this reason, it was important to hear what the head of the film crew had to say.

Filmmaker Geraldo Sarno explained that the footage shot in Meruri was part of a movie about Liberation Theology in Latin America, that they had already shot in Mexico and Peru, and that the CNBB had requested that they also film the events in Meruri. He further explained that this was not a commercial movie. He gave a detailed description of the hardships of obtaining sponsorship from the several agencies that funded the production and what his intentions were.

On his own initiative, he offered tickets, room, and board for three Bororo to travel to Rio de Janeiro when he began editing the film so they could share their views about the movie. He also offered the Bororo a 16-mm and a video copy of the movie. Sarno further pledged that, should the movie be commercialized, the Bororo would receive a percentage of the net revenue of all sales.

Frederico replied that these were only promises, and the Indians were weary of promises. The Bororo wanted something concrete and immediate, because they had long been waiting for FUNAI to send them pledged funds, and they needed money.

Father Thomas said he understood Frederico's position and even agreed with him. He suggested it would be interesting to hear the opinion of other meeting participants. He asked me to speak.

I talked about what I did and how I saw the role of the anthropologist. I said I knew anthropologists involved with the Indian cause to differing degrees, but that I had never met an anthropologist who had become rich off the Indians. I told them it was highly unlikely that the filmmakers were going to become millionaires off the movie they had just made. I agreed with Father Thomas when he said the time had come for the Indians to no longer bow their heads in submission and to demand their rights. For this very reason, I thought it was important that the Bororo demand action from the mayor of General Carneiro, who, without the Indians' permission, had built a bridge on reservation territory without offering any compensation. I said they should collect payment from farmers who grazed their cattle on Indian pastureland. They should "speak tough," as they themselves say, to the invaders of their lands and to all their enemies. I added that I didn't think they had any enemies in that room and that, although in general terms I agreed with their demands, I thought they had trained it on the wrong target.

Father Thomas suggested that the Indians gather in private to discuss and reach a consensus before presenting their claims. In the following day's meeting, the Bororo could speak directly to Antônio Brant, who, according to Father Thomas, had actually hired the film crew.

I left this first meeting dumbfounded and decided not to take part in any other. Among all the participants, I was the only one who had no connections with the church, and I guessed that the chain would break at its weakest link. I became even more certain of my decision when Father Thomas insisted on my attending the following day's meeting. I later found out that the Bororo had presented a list of claims that included everything they had not obtained from FUNAI (which for a long while had not released any funds) and everything else that they desired. I recall only a few items: a truck, a large quantity of diesel oil, fence wire, a tractor with implements, etc. As it was absolutely impossible for the filmmakers to meet these demands, they had no alternative but to hand over to the Bororo the reels of film.

During the meeting, I was called on by many Meruri Bororo. They came to tell me that, although the Bororo chief was trying to speak as their official spokesman, his words were not to be trusted because they conveyed only his personal opinion. A leader of the Garças village told me that the Indians were waiting for the departure of the *barae* (non-Indians) to depose the Meruri chief and replace him. (Two weeks after I returned to São Paulo I received a telephone call from the Bororo, who told me the chief had been overthrown and that the vice-chief was to hold his position until new elections.)

Analysis and Comments

The Theoretical Framework

My account does not exclude comments about and interpretations of the data. First, both the decoration of the bones in Garças and the mass and the urn burial in Meruri can be understood as a ceremony in the sense Dayan and Katz attributed to this concept. To these authors, a *ceremony* is both a spectacle and a festival. As a spectacle, a ceremony has a definite focus and a clear distinction for those who carry it out—performers—and for those who attend it—respondents—given that the latter are expected to answer in a specific, generally traditional, manner. As with celebrations, a ceremony implies an interaction between the audience and performers (Dayan and Katz, 1985: 17).

It is also interesting to focus on the concept of *social drama* as formulated by Victor Turner: "the 'social drama' concept is within the brackets of positive structural assertions; it is concerned mainly with relations between persons in their status-role capacity and between groups and subgroups as structural segments" (1974a: 45–46). Turner formulated this concept to deal with a processual analysis (which included, according to him, both cultural analysis and structural-functional analysis) whose main emphasis was the dynamics of social life itself. This perspective allows us to analyze *conflict* and its counterpoint—*cohesion*—from an angle that does not favor one side or the other. From this perspective, the *interests* of each group involved in the social drama must be deciphered.

Two other concepts are equally important for Turner's processual analysis: *metaphor* and *multivocal symbols*. In metaphor, "we have two thoughts of different things *active* together and supported by a single word, or phrase, whose meaning is a resultant of their *interaction*" (Richards, 1936: 93, in Turner, 1974a). Turner thus approaches I. A.

Richards's concept of *interaction view*. This view emphasizes the inherent dynamics of the metaphor, showing that "the two thoughts are active together, they 'engender' *thought* in their coactivity" (Turner, 1974a: 29).

In the metaphorical relationship thus conceived, the two elements are multivocal symbols with a systemic characteristic associated with a series of images, ideas, feelings, values, and stereotypes. The components of one system enter a dynamic relationship with the components of another; in this process, the characteristic implications of the subsidiary system are associated with the main system.

Symbols instigate social action while supporting temporal changes in social relations (Turner, 1974a: 55). According to Turner, ritual symbols are "multivocal," that is, susceptible to many meanings. Their references, however, tend to be polarized around physiological phenomena (such as blood) and the normative values of moral facts (reciprocity, generosity, respect for elders, obedience of authority, etc.). In ritual action there is an exchange between these two poles: the biological references are enabled and the normative referents are charged with emotional significance (1974a: chap. 1).

In a retrospective of the concept of culture as denoted throughout the development of anthropological theory, D'Andrade shows the pertinence of distinguishing between *meaning systems* and *symbol systems*. It becomes a matter of finding out where the meaning lies, whether it is inherent in the message, or whether it develops from "the interaction of a mind or a mechanism with a message. . . . Where does one look for meaning—in culturally produced messages of various sorts or in the minds of the people who interpret these messages?" (1984: 101–102).

These are the considerations that lead D'Andrade to distinguish between message and meaning through the ambiguity of the term *symbol*: "the term symbol can refer to either the physical thing that carries the meaning or to the meaning carried by the physical thing" (1984: 103). By the same token, if the meaning is not necessarily the message, "meaning systems need messages to keep themselves alive" (1984: 105).

D'Andrade's interpretation does not contradict Turner's; it merely introduces a greater sophistication. Because they are multivocal, as Turner states, symbols found in messages (ritual or other) can be interpreted in many ways and must be analyzed from the point of view of those who issue them and those to whom the messages are sent (and who can interpret them in different ways, as D'Andrade shows).

Another theoretical perspective—very close to the analysis proposed by Turner within the concept of social drama and the concept formulated by Van Velsen (1967) using the notion of social situation—was presented by Oliveira Filho (1988) in a work that addresses the relationship between the Ticuna and the tutelary system (i.e., SPI and FUNAI). This perspective deals with the different facets assumed by relations of power in interethnic contact. By taking up again Gluckman's analysis of more than 150 years of Zulu history (1939), Oliveira Filho points out Gluckman's interest in "capturing the different patterns of interdependence between the Zulu and the non-Indian, . . . an interdependence that does not imply a balanced reciprocity, a symmetry among the groups and persons involved" (1988: 57). The question of *intentionality*, of the interests and ideologies of the actors involved, is a fundamental step in understanding this interdependence.

Despite referring to the theoretical framework organized by Gluckman, Oliveira Filho prefers the expression *historical situation*—"a notion that does not refer to isolated events, but to models or schemes of distribution of power among several social actors" (1988). According to Oliveira Filho, this notion is sufficiently comprehensive to address situations in which politics is a sphere that specializes in events and activities contained in other domains of social life. Starting from the concept of *historical situation*, interethnic contact is thought of as "a set of relationships among social actors linked to different ethnic groups" (1988: 58). In the contact situation there is no automatic adherence to the actor's cultural code. From this point of view, there is a "denaturalization" of the cultural codes in which the person was socialized; standards of action appear as alternate conduct possibilities in which orientation values remain as components of alternative ideologies (1988: esp. 54–59).

I have identified the interests that were at play in Father Lunkenbein's funeral ceremony by deduction because, although I requested that the missionaries give me an interview, they refused.

The Salesians Strengthen a New Self-Image

We have already referred to the process that led the contemporary church, especially the more progressive branches linked to Liberation Theology, to make a "choice for the poor." Priests include Indians in the category of the "poor and oppressed" because of the historical process of domination to which they have been submitted and the plundering of their land.

Of the several orders and religious congregations active in Brazil, the Salesians have been regarded as the most conservative. After becoming a target of criticism,[4] the Salesians were interested in establishing a new image, especially in the eyes of the more progressive branches of the church. Thus, honoring Father Lunkenbein during the CIMI assembly ten years after his murder meant creating a strategic situation to publicize this new image among church members themselves. In order to understand the meaning and importance of conducting a Bororo funeral for the bones of a Salesian missionary, we must remember the words of the Salesians themselves while evaluating their Christian education work in 1925:

> Who could describe the *bakururu* [funeral rites and their many songs]? An evil spirit reigns over it, stimulates it, nourishes it: ignorance and savagery set it burning; superstition and fanaticism perpetuate and magnetize it. The *bari* (sorcerer) with cavernous voice intones the rhythmic symphony and a circle of comrades answer that bellowing, to that beastly howl in unison. As the terrible voice of the *bari* rises, the others join in like a band of threatened hyenas, in agony, then furious again, as they cruelly charge.[5]

Besides demonstrating a radical change in the Salesians' perception of this funerary ritual, the speeches proffered during the mass and burial of the urn clearly showed that the priest's death was closely related to the more contemporary context of land struggle and to the church's deep engagement in the country's land issues.

The Salesians' attempt to identify more closely with the Liberation Theologians implies, in my opinion, two necessary conditions: (1) alliance with those chosen by the progressive church: the poor and, in this case, the Bororo; (2) the symbolic identification between the Salesian missionaries and the Bororo that must become visible. This identification between missionaries and Indians was quite visible in all the speeches delivered by the priests and those given by the Bororo during mass. Lourenço spoke of "combining strengths" and the need for the Indians to be treated as "Christians." Genoveva recalled the close relationship that her brother had always had with the missionaries. Father Ochoa referred to Father Lunkenbein's mother as a woman well aware of the significance of her son's death, as someone who accepted the sacrifice of her son by forgiving his enemies.

Father Ochoa established the first relationship of identity among the actors involved in the ceremony, between the mother of Christ ("who looks down from heaven"), the mother of Father Lunkenbein ("who looks over from Germany"), and the mother of Simão (who, in the ceremony, represented both). In this context, the mother figure symbolizes the importance of a man who became a martyr. A man who dies is just an ordinary man, unless he dies for a noble cause (then he becomes a hero) or unless someone suffers deeply from the loss. Thus, it is the mother's loss of her son and her full acceptance of this loss that characterize the sacrifice as martyrdom. At the same time, it allows for the understanding of a man's acts from the viewpoint of martyrdom or self-sacrifice to legitimize certain ideas, beliefs, and attitudes: "To be a martyr one must be killed out of hate for Jesus Christ and His Church" (Balzola, 1932: 44). The Christian martyr is he who suffers for doing the work of Christ, which leads him, and the model he follows, to death.

As Turner (1974a: 122) demonstrates, history repeats the great myths of culture "generated in great social crises, at turning points of change." Although Turner is referring to central characters of the Mexican Revolution, his conclusions also pertain to the processes that allow us to view historical events as a great *social drama*, wherein actors must take on roles in which they act and speak in a suprapersonal, or "representative," way. This role playing is a preparation for the climax— a central myth of the death or victory of a hero or heroes.

Father Ochoa was extremely explicit when comparing event and myth. His comparison was also strategic in the sense of reinforcing the identification between Indians and missionaries. At the beginning of mass, he alluded to the image of Christ Our Lord, "a model that gave strength to our brothers and whose sacrifice will be validated during mass." He referred to Christ as a martyr and reminded everyone that Father Lunkenbein and Simão were also martyrs. Both Father Ochoa and the Reverend Pedro Casaldáliga used a vital symbol (in its literal and metaphorical sense)—blood—as a means of determining the social action through which Indians and missionaries might perceive themselves not as mere allies, but as one and the same person. How did the missionaries represent this union?

The murders of Father Lunkenbein and Simão led to *bloodshed*; furthermore, through scarification, Simão's relatives also inflicted on themselves a "sensitive wound," to which Father Ochoa made reference, as they mixed their blood with the blood of the dead. The Reverend Pedro Casaldáliga referred to the episode as a "blood bond." He associated the annatto dye, used by the Bororo for body painting, with blood.

The references to the "mother" figure are equally important in this process of creating mechanisms of identification. During mass, the association was extremely precise (see table 2).

There is a clear dignification of the biological referent—blood—and the attribution of an emotional meaning to the normative referent, as shown by Turner. First, in this metaphorical process the church's authority and the respect of its representatives is strengthened ("Believe in Father Lunkenbein. Believe that he helps—this is certain," Herman, the priest's brother, says). Second, what is strengthened is basically the identification, union, and need for alliance between Indians and mis-

Table 2. Identification Mechanisms

Christ	Missionaries	The Bororo
Blood of Christ	Blood shed by murderers	Scarification/ annatto dye
Mother of Christ	Mother of Rodolfo	Mother of Simão

sionaries (in this sense, the close of the Reverend Casaldáliga's speech is quite explicit in this regard). The essential element in the associations of blood/annatto dye, mother of Christ/mother of Rodolfo/mother of Simão is the possibility of identification among all actors involved, which allows the church, through the Salesians and the Bororo, to assume its Truth publicly and objectively.

Father Lunkenbein's biography speaks of a simple man who, through devotion and persistence, was able to overcome adversity to dedicate his life to an altruistic cause. Others painted him as a man devoted to his work, a friendly and sensitive person, "despite his size." The man described during the funeral ceremony was a man who fully represented the Christian ideal. In his brief life (this brevity is important for the analogy), Father Lunkenbein was identified as an archetype to be followed. "The Christ myth is here the model, not in a cognitive and bloodless way, but in an existential and bloody way," states Turner (1974a: 123) in a passage in which he could just as well be referring to the episodes we are discussing.

Still bearing in mind the manner in which the missionaries tried to act, according to their interests, I return to Dayan and Katz's concept of *ceremony*. As I have said, the ceremony had a definite focus: a tribute to a priest murdered ten years before. The ceremony also clearly distinguished between those who acted it out and those who watched it, although it was assumed that there was an interaction between these two groups. In this sense, the tribute to Father Lunkenbein strategically constituted a two-phase ceremony: during the decoration of the bones, the Bororo were "masters of ceremony," the performers. The missionaries played the role of "relatives of the dead," who watched and interacted with those who conducted the ceremony, according to the models defined by Bororo culture. The second phase of the ceremony comprised the mass celebrated by priests and bishops and attended by the Bororo community. In this sense, both the Indians and the missionaries participated in the ceremonies as assistants and performers, thus establishing, at least in the formal plan, an equality among the two groups. As I will show later, this equality may be of interest to both. The statement of this formal equality is important from the missionaries' point of view for the establishment of an alliance and a "union" between them and the Indians. In the missionaries' view, union (and this is a prized attribute in Christian discourse) is the true weapon of confrontation—not in terms of an armed struggle, which is contrary to Christian principles, but in terms of a joint battle. As the Reverend Casaldáliga put it, "United the native peoples among themselves, united the missionaries among themselves, united the missionaries and the Indians, if necessary until death, united in blood, united in the resurrection of Jesus." Just as the Bororo funeral, through the several phases of its rituals, promotes union among all members of its society (dead and living, mere mortals and heroes), the union that the Salesians established was not restricted to the Bororo who attended the ceremony, but was extended to Bororo society as a whole.

This union implies, as we have seen, total identification between Indians and missionaries, an identification that emphasizes not the obvious differences between these two groups, but the possibility of perceiving any underlying resemblance; such resemblance is fundamental if the groups are to act together. In missionary discourse, this resemblance is made explicit in the most vital symbol—the blood of martyrdom—which is, in every sense, the symbol of great transformation (life/death/resurrection; separation/union; oppression/liberation). Therefore, martyrdom is not only an element of identification between Indians and missionaries but, fundamentally, the possibility of expressing the Truth embodied by unity within the church. The messages contained in the declarations of the priests during the mass for Father Lunkenbein, as well as the symbols involved, were directed not only to the Bororo, but particularly to the church members who attended the ceremony.

The Celebrations from the Bororo Viewpoint

From the Bororo point of view, what was the meaning of Father Lunkenbein's funeral? The missions were established to concentrate the largest possible number of Indians under the missionaries' influence. This densely concentrated population, however, created problems, such as contagion during epidemics and difficulty in obtaining food.

Meruri, the village that is still most influenced by the missionaries, continues to house the largest number of Indians, and, although epidemics no longer occur, problems caused by population concentration persist. The assistance provided by missionaries continues to be the major attraction of the Meruri reserve. In addition to providing medical care that is far better than that received by Bororo groups outside mission territory, the Salesians fight the alcoholism that causes latent tensions and conflicts to surface, mainly in Meruri. The Bororo and the Salesians frequently mention the absence of powerful leadership as another major problem in Meruri.

During the census he conducted in twelve villages in 1910, Father Balzola counted 1,143 Bororo. The censuses conducted by Father Ochoa in October 1979 and by Master Mário Bordignon in 1986 produced the following figures (table 3). It should be noted that in 1979, around 40 percent (252) of all Bororo lived in Meruri, Garças, and Sangradouro, which are villages under the jurisdiction of the Salesian mission. By 1986, the Bororo population had increased by 12.7 percent to 706 individuals, of whom 54 percent (385) lived in the mission's territory.[6]

Table 3 shows us that, whereas the total Bororo population increased 12.7 percent in seven years, in areas under the influence of the missions, for example, in Meruri and Garças, it increased 56 percent and 64 percent, respectively. Jarudori, which was not a site of missionary work, was abandoned by 1986, and the population of all the others decreased, except for that of Córrego Grande (Gomes Carneiro), which increased only 0.6 percent.

The last census I took at nine Bororo villages, in July 1986, revealed a total population of 730, of which 292 lived in Meruri and 73 in Garças.[7] I visited the Indian reservation in Meruri in July 1972, January and February 1982, December 1983, July 1985, and July 1986. On those occasions, I was able to record several of the Bororo's statements and discussions. I was also able to follow over a period of years the progress of relations between Meruri and Garças and those between these two villages and the Salesians. At times the Indians asked that I record a message "to the government" or to someone qualified to act in their behalf. The following transcription of excerpts from a statement by a

Table 3. Salesian Censuses of the Bororo Population

Village	Population in 1979	Population in 1986
Meruri	163	260
Garças	61	101
Sangradouro	24	25
Jarudori	15	—
Tadarimana	105	73*
Gomes Carneiro	152	162
Perigara	102	86
Total	622	707

*Tadarimana's population includes Tadarimana, 48; Pobori, 15; and Paulista, 10.

chief of the Garças village, taped in December 1983, clearly shows the Bororo's struggle against the "eradication" to which they have been subjected throughout history:

> The so-called Bororo Indian is the authentic, original Indian, he is the first legitimate Brazilian, he is the Bororo . . . But it's amazing! Could it be that the silly whites, the government, are abandoning us? The whites want Indians to be without anything! Without anything, not a grain of sand, not a speck of dirt. By force, by resisting we are here in Brazil, our Brazil, our Mato Grosso. Then Mister Governor of the United States, Governor of São Paulo, Governor of another country, Germany, Italy, who should be helping us here, we know you are there and you should know we are here.
> The FUNAI staff here, the governor of Brazil here, no one is helping us. Because of our cries and our shouts we are finding something here in Mato Grosso, here in Brazil. Then we go looking for another idea; if the governor of Germany, Italy, the United States, São Paulo were only to help here in Mato Grosso [he is referring to the possibility of raising funds for projects submitted to foreign entities].
> Indians, we are Indians, I wish you would remember us. Never have we Indians been on television, on the radio, in the home of . . . of . . . the city, state, bus, truck, airplane, or anything. We are disappearing. Now other Indians appear: the Xavante and many more. And the Bororo who were first, [according to Indian myth, the Bororo were created first] . . .where are they? They should be remembered!

To become *visible* is fundamentally important in a competitive society. The Bororo know this and know that it is only as Indians that they can be regarded as a group and not merely as part of Brazil's population. I talked about this with an old Bororo in 1982 (he has since died). As we chatted on the verandah of the mission while waiting for mass to begin, he told me: "In the past we sneaked out to do Indian funeral. When Father João Falcon brought these, Indians from Pobojari, our culture got more animated. And they also live within the culture of the civilized—they plant, raise cattle, some are drivers. These here in Garças are conserving our culture. I sometimes go to Garças because I like to participate." This old Bororo was wise enough to recognize the advantages of assimilating new cultural patterns while preserving a culture that not only should remain alive but also should become visible to the surrounding society. He continued:

I used to like to come out in the picture, now I don't like it anymore; I guess it's because I'm getting old. But I only like to come
out in the picture when I have on full dress, when I am fully
decorated, like in the old days. I really like it, because I think it is
good for me and for the Bororo. Maybe someday it [his photograph]
will go public. Once I asked the priest why only the Xavante are
published. He said it's because the Xavante are many and the
Bororo are few. But it's for this reason that they should publish . . .

The Bororo are also deeply aware of the population imbalance that
characterizes the relations between them and Brazilian society. In 1985
a Bororo chief told me in Garças:

The *boe*, Bororo have tried to live like the whites. But there is no
way to do it. If they become like the whites, the *boe* disappear
among them. But if they study here, stay here without disappearing
among the whites, the Bororo will not turn white. The late Thiago[8]
fought hard to become a white. He went to school, then he went to
Germany and Italy, and he studied to become a priest. He came
back and did make it into the priesthood; he went back to being a
Bororo chief, to writing legends and stories. Here he can be big.

Royce shows that the most pertinent analyses of interethnic relations
necessarily revolve around three factors: power, perception, and purpose. In terms of power, "subordinate groups have been able to use the
fact of their subordination as a weapon in interaction with guilt-ridden
members of dominated groups" (1982: 4). In general, dominated groups
tend to be more fully aware of their situation. "The view from below is
quite different—to survive at all, to get ahead, requires a knowledge of
the subtleties of institutional structure, as well as knowledge of the
thoughts and values of the dominant group" (1982: 4). In this sense, I
believe we can understand the Bororo's participation in ceremonies held
to honor Father Rodolfo Lunkenbein as springing from their need to
secure their place—which in a broad sense comprises territorial integ-
rity, health care and education, financial resources, visibility and social
recognition, and so on—within the present structure of Brazilian society. The guarantee of this space necessarily implies (1) establishing
alliances with a few groups in the larger society that could have little or
no affinity among themselves, such as missionaries, anthropologists,
journalists, members of different agencies that support the Indian
cause, and so on; and (2) maintaining the Bororo's identity as a different
group.
    Located 12.5 miles from one another, the villages of Meruri and

Garças have the characteristics required for this strategy. Because of their easier contact with the *barae*, the Bororo of Meruri allied with the various outsiders who participated in the ceremony: missionaries, film-makers, tourists from Cuiabá, researchers, and participants in the CIMI assembly who had photographed or videotaped them. Given that the Bororo of Garças were the most knowledgeable about the traditions that comprise the intricate orchestration of the Bororo funeral, they were the only ones who could play their "Indian role" before a foreign audience. The Bororo know better than anyone else that their culture is their most precious asset, especially if we bear in mind that their society has been in contact with the region's non-Indian population since the early eighteenth century. For this reason, the Meruri Bororo view their proximity to the Garças village as strategic.

The Meruri Bororo are not always welcome in Garças, however, where they are discriminated against because they have not mastered the intricate codes of Bororo culture. In 1982, in Meruri, an old woman told me how she felt about the Bororo of Garças:

> I feel uncomfortable among them, because I don't know how to cry, i.e., perform the ritual wailing or sing. They say we are like the cicadas: we have no tears to cry. This hurts; it even hurts me who am old. Cicadas don't cry but they sing, don't they?
>
> Now the others, from the Garças village do not want to teach us and they keep scolding us. They say we cry like wolf cubs. They say "You are like the *baraedu,* civilized"—and this is a cuss word; it's offensive.

The funeral ceremonies held to honor a Salesian missionary (a "civilized" individual) and Simão, a Bororo Indian from the Meruri village, provided the young men of Meruri an excellent opportunity to be initiated and formally introduced as *boe*, thus leaving the ranks of *barae* (non-Indians). Rituals must be performed only by those who have an in-depth knowledge of the traditions; consequently, the celebrations gave the youth of Meruri access to the masters of the Garças village. This was also an opportunity for the Bororo to get the funds that had long been set aside but not disbursed by FUNAI. Their purpose was clearly shown when the Bororo charged the French tourists for attending a spectacle rather than a ceremony.

They attempted the same strategy to secure funds after the ceremonies, when the Bororo and the missionaries held discussions with the filmmakers and with me. Like the tourists, the filmmakers and I (as anthropologist) did not act as performer or as audience in the ceremony. As *reporters* of the ceremonies, we were to a certain extent able to show

Bororo village at the Meruri Salesian mission. *Sylvia Caiuby Novaes, 1986.*

it as a spectacle; for this reason, we should have *paid*. Obviously, the arguments we presented—that our records were critically important for the resistance strategy of the Bororo, a different society that should be duly respected as such—were not taken seriously.

Although Dayan and Katz's analysis focuses on the implications of certain ceremonies publicized on television, those ceremonies clearly demonstrate the reaction of the Bororo and (principally, though not explicitly) of the missionaries to them. In the first place, although at *spectacles* the audience is encouraged to participate, at no time is it allowed to become a defining element of the show. At a *ceremony*, which bears traces of both spectacle and festival, the interaction between *performers* and audience follows rules established by tradition:

> This interaction offers a *charismatic legitimization* of the proposed event. It *legitimizes* by being a "proper" reaction, and thus safe from the risk of "wrong" reaction. . . . By turning into a spectacle, an interactive ceremony undergoes an obvious impoverishment. The surprise is that, while television *represents* an occasion, and therefore flattens it into a spectacle, it gives itself a new mission: that of offering an equivalent to the lost participatory dimension. Thus, while destroying interaction by its very similarity to cinema,

television *performs* (or simulates) it anew. (1985: 23–24, original emphasis)

I believe these considerations clarify the reactions of both the missionaries and the Bororo, which I did not understand at the time. The recording of a ceremony (for video or television exhibition) shows the ceremony in its totality and excludes the specific participation of each group. Furthermore, the recording introduces a discerning narrator: while reporting on and publicizing the event, the narrator mentions its value and adds commentaries, thus transcending the event's original connotation and even the denotation of the records themselves.

The Bororo are ambiguous about the presence of someone who records and narrates the ceremony. If, on the one hand, they wish for it to be publicized (and, as I have shown, they need greater social visibility), the recording and commentaries are beyond their control, which radically changes the very nature of the event. As it reveals the content of a ceremony to a public that did not attend it, a video assumes the phatic function of communication,[9] thus creating, establishing, and maintaining contact with the viewer. Viewed from this perspective and in light of the thinking of these authors, the ceremony is no longer the locus of the particular semiotic practices of the involved groups. Furthermore, its diffusion allows spatial continuity where the script writing appears as a commentary intrinsic to the text itself.[10] If participants—the Salesians and the Bororo—cannot control what is said about it, they might regard any recording as transcending the reason for holding the ceremony.

Dayan and Katz show how television is replacing the "theatrical" nature of public events—where there is a real interaction between audience and performers (in, for example, ceremonies held in cathedrals, churches, halls of government, and courthouses)—with "a new mode of publicness based on the potential separation of performers and audiences, and on the rhetoric of narrative rather than the virtue of contact" (1985: 32). Much suspicion falls on the recorder, "since its [the ceremony's] dynamics lead to substitute simulation for representation, and since simulation, when endowed with authority, may turn into what Austin called 'performative,' and thus constitute a social reality" (1985: 32).

The possibility of infinite reproduction of all events or works, while abstracting from the original the primary intentions, leads in turn to the ever more frequent phenomenon of *simulacrum* (see chapter 2). The participating actors (missionaries, Indians, and even anthropologists) can acknowledge the simulacrum only as a *strategy* for the assertion of *truths* that belong in each of these groups, or categories. It is in essence a phenomenon devoid of any legitimacy for any of these three categories, all of which, not coincidentally, are domains of truth production.

Multifaceted Contact

Certain cultural domains—religious rituals in particular—may serve as "levers" for political displays. During the ceremonies held in honor of Father Lunkenbein, both the Bororo and the Salesians resorted to religious discourse to render an eminently political display. Although each of the groups in question had a different objective, they all were able to use the same model for action. And, as the ceremony was held in two parts—the Bororo funeral and the mass—it was also possible to avoid both confrontation and a "synchretized" ceremony.

The actors seem to have adopted a well-articulated strategy: to utilize their scheme of cultural references to express their own values. To the Bororo, the central issue was the possibility of asserting a different culture, with its own meanings, that could guide people in their relationship with life and death, and the recognition and visibility of this difference. The possibility of redefining the relationship between the Meruri Bororo (who knew less about the traditions of their society and were more liable to appropriate the code of the non-Indian world) and the Garças Bororo (the more "traditional" community) was also an important target, one that the Bororo reached.

To the missionaries, the ritual basically served to facilitate the assertion of a church that claims to be universal. It also served to assert an internal perspective for the church in terms of the Salesians' identification with the more progressive wing of the church. This strategy, in which both groups were interested, resulted in the strengthening of an alliance (between Indians and missionaries) that, at least formally, was manifested in the mutual recognition of the cultural standards of both groups and in the independence necessary to nurture this alliance. Although both groups had specific, individual interests, they shared this strategy and also successfully ensured their own space.

My analysis shows how the discourse of social agents involved in a specific historical situation and the meaning it conveys is a fundamental element for the constitution of the reality in which the agent's social practice is inscribed. My analysis also shows that the representations contained therein guide and confer a special meaning on the social praxis.[11] According to Maria Lúcia Montes, "There is no 'real' without a discourse that confers to it a specific 'reality,' just as there is no action on the real without its 'representation.'" She also affirms that "there is no political action outside the practice of social actors, and there is no practice except in the universe of ideology" (Montes, 1981: 62–63).

Montes goes on to show how, beginning in 1964, the military regime took away from the state the space in which the populist discourse that gave people their political identity had been articulated. This discourse must currently be found "in the most progressive sectors of the church." The church is another powerful influence on Brazilian society; from it "the voice that speaks for the humble people for whom God's kingdom has been reserved" is heard (1981: 75). Just as in the state's populist discourse prior to 1964, the church's discourse now operates "according to a contradictory logic, with a double meaning that is deciphered by the emitter and the receiver, . . . thus making room for the people at the same time that it tries to co-opt them, thus placing them at the service of class domination" (1981: 74).

The Person and Alterity

The anthropological literature about the Bororo shows that, in a society divided into two exogamic moieties (Tugarege and Ecerae), it is literally through the *other* (someone of the opposite moiety) that an individual exists socially and can, through ritual, become visible to society.

Eight clans make up the two moieties into which Bororo society is divided. The clans of the Tugarege moiety are the Iwagudu-doge, Aroroe, Apiborege, and Paiwoe. Those of the Ecerae moiety are the Bado Jebage Cebegiwuge, Kie, Bokodori Ecerae, and Bado Jebage Cobugiwuge. The relationship between these clans was defined in mythical times. It is a complex relationship that involves the various domains of social life. I have shown (1983) how—through the processes of manufacturing and circulating certain objects from Bororo material culture employed during the funeral—the need for the *other* in the constitution of the *social self* becomes clearly perceptible. From this standpoint, the *social self* among the Bororo manifests the transformation and transcendence of the individual as a "worldly object," that is, an empirical subject that talks and acts.[12] This model for constituting the social self is evident not only in the elaborate objects of Bororo material culture, but in numerous other instances.

In a society such as the Bororo, marked by exogamic moieties and matrilineal descent, the man of a specific clan contributes to the biological and social reproduction of a clan of the opposite moiety by means of a scheme of arranged marriages (which were also defined in mythical times). The model for production and reproduction of life in this society is the same as for handling death, when individuals of the opposite moiety to that of the deceased take care of dressing the corpse within the elaborate Bororo funeral system. Likewise, it is a man of the opposite moiety who will be appointed the deceased's social representative *(aroe-maiwu)* after his passing.

Among the Bororo, all chants and rituals (whether for funerals or not) are seen as the specific heritage of one of the eight clans of Bororo society.

The chants and rituals of a clan can be sung or performed only by members of a clan of the opposite moiety. The members of the clan who "own" these rituals must offer the necessary raw materials—annatto dye, genipap, and clay for face and body painting, specific types of feathers for manufacturing objects, and so on—for decorating the person (or persons) who will perform the ritual and render literally visible the deceased's social presence.[13]

If, as I have said, the assertion of the social self is necessarily an expression of an individual's transformation and transcendence as a "worldly object," that is, as an empirical subject who talks and acts, the church also thinks along similar lines in relation to the Christian individual. According to Dumont, "the brotherhood of love in and through Christ, and the consequent equality of all, an equality that exists purely in the presence of God. Sociologically speaking, the emancipation of the individual through a personal transcendence, and the union of outworldly individuals in a community that treads on earth but has its heart in heaven, may constitute a passable formula for Christianity" (1985: 99).

To Christians, relationships among people involve subjects made in God's image and who actually join him after their fleeting time on earth. It is precisely this totality, this union of all people, that the church symbolizes and presents as the first and universal truth. Without opposing this fundamental point of Christian faith, the progressive church attempts to lead people to become subjects of their own history. At the same time, it shows them that it is as collective individuals who recognize themselves in the other and come together in adversity that they will gather the necessary conditions to cope with their situation as politically dominated subjects.

Given that it is through the church that this union becomes feasible, that is, that these various others transcend themselves and act along new guidelines, there is an obvious compatibility between the logic of action and that of social assertiveness. This compatibility dictates the relationships between the Bororo and church representatives. It is precisely the need for transcendence of the self that, from different standpoints, brings together the mythical version that confers meaning on Bororo society and the sacred truth embodied by the church.

It is only at this ideological level that we can discuss contrastive identities, which are but two looking glasses positioned in such a way that the one who looks in the mirror can see only his or her own image (and own truth) reproduced infinitely. But unlike the mirror of Narcissus, which reflected his image until he was driven to despair and death, in a certain sense, the mirrors placed before Indians and missionaries offer them the possibility of life.

Notes

Preface

1. On the relationship between power and culture, see Maria Lúcia Montes (1981).

2. On the importance of the notion of individual and the ideology of corporality as fundamental elements in the understanding of South American Indian societies, see Seeger et al. (1979).

3. These authors base their findings on Gluckman (1958). A good review of this theoretical perspective is found in Oliveira Filho (1988).

4. Although Viertler (1979), Crocker (1977a, 1977b, 1985), and I (1983, 1986) have addressed the formation of the notion of person among the Bororo, we have not related this notion to the manner in which this society has always handled interethnic contact.

5. See, among others, Altenfelder (1949), Oberg (1949), and Galvão (1959).

6. Although I think conceptual precision is necessary to distinguish identity, self-image, and the notion of person, here I employ the term *identity*, as the most utilized term in the literature, to refer to these concepts in general.

1. Contemporary Anthropology and Studies of Identity and Social Change

1. See Kaplan and Manners (1981) and Herskovits (1965), among others.

2. Baudrillard goes even further to mock this paradox of anthropology: "It is most naïve to go and look for ethnology among the savages or in the Third World; it is here, everywhere, in the metropolises, among the whites, in a world that has been submitted to censuses, analyzed, and then *artificially resuscitated as real*, in a world of simulation, hallucinations of truth, extortions of reality, of the death of every symbolic form and its hysterical and historical retrospection, a death for which the savages, *noblesse oblige*, have paid the first price, but that long ago spread to all Western societies" (1978: 9–10, original emphasis).

3. See Beals's (1953) critical retrospective of acculturation studies conducted in the United States, Great Britain, and Germany.

4. See, among others, Wagley and Galvão (1955) on the Tenetehara; Wagley's comparison of the Tenetehara and the Tapirapé (1951); and Schaden (1954) on the Guarani. For judicious commentaries on these studies, see Viveiros de Castro (1986).

5. In 1936, Leslie Spier, editor of *American Anthropologist*, requested that American Anthropological Association members decide whether to publish articles on the acculturation issue in the magazine: "I believe such articles should be published in sociology journals or in periodicals devoted to contemporary living" (Beals, 1953: 622–623).

6. For an extremely careful analysis of these studies, see Oliveira Filho (1988).

7. "And, provided that the most dynamic and authoritative elements of the system tend to be those that integrate the more powerful subsystem (for example, Brazilian society), it could be said that the process in question means the Indians' integration into national society" (Cardoso de Oliveira, 1968: 343).

8. Although Lévi-Strauss does not appear in the bibliography of this collection, he remarks that the diversity of human cultures "is less a function of the isolation of groups than of the relations between them" (1960: 236).

9. "Humanity halts on the borders of the tribe, the language group, and, sometimes, even the village," says Lévi-Strauss (1960: 237).

10. To be fair, it must be said that in 1978 various authors, such as Laraia and DaMatta (1979), critically reexamined their own forecasts.

11. See, for example, the 1982 and 1986 editions of the *Anuário Antropológico*.

12. There are also a few processes, such as social and cultural change (associated with the different meanings of culture), and the processes of *motivation*, *perception*, and *cognition*, devised by psychology after the systematic observation of interaction, that can be seen only within certain concepts.

13. Although the conflict did not go unnoticed by functionalist authors such as Radcliffe-Brown (who did not accept the analogy between conflict and pathology proposed by Durkheim), this concept was not to be incorporated into anthropology until Gluckman (1949). Even so, Gluckman considered the concept to be an element that did not prevent the maintenance of social solidarity. The vision of culture as a symbolic system and the possibility of an interpretive analysis of behavior, carried out mainly by Geertz, had to wait until the humanistic sciences assimilated Lévi-Strauss's works.

14. In anthropology, the nonevolutionist investigation of the concept of human nature had to wait until 1949, when Lévi-Strauss published *Les Structures élémentaires de la Parenté*, thus inaugurating a new phase in the dialogue between anthropology, psychoanalysis, and linguistics.

15. Linton wrote, for example, "As a general term, *culture* means the social heredity of mankind, while as a specific term *a culture* means a particular strain of social heredity . . . ideas, habits, and techniques which have come down to them from their ancestors" (1937: 78, 69).

16. On the relationship between anthropology and psychoanalysis, see also Micela (1984).

17. "A social identity is an aspect of self that makes a difference in how one's rights and duties distribute to specific others" (1969: 313).

18. The concepts of self and identity have different origins. The concept of self as a central archetype, an organizer of personality, is associated with Jung's work and the process of individuation with its biological, psychic, and social implications. The concept of identity, found mainly in Erikson's work, seeks to situate the feeling of identity as "an individual's progression through the life cycle, always modified by the historical context" (Bock, 1988: 128). However,

both *self* (which in German is *Selbst*, i.e., "the same") and *identity* denote the perception of that which is the same, equal. This perception becomes possible only through the perception of the difference, the other, as Bateson has clearly demonstrated. In turn, self and identity are absent in Freud's work, where the focus is on the analysis of the ego, the superego, and the id. "According to C. Thompson, Freud made a big mistake by taking for biological the cultural phenomena" (in Micela, 1984: 116).

2. Identity in the Broad Sense: The Other as Model

1. In the classical definition of sign as proposed by Saussure there is a balance, if not a symmetry, between signifier (expression) and signified (content): "at the level of sign, the distinction between signified and signifier remains indispensable and J. Derrida claims that if the *supremacy of the signifier* meant that there were no place for a difference between it and the signified, the term *signifier* itself would lose all meaning. He claims, on the contrary, that something works as signifier even in meaning: such is the role of trace" (Ducrot and Todorov, 1988: 314, my emphasis).

2. I have heard militant homosexual men call for a "virile and macho" role in relationships with partners.

3. In 1973 Foucault conducted an extremely interesting analysis of similarity and similitude.

3. Literature as Mirror: Different Views of Social Change in Bororo Society

1. Nor does Viertler present any systematic research on when and how the Bororo turn to the regional market, which would be indispensable for the verification of her conclusions.

2. In 1979 Sahlins produced what I consider the best criticism of anthropological approaches that regard human cultures as based on a practical and utilitarian activity.

3. In his review of Crocker's book, Viveiros de Castro offers the following commentary on the foregoing excerpt: "The presentation of the question as one of 'choice' barely conceals a largely *passive* conception of Bororo society because the choice ends up being, in Crocker's terms, between dying or dying, since for the author 'acculturation' means cultural death" (Viveiros de Castro, 1988: 13).

4. "One novel Brazilian good seems to have summarized all the attractive lethalty, the irreversible entropic decline, the cancerous blossoming of indigenous social tensions, brought about by sustained contacts between the two societies. This was alcohol, or in the form most commonly known to the Bororo, cachaça, sugar-cane brandy or rum, locally called *pinga*" (Crocker, 1985: 328).

5. Although Crocker published a few articles on the Bororo, his 1985 monograph is the only text in which he extensively addresses the issue of change.

4. Self-Image as Formed in the Play of Mirrors: Structural Distance and Reference Values

1. The term "alteration" must be understood here in its literal sense, that

is, as formed from *alter* + *action*, meaning the actions one takes because of an other.

2. In an extremely interesting article, Umberto Eco shows that "the magic of mirrors springs from their extensively intrusive nature, which allows us not only to take a closer look at the world but also to see ourselves as we are seen by our beholders: this is a unique experience, and humankind knows no other similar experiences" (1989: 13). I am employing the mirror in this sense, as an analytical metaphor, for "the essence of metaphor is understanding one thing in terms of another" (Lakoff and Johnson, 1980: 5, in Smith, 1985: 69).

3. "The 'me' that I think another sees, can be cognitively created only in conjunction with the basic structure of the 'me' that I perceive. This meta-identity is woven into the fabric of self-identity, as self-identity is woven into the fabric of meta-identity" (Laing, 1966: 7).

4. Although I refer more to the level of representation, I emphasize that the created images generate repercussions in the form of action. I shall demonstrate this for a few cases.

5. One of these groups remained at the location that today is known as São Marcos. The other group settled in Sangradouro, which is still occupied by the Xavante and the five Bororo families who decided to stay.

6. The informant refers to the deaths of the Reverend Fuchs and the Reverend Sacillotti, two missionaries murdered by the Xavante in 1934. *Dogue* is a suffix used to designate the plural; *padredogue* means priests.

7. By analyzing the status of the Pancararé at Brejo do Burgo (State of Bahia), Omar da Rocha shows how the same argument—that, to satisfy their professional interests, anthropologists would have created the "Indians"—was disseminated throughout the region. This argument was adopted by the "non-Indians" to stop the Indians, who wanted a reservation, from "taking over" their land and their homes (Rocha, Jr., 1982b: 3).

8. Interestingly, this opinion is shared by sugarcane field laborers in the hinterland of the state of Pernambuco, as revealed by Lygia Sigaud (1978).

9. During the Sarney administration (1984–1989), FUNAI had six chairmen.

10. The Bororo are not sure whether they like the tutelage. The following statement underscores the Bororo's uncertainty about the tutelary nature of the relationship: "If only there were another agency, we could become independent from FUNAI and from the priests. One bank plus the Franciscans or Jesuits. It would not be wise for the Bororo to boss themselves alone, because our land is highly coveted by the non-Indians and no land title has been issued for the reservation yet. Sangradouro and São Marcos already have a name [they have been demarcated], but our reserve [Meruri] has not been granted indemnity yet. From what we can see, FUNAI doesn't have good intentions toward us. Like other people who have taken land from the Indians, FUNAI sells Indian land. But the Bororo cannot defend their own land, because the Bororo are very few" (Meruri, 1982).

11. "The delimitation and the removal, the outline of a territory, not by the tribe but by the state, introduce the mediation of the market and the land as a commodity in man's relation with the environment" (Martins, 1986: 35).

12. "The Indian is a federal subject," says Enéas Pankaré. "From the Indians' viewpoint, this issue is permeated by the concept of 'justice': after being

discriminated against by local power with respect to access to municipal health and education services, and being denied their historical rights to the territory on which they live and to their own identity, the only way the Indians can reach a balance in relation to regional society is to rely on an agency hierarchically superior to the municipal administrations—FUNAI. 'The Indian is a federal subject,' and for this reason should abide by specific laws and need an agency to oversee them" (Rocha, Jr., 1982a: 7).

13. According to Sartre, "It is not what man has been made of that is essential, but what he has done with the man into which he was made."

14. It should be noted that, when productivity per square yard is taken into consideration, the traditional farming systems are more productive than the backwoods plantations introduced as part of the FUNAI project (cf. Serpa, 1988: 294).

15. See Viertler (1982) for an analysis of the Bororo funeral from the cultural ecology perspective.

5. The Salesian Missions in Mato Grosso

1. Bordignon (1987) furnishes an excellent summary of the historical relations between the Bororo and the non-Indians, as well as of the numerous conflicts in which they were involved between the seventeenth and the nineteenth centuries. Besides the writings that this Salesian teacher produced for the young Bororo, the history of interethnic contact between the seventeenth century and the 1970s is discussed in the first part of Viertler (1982). Viertler collected data scattered in different historical documents, but did not interpret them.

2. When referring to the eagerness for knowledge about the Far East, which Said calls Orientalism, he writes, "The imaginative examination of things Oriental was based more or less exclusively upon a sovereign Western consciousness out of whose unchallenged centrality an oriental world emerged, first according to general ideas about who or what was an Oriental, then according to a detailed logic governed not simply by empirical reality but by a battery of desires, repressions, investments and projections" (Said, 1979: 8). With respect to missionary work, see Gambini (1988) about the Jesuit missions as a projection. About modernity in the jungle and the nature of world expositions, see Foot Hardman (1988).

3. The Salesian mission in Mato Grosso and Goiás celebrated its fiftieth anniversary in 1944.

4. "The Bororo say that the *bope* cause all things to die. They are therefore the principle of all organic transformation, of fructification, growth, death and decay, the spirits of metamorphoses" (Crocker, 1985: 36). It is interesting to note that the authors of *Enciclopédia Bororo*, vol. I, translate *bope* as "evil spirit" (Albisetti and Venturelli, 1962a: 511).

5. *Revista Santa Cruz* 12, no. 2 (November 1908): 67.

6. Ibid.: 70.

7. Ibid.: 72.

8. "In the first, the overdevelopment of administrative bodies and framework takes the place of mobility or reflux of convictions among militants. In the

second, on the contrary, institutions in the process of decaying or of isolating themselves allow the beliefs that they had long fomented, maintained and controlled to become dissipated" (1985: 149).

9. *Bollettino Salesiano* 32, no. 4 (April 1908): 116.

10. Ibid.

11. Year 14, vol. 6, no. 2 (March–April 1915):47–48.

12. Ibid.: 47.

13. Ibid.: 48.

14. More information about this episode is found in *Missioni Salesiane, Prelatura di Registro di Araguaya*, Turin, 1925.

15. *Bolletino Salesiano* 8, no. 6 (November–December 1917): 152–162.

16. *Missões Salesianas em Matto Grosso* (1912): 9.

17. Ibid.

18. Ibid.: 31–32.

19. *Missioni Salesiane* (1925): 97–99.

20. See *Bollettino Salesiano* 59, no. 1 (January 1935).

6. The Salesians and the Progressive Church: The Reshaping of an Image

1. See chaps. 2 and 3 in Davis (1978) on these development programs and their effects on the living conditions of populations in the region. See chap. 1 in Martins (1986) on the effects of these programs on the Indian populations.

2. One such case involved land in Bororo territory (the Teresa Cristina reservation) purchased by a farmer named Figueiredo Ferraz, from São Paulo, who obtained a certificate from FUNAI attesting that said land did not belong to the Indians. To date the area in question has not been returned to the Bororo.

3. *Folha de São Paulo* (16 July 1976), p. 7. See also Bordignon (1987: 36–38) on the Meruri bloodshed.

4. Ibid. (17 July 1976), p. 1.

5. Ibid. (19 July 1976), p. 10.

6. Father Venturelli was co-author of the *Enciclopédia bororo*, a comprehensive compilation of data collected by Father César Albisetti, who worked among the Bororo for nearly forty years.

7. Buarque de Hollanda (1975: 1165–1166). See also Albisetti (1925: 119): "As soon as the missionary got in touch with the Bororo, his first thoughts were to dress those miserable children of Adam with that which he had received from the charity of so many generous souls. In so doing, his goal was not to give them a veneer of civilized life, but to stimulate shame, until then not cared about."

8. I collected the following description of the women (*aredu-baito*) who usually came to the central house on site (Tadarimana, 1985) from an old woman of the Baadojeba clan. It shows why the Salesians were so disgusted with this place: "In the old days the *ipare* [guys] slept on straw mats lined up inside the central house. Then a man of the Tugarege moiety went out to seek a woman of the Ecerae moiety. In the central house she lay down with all the Tugarege men, one at a time, but they did not mess with her; they just lay there. The man who had gone to get her waited outside. Only after she had lain with all the men did he enter the central house and sleep with her all night. The following day the

woman was adorned by all the men with whom she had lain. After that they went out hunting or fishing, and they all brought her some meat. If the woman got pregnant, the child would belong to all the men, but the actual father would be the man whose clan maintained a *iorubadare* relationship with the woman's clan. (An *iorubadare* relationship allows marriage between members of clans. *Iorubadare* also means 'godfather' and applies when a man from one clan initiates a boy from a clan in the opposite moiety.) Whenever a man and a woman engaged in a stable and exclusive relationship, the man stopped sleeping in the central house and, after announcing that he was taking the woman as his wife, he moved to her house."

9. *Missões Salesianas em Mato Grosso*, 1912: 30.

10. Ibid.: 20–21.

11. *Sedoc* (July–August 1974): 107, in Menezes (1984): 72.

12. *CIMI Bulletin* no. 7, in Ricardo (1980): 6.

13. The acculturation process that Pope Gregory I supported was to be conducted through "the reinterpretation of rites and beliefs, without disrupting the institutional settings and unnecessarily replacing the cultural materials that may be assimilated" (Azevedo, 1976: 367).

14. Previously I tried to reconstruct the history of the missions using data I collected from the Salesian files; here I utilize data that I collected during my several research trips to the missions between 1972 and 1987. In addition to the data I collected on site, I have gathered information through letters and telephone calls exchanged with the Salesians working in Meruri, whom I also met during their visits to São Paulo.

15. Letter from Master Mário Bordignon, 25 May 1989.

16. *Ki* = slenderness; *ogwa* = lack; *ro* = suffix designating action. In other words, that which leads to lack of slenderness—good health or well-being. *Kiogwaro* is the generic name given to the plume and feather adornment made by a father to be worn by his child during the naming ritual.

17. The manufacture of traditional Bororo objects, especially those articles made with feathers and plumes, has become increasingly difficult. The intricate design involves arranging patterns according to clan principles. In addition, this type of handicraft is affected by the lack of raw materials, since the birds from which said feathers and plumes are extracted are now rare. See Ferraro Dorta (1981) for Bororo feather art and, particularly, the intricate design and manufacturing of the plume headdress called *pariko*.

18. A similar attitude was adopted by the Salesians at the turn of the century, when they kept in their possession the Indians' Sunday clothes. After wearing the clothing, the Indians handed it to the Salesians, who laundered it and had it ready for the next use.

7. Missionaries and Indians: Identification Created through Martyrdom

1. On the Bororo burial ceremony, see Viertler (1982), Bloemer (1980), and Caiuby Novaes (1983, 1986).

2. The Bororo usually play a lot in their own funeral rites. The Salesians did not want this attitude in Father Lunkenbein's funeral.

3. Given the tense environment at the meeting, I decided against taping it; thus, the description that follows is reconstructed from my own recollections.

4. In April 1981, the *Folha de São Paulo* published a series critical of the Salesians' work among the Indians at the Negro River. Similar articles were published in other newspapers. Concerning the violence at the Salesian mission in the Upper Negro River region, see *Aconteceu Especial*, issue 10 (April 1982), p. 91, for a statement by Salesian missionary Eduardo Lagório, who worked in that region for thirty-eight years.

5. *Missioni Salesiani* (1925: 94).

6. Comparative data on the distribution of the Bororo are found in Bordignon (1986), from which I have extracted my data, and in Serpa (1988). In the last available census (1994), the Bororo numbered 914 (Ricardo, 1996: vi).

7. Since 1970 I have conducted a number of surveys on the Bororo population. Meruri has always had the largest population:

Village	Date of Census	Population
Perigara	July 1971	90
	July 1986	99
Meruri	July 1972	201
	July 1982	292
Garças	January 1982	69
	July 1982	101
	July 1985	87
	July 1986	73
Tadarimana	October 1975	48
	February 1985	50
	July 1986	39
Pobori	July 1986	24
Paulista	July 1986	13
Jarudori	July 1977	25
Córrego Grande	July 1970	104
	July 1971	70
	September 1973	139
	November 1975	116
	July 1977	143
	July 1985	114
	July 1986	126
Piebaga	July 1986	42

8. Thiago Marques Aipobureu was a Bororo raised by the Salesian missionaries. His history is reviewed by Fernandes (1946) and Baldus (1979).

9. Dayan and Katz (1985: 29–31) refer to the three functions of communication as the referential (which concerns the content of the message), the emotive (which concerns the speaker), and the conative (which concerns the effect of a message on the addressee). Jakobson (1960) introduces three other functions: the metalinguistic (a function of actually identifying the communication code that is being used), the poetic (the function of assessing the intrinsic value of the message in its material structure), and the phatic (the function of establishing

social contact and keeping the channels of communication open, which is central to human relationships). On functions and factors of communications, see Ducrot and Todorov (1988).

10. In a sense, this corresponds to what we have just accomplished by analyzing the ceremony.

11. See Geertz (1978: esp. 15, 27, 57, and 64) on the relationship between action and representation as well as on culture as a system of symbols by means of which individuals guide and confer meaning on their actions.

12. See Dumont (1985) on the two denotions of the term "individual," as (a) the empirical being present in all human societies who speaks, thinks, and desires; and, (b) the individual as value, independent moral being, and bearer of supreme values, as defined by the contemporary ideology of people and society.

13. On this subject, see Crocker (1969, 1977a, 1977b, and 1985) and Caiuby Novaes (1983).

Bibliography

Archives and Journals

Aconteceu: povos indígenas no Brasil/1981, no. 10 (April 1982).
Boletim Salesiano, São Paulo, 1902–October 1989.
Bollettino Salesiano, Turin, 1877–December 1988.
Revista Santa Cruz, 1908.

Books, Articles, Manuscripts

Aberle, David. "The Influence of Linguistics on Early Culture and Personality Theory." In R. Manners and D. Kaplan (eds.), *Theory in Anthropology*, pp. 303–317. Chicago: Aldine-Atherton, [1957] 1971.

Albisetti, César. *Mottogéba, uma flor da floresta*. Niterói: Escola Industrial Dom Bosco, 1944.

Albisetti, César, and A. J. Venturelli. *Enciclopédia bororo*. Vol. 1. Campo Grande: Museu Regional Dom Bosco, 1962a.

———. *Enciclopédia bororo*. Vol. 2. Campo Grande: Museu Regional Dom Bosco, 1962b.

———. *Enciclopédia bororo*. Vol. 3. Campo Grande: Museu Regional Dom Bosco, 1976.

Altenfelder Silva, Fernando. "Mudança cultural dos Terêna." *Revista do Museu Paulista*. N.s., 3 (1949): 271–379.

Anchieta, José. *Cartas inéditas do Padre José de Anchieta copiadas do Archivo da Companhia de Jesus*. São Paulo: Typ. da Casa Ecléctica, [1584] 1900.

Azanha, Gilberto. "Projeto krahô: uma avaliação." São Paulo: Centro de Trabalho Indigenista, 1985. Mimeo.

Azanha, Gilberto, and Sylvia Caiuby Novaes. "O CTI e a antropologia, ou o antropólogo como "agente." 5ª Reunião Anual da ANPOCS. Freiburg, October 1981. Mimeo.

Azevedo, Thales de. "Catequese e aculturação." In Egon Schaden (org.), *Leituras de etnologia brasileira*, pp. 365–384. São Paulo: Cia. Ed. Nacional, [1966] 1976.

Baldus, Herbert. *Ensaios de etnologia brasileira*. São Paulo: Cia. Ed. Nacional—INL/MEC, [1937] 1979.

Balzola, Giovanni. *Fra gli Indi del Brasile. Note autobiografiche e testimonianze*

raccolte da D.A. Cojazzi. Turin: Società Editrice Internazionale, 1932.
Barnow, Victor. Cultura y personalidad. Buenos Aires: Ediciones Troquel, 1963.
Barth, Fredrik (ed.). Ethnic Groups and Boundaries: The Social Organization of
     Culture Difference. Boston: Little, Brown, 1969.
Barthes, Roland. O rumor da língua. São Paulo: Editora Brasiliense, 1988.
————. The Rustle of Language. São Paulo: Editora Brasiliense, 1986.
Bateson, Gregory. "Difference, Double Description and the Interactive Designa-
     tion of Self." In F. A. Hanson, ed., Studies in Symbolism and Cultural
     Communication. Publications in Anthropology, no. 14. Lawrence: Univer-
     sity of Kansas, 1982.
Baudrillard, Jean. "La précession des simulacres." Traverses, no. 10 (1978): 2–37.
Beals, Ralph. "Acculturation." In A. L. Kroeber, org., Anthropology Today, pp.
     621–641. Chicago: University of Chicago Press, 1953.
Benedict, Ruth: Padrões de cultura. Lisbon: Livros do Brasil., n.d. (English ed.
     1934).
Beozzo, Fr. José Oscar. "História da Igreja Católica no Brasil." Cadernos do ISER,
     no. 8 (April 1979): 3–10.
Biren, J. "Lesbian Photography: Seeing through Our Own Eyes." Studies in
     Visual Communication 9, no 2 (spring 1983): 81–96.
Bloemer, Neuse. "Itaga: Alguns aspectos do funeral bororo." M.A. thesis,
     University of São Paulo, 1980.
Bock, Philip. Rethinking Psychological Anthropology: Continuity and Change
     in the Study of Human Action. New York: Freeman & Company, [1980]
     1988.
Bordignon Enawuréu, Mário. Os Bororos na história do centro oeste brasileiro
     1716–1986. Campo Grande: Missão Salesiana de Mato Grosso, CIMI MT,
     1987.
Buarque de Holanda Ferreira, Aurélio. Novo dicionário da língua portuguesa.
     Rio de Janeiro: Editora Nova Fronteira, 1975.
Caiuby Novaes, Sylvia. Mulheres, homens e heróis—dinâmica e permanência
     através do cotidiano da vida bororo. Série Antropologia, no. 8. São Paulo:
     FFLCH–USP, 1986.
————. "Os índios vão à justiça." Folha de São Paulo (22 April 1983), p. 3.
————. "Tranças, cabaças e couros no funeral Bororo—a propósito de um
     processo de constituição de identidade." Revista de Antropologia 24 (1981):
     25–36.
Cardoso, Ruth (org.). A aventura antropológica. Rio de Janeiro: Paz e Terra, 1986.
Cardoso de Oliveira, Roberto. Identidade, etnia e estrutura social. São Paulo:
     Livraria Pioneira Editora, 1976.
————. Preface. In R. Laraia, and da R. Matta, eds., Índios e castanheiros: a
     empresa extrativa e os índios do Médio Tocantins, pp. 35–47. 2nd ed. Rio de
     Janeiro: Editora Paz e Terra, 1979.
————. "Problemas e hipóteses relativos à fricção interétnica: sugestões para
     uma metodologia." América Indígena 28, no. 2 (1968): 339–388.
Carneiro da Cunha, Manuela. "Etnicidade: da cultura residual mas irredutível."
     In Antropologia do Brasil, pp. 97–108. São Paulo: Editora Brasiliense, 1986.
————. Negros, estrangeiros—os escravos libertos e sua volta à África. São
     Paulo: Ed. Brasiliense, 1985.

Casaldáliga, Pedro. "Uma igreja da Amazônia em conflito com o latifúndio e a marginalizão social." Mato Grosso: N.p., n.d.

Chaui, Marilena. *Conformismo e resistência.* São Paulo: Editora Brasiliense, 1986.

———. "Os trabalhos da memória." In Ecléa Bosi (ed.), *Lembranças de velhos,* pp. xvii–xxxii. São Paulo: T. A.Queiroz, 1983.

———. "Participando do debate sobre mulher e violência." In Cardoso et al., *Perspectivas Antropológicas da Mulher,* no. 4, pp. 23–62. Rio de Janeiro: Zahar, 1985.

Clifford, James. "Fieldwork, Reciprocity and the Making of Ethnographic Texts: The Example of Maurice Leenhardt." *Man* 15, no. 3 (1980): 518–532.

Cohen, Abner. *Custom and Politics in Urban Africa.* London: Routledge & Kegan Paul, 1969.

——— (ed.). *Urban Ethnicity.* London: Tavistock Publications, 1974.

Colbacchini, A., and C. Albisetti. *Os bororos orientais orarimogodugue do planalto oriental de Mato Grosso.* São Paulo: Editora Nacional, 1942.

Colbacchini, Fr. Antonio. "Trinta e quatro annos entre os Indios Borôros." *Revista de Ribeirão Preto,* no. 4 (December 1939).

Crocker, Jon. "My Brother the Parrot." In E. Sapir and J. Crocker, *The Social Use of Metaphors: Essays on the Anthropology of Rhetoric,* pp. 164–192. Philadelphia: University of Pennsylvania Press, 1977a.

———. "Reciprocidade e hierarquia entre os Borôro orientais." In E. Schaden, ed., *Leituras de etnologia brasileira,* pp. 164–185. São Paulo: Cia. Editora Nacional, 1976.

———. "Reciprocity and Hierarchy among the Eastern Bororo." *Man* 4, no. 1 (1969): 44–58.

———. "Les Réflexions du soi." In C. Lévi-Strauss, org., *L'Identité,* pp. 157–179. Paris: Bernard Grasset, 1977b.

———. "Selves and Alters among the Eastern Bororo." In D. Maybury-Lewis, ed., *Dialectical Societies: The Gê and Bororo of Central Brazil.* Cambridge: Harvard University Press, 1979.

———. *Vital Souls: Bororo Cosmology, Natural Symbolism, and Shamanism.* Tucson: University of Arizona Press, 1985.

D'Andrade, Roy. "Cultural Meaning Systems." In R. Shweder et al., eds., *Culture Theory: Essays on Mind, Self and Emotion,* pp. 88–119. Cambridge: Cambridge University Press, 1984.

Davis, Shelton. *Vítimas do milagre—o desenvolvimento e os índios do Brasil.* Rio de Janeiro: Zahar Eds., 1978.

Dayan, Daniel, and Elihu Katz. "Electronic Ceremonies: Television Performs a Royal Wedding." In M. Blonsky (ed.), *On Signs.* Baltimore: Johns Hopkins University Press, 1985, pp. 16–32.

De Certeau, Michel. "The Jabbering of Social Life." In M. Blonsky, ed., *On Signs,* pp.146–154. Baltimore: Johns Hopkins University Press, 1985a.

———. "What We Do When We Believe." In M. Blonsky, ed., *On Signs,* pp.192–202. Baltimore: Johns Hopkins University Press, 1985b.

Della Cava, Ralph. "A igreja e a abertura, 1974–1985." In P. Krishke and S. Mainwaring, *A igreja nas bases em tempo de transição (1974–1985),* pp. 13–45. Porto Alegre: LPM and CEDEC, 1986.

————. "A teologia da libertação no banco dos Réus." *Lua Nova* 2, no. 2 (July–September 1985): 44–49.

"Diretório da missão salesiana de Mato Grosso para a atividade missionária junto às populações indígenas." Campo Grande, Mato Grosso, 18 January 1977. MS.

Ducrot, Oswald, and Tzvetan Todorov. *Dicionário enciclopédico das ciências da linguagem.* São Paulo: Editora Perspectiva, [1972] 1988.

Dumont, Louis. "A Modified View of Our Origins: The Christian Beginnings of Modern Individualism." In M. Corrithers, S. Collins, and S. Lukes (eds.), *The Category of the Person: Anthropology, Philosophy, History,* pp. 93–122. Cambridge: Cambridge University Press, 1985.

Durkheim, Émile. *Sociologia e filosofia.* Rio de Janeiro, Ed. Forense, 1970.

Duval, Shelley, and R. A. Wicklund. *A Theory of Objective Self-Awareness.* New York: Academic Press, 1972.

Dyer, Richard. "Seen to Be Believed: Some Problems in the Representation of Gay People as Typical." *Studies in Visual Communication* 9, no. 2 (1983): 2–19.

Eco, Umberto. "Sobre os espelhos." In *Sobre os espelhos e outros ensaios,* pp. 11–37. Rio de Janeiro: Editora Nova Fronteira, 1989.

Eliade, Mircea. *Myth and Reality.* New York: Harper & Row, 1963.

Evans-Pritchard, E. E. *The Nuer: A Description of the Modes of Livelihood and Political Institutions of a Nilotic People.* New York: Oxford University Press, [1940] 1972.

Fernandes, Florestan. "Tiago Marques Aipobureu: um bororo marginal." In *Investigação etnológica no Brasil e outros ensaios,* pp. 84–115. Petrópolis: Ed. Vozes, [1946] 1985

Ferraro Dorta, Sonia. *Pariko—Etnografia de um artefato plumário.* Série Etnologia, no. 4. São Paulo: Coleção Museu Paulista, 1981.

Ferreira dos Santos, Jair. *O que é pós-moderno?* São Paulo: Ed. Brasiliense, 1986.

Foot Hardman, Francisco. *Trem fantasma—a modernidade na selva.* São Paulo: Companhia das Letras, 1988.

"A formação dos Salesianos de Rev. Bosco—Princípios e normas." Ratio Fundamentalis et Studiorum. MS, n.d.

Foucault, Michel. *Isto não é um Cachimbo.* São Paulo: Ed. Paz e Terra, [1973] 1988.

Freud, Sigmund. *Totem and Taboo.* London: Routledge & Kegan Paul, 1950.

Fry, Peter, and Edward MacRae. *O que é homossexualidade?* São Paulo: Editora Brasiliense, 1983.

FUNAI. *O conflito do Merure na imprensa diária—análise morfológica e de conteudo.* Brasília: Assessoria de Comunicação Social, 1976.

Galvão, Eduardo. "Aculturação indígena do Rio Negro." *Boletim do Museu Paraense Emílio Goeld.* N.s., Antropologia, no. 7 (1959).

————. "Estudos sobre a aculturação dos grupos indígenas do Brasil." In E. Galvão, *Encontro de sociedades,* pp. 126–134. Rio de Janeiro: Ed. Paz e Terra, [1953] 1979.

Gambini, Roberto. *O espelho índio—os jesuitas e a destruição da alma indígena.* Rio de Janeiro: Espaço e Tempo, 1988.

Geertz, Clifford. *A interpretação das culturas.* Rio de Janeiro: Zahar Ed., 1978.

———. *The Interpretation of Cultures.* New York: Basic Books,1973.

———. "Ritual and Social Change: A Javanese Example." *American Anthropologist* 59, no. 1 (1957): 32–54.

Ginzburg, Carlo. *Mitos, emblemas, sinais.* São Paulo: Cia. das Letras, 1989.

———. "Signes, traces, pistes: racines d'un paradigme d l'indice. *Le Débat,* no. 6 (November 1980): 3–44.

Gluckman, Max. *Analysis of a Social Situation in Modern Zululand.* The Rhodes Livingstone Papers, 28. Manchester: Manchester University Press, 1939.

———. "The Kingdom of Zulu of South Africa." In M. Fortes and E. E. Evans-Pritchard, eds., *African Political Systems.* London: Oxford University Press, 1949.

Goodenough, Ward. "Rethinking 'Status' and 'Role': Toward a General Model of the Cultural Organization of Social Relationship." In M. Banton, ed., *The Relevance of Models for Social Anthropology,* pp. 1–24. A.S.A. Monographs 1. London: Tavistock, 1969.

Harris, Marvin. *The Rise of Anthropological Theory: A History of Theories of Culture.* New York: Harper & Row, 1968.

Hartmann, Thekla. "Aculturação dos Bororo do São Lourenço—12 anos depois." 1964. MS.

———. "A contribuição da iconografia para o conhecimento de índios brasileiros do século XIX." Série de Etnologia, no. I. São Paulo: Coleção Museu Paulista, 1975.

———. "Dados históricos sobre os Bororo." N.d. MS.

Herskovits, Melville. "A Genealogy of Ethnological Theory." In Melford Spiro, ed., *Context and Meaning in Cultural Anthropology,* pp. 403–415. New York: Free Press, 1965.

Huestis, Esther. "Bororo Spiritism as Revitalization." *Practical Anthropology* 10, no. 4 (1963): 187–189.

Jakobson, R. "Linguistics and Poetics." In Thomas Sebeok, ed., *Style in Language,* pp. 350–377. New York: Wiley.

Kaplan, David, and Robert Manners. *Teoria da cultura.* 2nd ed. São Paulo: Ed. Zahar, 1981.

Kroeber, A. L. "A Half-Century of Anthropology." In *The Nature of Culture,* pp. 139–143. Chicago: University of Chicago Press, [1950] 1952a.

———. "*Totem and Taboo* in Retrospect." In *The Nature of Culture,* pp. 306–309. Chicago: University of Chicago Press, [1939] 1952b.

Kuhn, Thomas S. *The Structure of Scientific Revolutions.* Chicago: University of Chicago Press, 1962.

Lacan, J. "Stade du miroir comme formateur de la fonction du je telle qu'elle nous est révélée dans l'expérience psychanalytique." In *Écrits,* pp. 93–100. Paris:. Editions du Seuil, 1966.

Ladeira, Maria Inês. "Projeto Guarani SP, primeiro relatório." São Paulo: Centro de Trabalho Indigenista, 1981. Mimeo.

Laing, R. D. *The Divided Self: An Existential Study in Sanity and Madness.* London: Penguin Books, 1971.

———. *Interpersonal Perception: A Theory and a Method of Research.* New York: Harper & Row, 1966.

Laraia, Roque de Barros, and Roberta DaMatta, eds. *Índios e castanheiros: a empresa extrativa e os índios do Médio Tocantins*, pp. 35–47. 2nd ed. Rio de Janeiro: Editora Paz e Terra, 1979.

Lasagna, Dom Luis. "Cartas." Vol. 1 (1873–1881). Trans. A. S. Ferreira. São Paulo, 1985. Mimeo.

Lévi-Strauss, Claude. "A crise moderna da antropologia." *Revista de Antropologia* 10, nos. 1, 2 (June, December 1962): 19–26.

———. "A estrutura dos mitos." In Lévi-Strauss, *Antropologia estrutural*, pp. 237–265. Rio de Janeiro: Tempo Brasileiro, 1967.

——— "Raça e história." In Juan Comas et al., eds., *Raça e ciência*. Vol. 1, pp. 231–270. São Paulo: Editora Perspectiva, [1952] 1960.

——— (org.). *L'Identité*. Paris: Presses Universitaires de France, 1977.

Linton, Ralph. *O homem. Uma introdução à antropologia*. São Paulo: Livraria Martins Editora., n.d.

———. *The Study of Man: An Introduction*. New York: D. Appleton–Century Company, 1937.

Lorenz, Sônia, and Sylvia Caiuby Novaes. "Fatos e não Boatos." *Folha de São Paulo* (May 1984), p. 3.

Macedo, Carmem Cinira. *Tempo de Gênesis—o povo das comunidades eclesiais de base*. São Paulo: Editora Brasiliense, 1986.

Marcigaglia, Fr. Luis, S.D.B. *Os Salesianos no Brasil: ensaio de crônica dos primeiros vinte anos da obra de Dom Bosco no Brasil*. São Paulo: Cia Editôra Nacional, 1955.

Martins, José de Souza. *Não há terra para plantar neste verão—o cerco das terras indígenas e das terras de trabalho no renascimento político do campo*. Petrópolis: Ed. Vozes, 1986.

Mauss, Marcel. "Une catégorie de l'esprit humain. La notion de personne, celle de 'moi.'" In *Sociologie et Anthropologie*, pp. 331–362. Paris: Presses Universitaires de France, 1968.

Mead, George. *Mind, Self, and Society*. Chicago: University of Chicago Press, 1934.

Mead, Margaret. *Coming of Age in Samoa: A Psychological Study of Primitive Youth for Western Civilization*. New York: William Morrow, 1928.

———. *Growing Up in New Guinea: A Comparative Study of Primitive Education*. New York: William Morrow, 1930.

———. *Sex and Temperament in Three Primitive Societies*. New York: William Morrow, 1935.

Melo Franco, Afonso Arinos. *O índio brasileiro e a Revolução Francesa—as origens brasileiras da teoria da bondade natural*. Rio de Janeiro: Livraria José Olympio Editora/MEC, [1937] 1976.

Menezes, Claudia. "Missionários e índios em Mato Grosso (Os Xavante da Reserva de São Marcos)." PhD diss., Universidade de São Paulo, 1984.

Mezan, Renato. "Identidade e cultura." In *A Vingança da esfinge*, pp. 252–270. São Paulo: Editora Brasiliense, 1988.

Micela, Rosaria. *Antropologia e psicanálise—uma introdução à produção simbólica, ao imaginário e à subjetividade*. São Paulo: Ed. Brasiliense, 1984.

Missioni Salesiane: Prelature di Registro di Araguaya. Turin: Tip. della Società

Editrice Internazionale, 1925.

Missões salesianas em Matto Grosso. Rio de Janeiro: Typ. d'A União, 1912.

Montes, Maria Lúcia. "O discurso populista ou caminhos cruzados." In José Marques de Melo, ed., *Populismo e comunicação*, pp. 61–75. São Paulo: Cortez Editora, 1981.

———. "O poder e a cultura. Novos temas, velhas reflexões ou pode a emoção ensinar a obediência política?" Paper presented at ANPOCS, Caxambu, Brazil, 1981.

Nadel, Jacqueline. "Rôle du milieu dans la conception wallonienne du development: l'équilibre fonctionel et la distinction entre fonction et activité." *Enfance*, no. 5 (1979): 363–372.

Oberg, Kalervo. *The Terena and the Kadureo of Southern Mato Grosso, Brazil*. Publication no. 9. Institute of Social Anthropology. Washington, D.C.: Smithsonian Institution, 1949.

Oliveira Filho, João Pacheco. *"O Nosso Governo"—Os Ticuna e o regime tutelar*. Brasília: Editora Marco Zero, MCT, CNPq, 1988.

Orlandi, Eni. "Uma retórica do oprimido—os discursos de representantes indígenas." *Encontros de Sociolinguistica e Análise do Discurso* (1984).

Paoli, Maria Célia. "Mulheres. Lugar, imagem, movimento." In Cardoso et al., *Perspectivas antropológicas da mulher*, no. 4, pp. 63–99. Rio de Janeiro: Zahar Editores, 1985.

Ribeiro, Darcy. "Convívio e contaminação." *Sociologia* 18 no. 1 (1956): 3–50.

———. "Culturas e línguas indígenas do Brasil." *Educação e Ciências Sociais*, no. 6 (1957): 5–102.

Ricardo, Carlos Alberto. *Povos indígenas no Brasil: 1991–1995*. São Paulo: Instituto Socioambiental, 1996.

Ricardo, Fany. "O Conselho Indigenista Missionário—CIMI: cronologia das transformações recentes da pastoral indigenista católica no Brasil, 1965–1979." *Cadernos ISER*, no. 10 (1980): 1–25.

Richards, I. A. *The Philosophy of Rhetoric*. London: Oxford University Press, 1936.

Rocha Júnior, Omar. "O índio é federal (O INTERBA no caso pankararé)." Paper presented at VI Encontro Anual da ANPOCS, Caxambu, Minas Gerais, 1982a.

———. "A política dos brancos." Centro de Trabalho Indigenista. São Paulo, 1982b. Mimeo.

Royce, Anya Peterson. *Ethnic Identity, Strategies of Diversity*. Bloomington: Indiana University Press, 1982.

Saake, Fr. Guilherme, S.V.D. "A aculturação dos Bororo do Rio São Lourenço." *Revista de Antropologia* I, no. 1 (June 1953): 43–52.

Sahlins, Marshall. *Cultura e razão prática*. Rio de Janeiro: Zahar Ed., 1979.

Said, Edward W. *Orientalism*. New York: Vintage Books, 1979.

Schaden, Egon. "Aculturação indígena—ensaio sobre fatores e tendências da mudança cultural de tribos índias em contacto com o mundo dos brancos." *Revista de Antropologia* 13 (1965).

———. *Aspectos fundamentais da cultura guarani*. São Paulo: EPU and EDUSP, 1974 (1954).

Seeger, A., R. da Matta, and E. A. Viveiros de Castro. "Construção da pessoa nas sociedades indígenas brasileiras." *Boletim do Museu Nacional*, n.s., no. 32 (1979): 2–19.

Serpa, Paulo. "Boe Epa—O cultivo de roça entre os Bororo de Mato Grosso." MA thesis, Universidade de São Paulo, 1988.

Sigaud, Lygia. "A morte do Caboclo—um exercício sobre sistemas classificatórios." *Boletim do Museu Nacional*, no. 30 (1978): 1–29.

Smith, M. B. "The Metaphorical Basis of Selfhood." In A. Marsella et al., eds., *Culture and Self: Asian and Western Perspectives*, pp. 56–88. New York: Tavistock Publications, 1985.

Turner, Terence. "From Cosmology to Ideology: Resistance, Adaptation and Social Consciousness among the Kayapo." Paper presented at Associação Brasileira de Antropologia, Belem, 7–10 December 1987.

Turner, Victor. *Dramas, Fields and Metaphors: Symbolic Action in Human Society*. Ithaca: Cornell University Press, 1974a.

———. *O processo ritual*. Petrópolis: Ed. Vozes, 1974b.

Vangelista, Chiara. "Espaço índio e espaço cristão nas missões salesianas." In A. Aderle, ed., *Iglesia, religión y sociedad en la historia latinoamericana, 1492–1945*, pp. 185–203. Szeged, Hungary: Universidad Josef Attila, 1986.

Van Velsen, J. "The Extended-Case Method and Situational Analysis." In A. Epstein, ed., *The Craft of Social Anthropology*, pp. 129–149. London: Tavistock Publications, 1967.

Viertler, Renate. "Aroe J'Aro—implicações adaptativas das crenças e práticas funerárias dos Bororo do Brasil Central." Thesis, Universidade de São Paulo, 1982.

———. "Córrego Grande revisitada." *Revista da Universidade de São Paulo*, no. 4 (March 1987): 119–142.

———. "A noção de pessoa entre os Bororo." *Boletim do Museu Nacional*, n.s. no. 32 (May 1979): 20–30.

Viveiros de Castro, Eduardo. *Araweté: os deuses canibais*. Rio de Janeiro: Ed. Zahar/ANPOCS, 1986.

———. "Por uma antropologia mais real—a responsabilidade social do etnólogo." Paper presented at 4ª Reunião Anual da ANPOCS, Rio de Janeiro, 1980.

———. "Spirits of Being, Spirits of Becoming: Bororo Shamanism as Ontological Theatre." *Reviews in Anthropology* 15, no. 4 (1988): 77–92.

Wagley, Charles. "Influências culturais sobre a população: uma comparação entre duas tribos tupi." Trans. Thekla Hartmann. *Revista do Museu Paulista*. N.s., V (1951): 95–104.

Wagley, Charles, and Eduardo Galvão. *Os índios tenetehara*. Serviço de Documentação, Rio de Janeiro: MEC, 1955.

Wallon, Henry. "Le rôle de 'l'autre' dans la conscience du 'moi.'" *Journal Egyptien de Psychologie* 2, no. 1 (1946): 87–93.

Zavattaro, Felix. "O Decreto 'Ad Gentes' e a problemática missionária." N.d. Mimeo.

Index

Aberle, David, 10

Ação Católica (Catholic Action), 105

Acculturation studies: and contact relationships, xv; and cultural traits inventory, 6; and functionalist approach, 1–5; of Indians of Brazil, 2, 5, 27; and work habits, 30

Action: and Baldus's concept of culture, 29; and belief, 74; and contact relationships, xvi; and identity, xi, xii; and the other, 14; and reflected images, 46, 47; Salesian model of, 95; and value systems, 11

Africa, 1, 7

African Americans, 7

Afro-Brazilians, x, xii

Agrarian reform, 101

Agribusiness, 102, 103. *See also* Farming

Aije ceremony (male initiation ceremony), 37, 85–86, 120–122

Aijeri village, 101

Albisetti, César: and Bororo Indian family life, 108; census figures of, 101; and Sangradouro mission, 98, 100; writings of, 32, 66, 69, 94

Alcohol consumption, 36, 71, 135–136, 147n.4

Alliances: of Bororo Indians with Salesian missionaries, 133–135, 142; of Bororo Indians with whites, 58–59, 138; with non-Indian groups, 43; strategy for, 42;

and structural relativity, 53; and territorial defense, 58; of young Bororo Indians, 34

Alter, 8, 147–148n.1. *See also* Other

Ambivalence, 8, 9

Anchieta, José de, 91–92

Anthropology and anthropologists: and contact relationships, xv; functionalist approach, 1–5, 11, 30; and identity, x–xi, 7, 44; and linguistics, 7–16; literature of, as mirror, 37–44; and person, xiv; political actions of, 41, 43; and psychology, 7–16, 146n.14; purpose of, 1–2, 11, 41–43, 128, 145n.2; Viertler's view of, 34; Xavante Indians' image of, 52

Aragarças, 52

Araguaia River village, 78

Aroe-etawara-are (master of the soul's way), 36

Aroe-maiwu (social representative of the dead), xvi, 120, 123, 143

Asian societies, 26–27

Associação Brasileira de Antropologia (Brazilian Anthropology Association), 18

Augustine, Saint, 80

Azanha, Gilberto, 61

Azevedo, Thales de, 84

Backwoods plantations, 62, 63, 149n.14

Baito (men's house), 75, 92–93, 108, 115–116, 150–151n.8

Baldus, Herbert, 2, 27–30, 37
Balzola, Giovanni: and attacks on
    Bororo Indians, 78–79; and Bororo
    Indians' dependent relationship,
    79; and Bororo Indians'
    impression of Salesian missionar-
    ies, 75; census figures of, 136;
    civilization efforts of, 67; and
    clothing for Bororo Indians, 77;
    and funeral ceremonies, 81–83;
    and male initiation ceremony, 86;
    mori system translated to charity,
    76; and Negro River region, 94;
    recruitment efforts of, 74–75; and
    Sagrado Coração de Jesus, 75, 90;
    as Teresa Cristina colony
    director, 66, 70–73
Barae (civilized), 49, 51
Barbados statement, 105
Barbarism, ix, 67, 95
Bari: and Bororo Indian band, 87;
    health care of, 72–73, 85;
    leadership of, 31; and male
    initiation ceremonies, 86; and
    men's house, 93; power of, 54, 85;
    and Salesian missionaries, 54, 72–
    73, 75, 132
Barra do Garças, 52, 103
Barreiro, 75
Barreiro River region, 94
Barth, Fredrik, xv, 5–6, 7
Barthes, Roland, 8
Basic Christian Communities, 106–
    107
Bateson, Gregory, 14–15
Baudrillard, Jean, 8, 23, 27, 89,
    145n.2
Behaviorism, 14
Belief, and the other, 74, 84–85
Benedict, Ruth, 9, 10
Bento, Divina, 126
Bilreiro Indians, 58
Biren, J., xii
Blood, as symbol, 133–135
Boarding schools, 85, 95, 97, 100,
    114–115
Boas, Franz, xvii, 9–12, 28
Bock, Philip, 12

Body malformations, ix
Boe, 51, 122, 138, 139
Bokodori Ecerae, 121
Boletim Salesiano, 66, 77, 92
Bollettino Salesiano, 66
Bone basket, xvi, 121, 125
Bone ornamentation, xvi, 122, 123,
    129, 134
Bope, 85, 149n.4
Bordignon Enawuréo, Mário, 43, 69,
    116, 126, 136
Bororo Indians: analysis of, 4;
    attacks on, 77–79; autonomy of,
    64; Baldus on, 2, 27–30, 37; and
    Brazilian government, 55–56, 137;
    and Christian names, 83, 85, 114;
    clothing for, 76–77, 86, 94, 98,
    107; demographic density of, 50;
    dependency of, 56–64, 79, 84,
    148n.10; elderly Bororo Indians,
    34–35, 37, 43; eternal return
    ideology, 27, 35–36, 116; family
    life of, 27–28, 30, 107–108, 113–
    114; government of, 55; land
    demarcation, 103; Mato Grosso
    government's movement of, 70,
    137; men's house of, 75, 92–93,
    108, 115–116, 150–151n.8; and
    music, 86–87, 89, 122; national
    society's relationship with, 32,
    47, 56, 64, 138; non-Indians
    alliances with, 43; non-Indians'
    relationship with, 104, 149n.1;
    and notion of person, xv, xvi;
    payment of, 122, 127–129, 139–
    140; poverty of, 54–56, 61;
    representation of self, x; self-
    image of, xvi, 47–54, 59–60, 63–
    64, 104; social organization of, 26,
    113; territorial defense of, 58–59,
    64, 115; value system of, 69, 84–
    85, 93, 110, 142; villages of, 77,
    100, 101, 136, 152n.7; visibility
    of, 137, 138, 141; whites'
    alliances with, 58–69, 138;
    whites' conflicts with, 78–79; and
    Xavante Indians' image, 49–52;
    Xavante Indians' relationship

with, xvii, 47–49, 51–54, 65, 100;
young Bororo Indians, 34, 35, 37,
43, 85–86. *See also* Bororo-
Salesian relationship; Religious
education
Bororo-Salesian relationship: and
agricultural projects, 61; alliances
between, 133–135, 142; and *bari*,
54, 72–73, 75, 132; and Bororo
Indian clans, 27, 107, 108; and
Bororo Indians' autonomy, 64;
and Bororo Indians' behavioral
changes, 27, 83–85, 107; and
Bororo Indians' culture, 69, 71–
72, 112–116; and Bororo Indians'
dependence, 79; Bororo Indians'
identification with Salesians, 47;
Bororo Indians' image of Xavante
Indians, 52; Bororo Indians'
loyalty to Salesian missionaries,
117–118; Bororo Indians' self-
image, xvi, 49; civilization efforts
of, 67, 74, 80; and funeral
ceremonies, 32, 64, 81–82, 132,
134, 135–141; Jesuits compared
to, 91–92; and land conflicts, 59,
69; and Lunkenbein's assassination, 104; and Lunkenbein's
funeral ceremony, 134, 135–141;
mutual dependency of, 84; and
religious education, 118; Salesian
influence in Meruri, 48; Salesian
missionaries as protector from
enemy tribes, 75, 79, 84, 100;
Salesian missionaries' assessment
of progress in, 94–101; Salesian
missionaries' attitude toward
Bororo culture, 69, 71–72, 112–
116; Salesian missionaries'
identification with Bororo
society, 119, 132–135; Salesian
missionaries' image of Bororo
Indians, 68, 69, 74, 75–76, 89, 91,
95, 97; Salesian missionaries'
promotion of Christian morality,
69, 80, 89, 107; Salesian
missionaries' study of Bororo
Indians, 28, 32, 69, 71–72, 90–91,

94, 111; and simulacrum, 90; and
territorial boundary issues, 42;
Vatican II effects on, 113–119;
and young Bororo Indians, 85–86
Bosco, Reverend, 67, 83, 92, 95
Boundary, Bateson's concept of, 14–
15
Braiding of mourners' hair, xvi
Brant, Antônio, 128
Brazilian Anthropology Association
(Associação Brasileira de
Antropologia), 18
Brazilian government: and Bororo
Indians, 55–56, 137; economic
policy of, 102, 105; Indian policy
of, 41, 43, 102; and Lunkenbein's
assassination, 104; military rule
of, 102, 105–106, 142; political
freedom of mid-1970s, xi; and
Salesian missionaries, 67, 75, 78;
and territorial issues, 57
Brazilian Indians. *See* Indians of
Brazil; *names of specific tribes*

Campo Grande research center, 94
Cannibalism, ix
Capitalist society, 33, 61, 63
Cardoso de Oliveira, Roberto, 5, 6, 7,
46, 51
Carmelites, 94
Carrano, Guilherme, 50
Casaldáliga, Pedro, 103, 125, 126,
133–135
Catastrophic perspective, 3, 5, 38
Catechism. *See* Religious education
Catholic Action (Ação Católica), 105
Cattle ranching, 100, 102–103
Causal-functional integration, 4
CEBs (Comunidades Eclesiais de
Base), 106–107
Cemeteries, 82
Center for Native Work, 18, 41
Central house. *See* Men's house
(*baito*)
Centro de Trabalho Indigenista
(CTI), 18, 41
Ceremony, definition of, 129, 134,
140–141. *See also* Funeral

ceremonies; Rituals

Change. *See* Social changes

Charismatic legitimization, 140

Charity, *mori* system translated to, 76

Chauí, Marilena, 51, 63, 64

Chiefs: double chieftaincy, 32; First Assembly of Indian Chiefs, 125; influence of, 31; role of, 55, 62

Children: and boarding school, 97, 114; and human behavior, 13; of Turin, Italy, 67. *See also* Young Bororo Indians

Chit system, 60–61, 110

Christian morality: and family life, 108; and religious education, 79; Salesian missionaries' promotion of, 69, 80, 89, 107; and women, 107

Christian names, 83, 85, 114

Christian values, 49, 67–68, 84, 91, 110

CIMI (Conselho Indigenista Missionário): establishment of, 106; and Indian support, 18; and Lunkenbein's funeral ceremony, 120, 123, 131–132; and oppressed groups, 107; and recording of ritual, 127; and tribal beliefs, 112

Citizenship: of Indians of Brazil, 67; and religion, 89; Salesian missionaries' promotion of, 69, 79; and work habits, 108

Civilization: Europe's efforts toward, 68, 74; Salesian missionaries' efforts toward, 67, 74, 80

Clans: and Bororo-Salesian relationship, 27, 107, 108; and rituals, 143–144; role of, 113–114, 143, 151n.8

Climate, 77

Clothing, for Bororo Indians, 76–77, 86, 94, 98, 107

CNBB (Conferência Nacional dos Bispos do Brasil), 106, 127

Cohen, Abner, xv, 7

Cohesion, processual analysis of, 129

Colbacchini, Fr. Antonio: and *bari*, 73; Bororo Indian writings of, 28, 32, 90–91, 94; and Bororo Indians' image, 68, 91; and Bororo Indians' impression of Salesian missionaries, 75; Indian language study, 69; and men's house, 92–93, 115; recruitment of, 74; and Sagrado Coração de Jesus colony, 90–91; and treatment of Bororo Indians, 91–92

Collective representation, 8

Comissão Pastoral de Terra (CPT), 106, 107

Comissão Pró Indio (CPI), 18

Commission for Indians, 18

Communication, functions of, 141, 152–153n.9

Comparative historical method, 13

Comunidades Eclesiais de Base (CEBs), 106–107

Confederação dos Trabalhadores Agrícolas (CONTAG), 18

Confederation of Farm Workers, 18

Conferência Nacional dos Bispos do Brasil (CNBB), 106, 127

Conflict: processual analysis of, 129; in psychoanalysis, 8, 9

Conformity, and resistance, 63

Conselho Indigenista Missionário. *See* CIMI (Conselho Indigenista Missionário)

Contact relationships: and anthropology, xv; of Bororo Indians, xvi, 27; cultural dimensions of, 6; and cultural ecology, 32; effects of contact, 3; and identity fabrication, 20; and interethnic relations, xv, 5; of Kayapó Indians, 39–40; and notion of person, xiv–xv, xvi, 145n.4; and psychology, 16; and religion, 3; and representation of other, xv–xvi; and self-image, xiv, 6; and social changes, xv, xvi; and territorial defense, 56–58. *See also* Bororo-Salesian relationship; Interethnic relations

CONTAG (Confederação dos Trabalhadores Agrícolas), 18

Context, and interpersonal relationships, 15

Contextualization, 11

Córrego Grande village, 31, 32, 36, 38, 41, 152n.7

Correia, Pero, 78

Correio Paullistano, 94

Couto Magalhães, 103

CPI (Comissão Pró Indio), 18

CPT (Comissão Pastoral de Terra), 106, 107

Creeds, 74, 84

Crocker, Jon, xv, 32, 36–37, 145n.4, 147n.3

Cross, as sign, 93, 115–116

CTI (Centro de Trabalho Indigenista), 18, 41

Cuiabá, 66

Cuiabá Indians, 59

Cultural change studies. *See* Acculturation studies; Social changes

Cultural decharacterization, 31–32

Cultural disintegration, 3, 5, 36

Cultural dynamics, 2

Cultural ecology, 32

Cultural integration: and dependency, 63–64; and interethnic friction, 5, 146n.7; of Kayapó Indians, 39; at markets, 33; and social changes, 4; and work habits, 31

Cultural standards, xiv, 31

Cultural traits, 6, 11, 38, 85

Culture: and Bororo Indians' self–image, 54; changes in, 29; coexisting cultures, 86; conception of, 3, 8, 11, 14, 130, 146n.15; and contact relationships, 6; and contextualization, 11; diacritical cultural signs, xii, xiii, 24; discrepancies among cultures, xv; as dynamic, 4, 35; ethnologists' view of, 29; folklorization of cultural traditions, 34; Geertz on, 4, 16; Indians compared to non-Indians, ix; and linguistics, 10; and nature, 10; and power, xiii, 6; and psychology, 9–10; Roman Catholic Church's view of, 111; Salesian missionaries' study of, 28, 32, 69, 71–72, 90–91, 94, 111; and social structure, 4–5; and universal human nature, 9

D'Andrade, Roy, 14, 130

Data collection and analysis, 9, 11

Davis, Shelton, 100, 102

Dayan, Daniel, 129, 134, 140, 141, 152n.9

De Certeau, Michel, 74, 84, 89, 93

Della Cava, Ralph, 106

Demographic density, Bororo compared with Xavante, 50

Derrida, J., 147n.1 (chapter 2)

Diacritical cultural signs, xii, xiii, 24

Difference: Bateson's use of, 14–15; between Indians of Brazil, 19; maintenance of preestablished differences, 20–24

Diffusionism, xv

Dinka Indians, 52–53

"Diretório da missão salesiana de Mato Grosso para a atividade missionária junto às populações indígenas," 110–112

Dominating society, 6–7, 17, 24. *See also* National society

Dos Santos, Joaquim Manoel, 77

Double chieftancy, 32

Double description, Bateson's use of, 14–15

Doyle, Conan, 20

Duarte, Antônio José, 70

Dumont, Louis, 144

Durkheim, Émile, 8, 47, 48

Duval, Shelley, 12

Ecerae moiety, 121, 143
Eco, Umberto, 148n.2
Economic dependence, 62–64
Education. *See* Boarding schools;
    Religious education
Egyptian government, 53
Elderly Bororo Indians, 34–35, 37, 43
Eliade, Mircea, 36
Ends and means, relationship
    between, 13
Enemies, Salesian missionaries as
    protection from, 75, 79, 84, 100
England, 2, 9, 80
Environment, individuals'
    adaptation to, 13
Environmental values, 40
Epidemics: and *bari,* 72; and funeral
    ceremonies, 82; and population
    concentration, 73, 135; of Rio de
    Janeiro, 87; Salesian missionaries'
    protection from, 59; at Sangra-
    douro mission, 73. *See also*
    Health care
Equality: and identity, xi; between
    Salesian missionaries and Bororo
    Indians, 134–135
Erikson, Erik, 8, 15, 146n.18
Eternal return ideology, 27, 35–36,
    116
Ethnicity, 5–7. *See also* Interethnic
    relations
Ethnology, purpose of, 29, 36
Europe: civilization efforts of, 68,
    74; and Indians of South America,
    69, 74; research projects of, 17;
    social visibility of groups in, xii
Evans-Pritchard, E. E., 52
Evolutionism, 9, 17, 107, 146n.14

Falcon, João, 137
Family life, of Bororo Indians, 27–28,
    30, 107–108, 113–114
Far East, 68, 149n.2
Farmers: Bororo Indians' conflicts
    with, 100, 103, 128; Bororo
    Indians' identification with, 47
Farmhands, 102–103
Farming: backwoods plantations, 62,

63, 149n.14; and economic
    dependence, 62–63; and rituals,
    63, 82; Salesian missionaries'
    introduction of, 70–71; and
    subjugation to labor, 60–61;
    support from, 77, 88
First Assembly of Indian Chiefs, 125
First Meeting of Indigenous Peoples
    in Brazil, 18
Fishing. *See* Subsistence activities
Folklorization of cultural traditions,
    34
Frazer, Sir James George, 9
Frederico (Bororo Indian), 127–128
Freud, Sigmund, 8, 9–12, 20,
    147n.18
Fuchs, Father, 95, 148n.6
FUNAI (Fundação Nacional do
    Indio): and agricultural projects,
    61, 149n.14; and Bororo as other,
    xvii; Bororo Indians' identifica-
    tion with, 47; and Bororo Indians'
    poverty, 55; Bororo Indians'
    relations with, 56, 64, 118, 128,
    137, 139, 148n.10; and Bororo
    Indians' rituals, 82; and Bororo
    Indians' self-image, 48; Bororo
    Indians' subordination to, 100;
    and land demarcation, 103; and
    Lunkenbein's assassination, 104;
    and official Indian policy, 41, 42,
    103; and Primerio Encontro dos
    Povos Indígenas no Brasil, 18–19;
    and traditional economic order,
    63; and Xavante Indians' self-
    image, 52
Functionalist approach, 1–5, 11, 30
Fundação Nacional do Indio. *See*
    FUNAI (Fundação Nacional do
    Indio)
Funeral ceremonies: and Bororo
    Indians' autonomy, 64; and
    Bororo-Salesian relationship, 32,
    64, 81–83, 132, 134, 135–141;
    Crocker on, 36–37; for
    Lunkenbein, 120–123, 129–131,
    139; and men's house, 93; and
    notion of person, xvi; prohibition

of, 32; purpose of, 37, 143; and subsistence activity, 62; theoretical framework for, 129–131; and tribal cohesion, 31; Viertler's analysis of, 32–33; women's role in, 28, 120–122

Galvão, Eduardo, 2, 41
Garças village: author's study of, 41; cultural preservation in, 137; and Lunkenbein's funeral ceremony, 120, 122, 129, 139; and Meruri, 139, 142; population of, 136, 138, 152n.7
Geertz, Clifford, 4–5, 16, 146n.13
General Carneiro, 104, 128
Genoveva (Simão's sister), 125, 132
Germany, 137
Ginzburg, Carol, 20–21, 23
Gluckman, Max, 131, 146n.13
Gomes Carneiro, 136
Gonçalves, Clarismundo, 78
Goodenough, Ward, 14, 15
Goods distribution, and Salesian missionaries, 78, 110
Government functionaries, corruption of, 55
Gregory I, 80, 113, 151n.13
Group mind, and identity, xi, xii
Groups. *See* Minority groups; Social groups
Grunberg, Georg, 105
Guaicuru Indians, 58
Guarani Indians, 18, 62
Guató Indians, 3

Handicrafts, 30, 116, 151n.17
Hartmann, Thekla, ix, 35, 58–59
Health care: of *bari*, 72–73, 85; of Salesian missionaries, 59, 72–74, 75, 79, 85, 110, 135; as strategy, 83–84. *See also* Epidemics
Herskovits, Melville, xv
Hispanics, 7
Historical data, 10
Historical empiricism, xv
Historical particularism, 10
Historical situation, 131, 142

Homosexuals, xi–xii
Huestis, Esther, 2, 31–32, 38
Human behavior, 7–10, 13
Humanitarian values, 40
Human rights, and Roman Catholic Church, 106
Hunting. *See* Subsistence activities

"I", formation of, 12, 13, 14
Iconography, of Brazilian Indians, ix
Identity: and anthropology, x–xi, 7, 44; Bateson on, 15; conception of, 25; ethnic identity, 6; fabrication of, 17–20; and group mind, xi, xii; and imitation, 21, 23; of Indians, xvi, 21; and interethnic relations, 5–7, 51; Lévi-Strauss on, x–xi; and Lunkenbein's funeral ceremony, 132–134; meta-identity, 46–47, 148n.3; Mezan on, 15–16; and minority groups, xi, xiii; and play of mirrors, 46, 144; in psychology, 8; and self, 146–147n.18; and self-image, xiii–xiv; and social changes, xv; of social groups, xi–xiii; study of, xvi
Image, and simulacrum, 89–93
Imaginary self, 46
Imitation: and dereferentialization of reality, 19; and identity, 21, 23; of other, 35
Inácio, Manuel, 78
Indian language, 19, 69, 111, 115, 116
Indian Protection Service, 2, 41, 64, 100
Indians of Australia, 1
Indians of Brazil: acculturation studies of, 2, 5, 27; catastrophic predictions for, 3, 5, 38; and contact relationships, xiv–xv; cultural differences from non-Indians, ix; diacritical cultural signs of, xii; dominating society's differences from, 6–7; economic dependence of, 62–63; ethnicity of, 7; iconography of, ix; identity construction of, xvi, 17–20; and

Jesuits, 78; maintenance of preestablished differences, 20–24; and military rule, 102; and notion of person, xiv; official policy on, 41, 43, 102; and Protestant religious movements, 106; recognition of, 18; Roman Catholic Church's support of, 105; Salesian missionaries' image of, 66–69; social visibility of, xii

Indians of New Guinea, 1

Indians of North America, 1

Indians of South America, 1, 36, 69, 74

Individuals: environmental adaptation of, 13; in funeral ceremonies, xvi; resistance to change, 28; role of, in Roman Catholic Church, 118; and social self, 143–144. *See also* Person, notion of

Intentionality, 131

Interaction view, 130

Interdependent relationships, ix–x, 131

Interethnic relations: and Bororo funeral ceremonies, 33; and contact relationships, xv, 5; Crocker on, 38; and identity, 5–7, 51; and power, 131, 138; Viertler on, 38; and Xavante Indians, 65; young Bororo Indians' attitudes toward, 43. *See also* Bororo-Salesian relationship; Contact relationships

Interlocutors, xiii, 48, 55

Interpersonal relationships, 15, 46, 76

Intertribal acculturation, 2

Investigation of Interethnic Areas in Brazil Project, 5

Isabel colony, 59, 70

Italy, 74, 137

Ivo (Bororo Indian), 127

Jarudori village, 41, 101, 136, 152n.7

Javanese funeral rite, 4

Jesuits, 59, 78, 92, 111

Jews, 7

João VI, 86

Joaquim, chief of Bororo Indians, 75, 78

Juiz de Fora, 94

Jung, Carl Gustav, 9, 146n.18

Just Wars, 59

Katz, Elihu, 129, 134, 140, 141, 152n.9

Kayapó Indians, 39–40, 52, 58, 78, 79

Kioguaros, 116

Kodo, 121

Kraho Indians, 61

Kroeber, A. L., 9, 11

Labor organization: changes in, 30, 61; Salesian missionaries' goals for, 67, 70–71, 77, 79–80, 110; subjugation to labor, 60–61, 64. *See also* Subsistence activities; Work habits

Lacan, J., 46

Ladeira, Maria Inês, 62

Laiane Indians, 3

Laing, R. D., 24, 46

Land. *See* Territorial issues

Language: and contextualization, 11; and graphic representation, ix; Indian language, 19, 69, 111, 115, 116; and linguistics, 10; unconscious nature of, 8

Lasagna, Dom Luis, 66, 69–70

Latin Amerian Episcopate, Second General Conference of, 105

Leo XIII, 70, 83

Lévi-Strauss, Claude: and Bororo Indian social organization, 28; films of, 125; and incest taboo, 10; on identity, x–xi; and paradox of anthropology, 1–2

Lévi-Strauss, Dina, 125

Levy-Bruhl, Lucien, 26

Liberation Theology, 131–132

Liceu Coração de Jesus, 70

Linguistics, 7–16, 18

Linton, Ralph, xv, 11, 146n.15

Logico-meaningful integration, 4
Lourenço (Bororo Indian), 124, 132
Luciara, 103
Lunkenbein, Fr. Rodolfo: assassination of, 53, 103–104; Bororo Indians' view of funeral, 134, 135–141; funeral ceremony for, 120–123, 129–131, 139; as martyr, 133; mass for, 123–127, 129; relatives of, 121–124; rituals held in honor of, 115; Salesian missionaries' view of funeral, 131–135

Macedo, Carmem Cinira, 106, 118
Malan, Reverend, 77, 78, 86–89, 94
Malaria, 72–73
Male initiation ceremonies, 37, 85–86, 120–122
Malinowski, B. K., 1, 10, 30
Manaus-Boa Vista Highway, 102
Marcigaglia, Fr. Luis, 66
Marinoni, JosÈ, 126
Marques, Thiago, 28–29, 152n.8
Marriage bond, 108, 113–114. *See also* Family life
Martins, José de Souza, 100, 102, 103
Martyrdom, 124, 132–133, 135
Mass: Bororo Indians' attendance, 83, 85; in Indian language, 115; for Lunkenbein, 123–127, 129
Material culture, 29
Mato Grosso: and Bororo Indians' movement, 70, 137; land conflicts in, 69, 103; Salesian missionaries in, 65, 70
Mato Grosso Salesian Mission Directory of Missionary Work with Native Populations, 110–112
Mauss, Marcel, xiv–xv, 8
Mead, George, 8, 12
Mead, Margaret, 9
Meaning systems, 130
Means and ends, relationship between, 13
Médici, Emílio, 102

Menezes, Claudia, 65
Men's house (*baito*), 75, 92–93, 108, 115–116, 150–151n.8
Meruri: author's study of, 41; and Baldus, 27; and Bororo Indians' culture, 115; and Bororo Indians' self–image, 54; census of, 136, 152n.7; cultural reinvigoration of, 43; and Lunkenbein's assassination, 103–104; and Lunkenbein's funeral ceremony, 120–123, 138; and Lunkenbein's mass, 123–127; population concentration of, 135; and Salesian missionaries' influence, 48, 135–136; and Xavante Indians, 53
Metaidentity, 46–47, 148n.3
Metaperspective, 46
Metaphor, and processual analysis, 129–130
Metaphorical processes, xvi, 133–134
Metonymical processes, xvi
Mexican Revolution, 133
Mezan, Renato, 15–16
Minas Gerais, 94
Mineiro, João, 103, 120
Mining industry, 100, 102
Minority groups, x, xi, xiii, 2
Mirror. *See* Play of mirrors
Missioni Salesiane, 98
Montes, Maria Lúcia, 142–143
Morellli, Giovanni, 20, 21
Mori (reciprocity), 76
Mortes River village, 73, 95
Mortuary gourd production, xvi
Moschin, José, 126
Mothers, as symbol, 132–134
Multivocal symbols, 129–130
Murtinho, Manoel, 70
Music, 86–87, 89, 122

National Conference of Brazilian Bishops, 106, 127
National Indian Foundation. *See* FUNAI (Fundação Nacional do Indio)
National Integration Program, 102

National society: Bororo Indians'
    relationship with, 32, 47, 56, 64,
    138; Kayapó Indians' relationship
    with, 39–40; resistance to, 43; and
    Roman Catholic Church, 143;
    and territorial issues, 38, 56–58,
    131. *See also* Contact relation-
    ships; Interethnic relations
Native Missionary Council. *See*
    CIMI (Conselho Indigenista
    Missionário)
Natural endowments, of individuals,
    28, 29
Nature, and culture, 10
Negro River region, 94
Nekretch (traditional ritual items),
    39
Niterói, Brazil, 70
Non-Indians: attacks on Bororo
    Indians, 77–78; and boarding
    schools, 97, 100, 114; Bororo
    Indians' alliances with, 43; Bororo
    Indians relationship with, 104,
    149n.1; and Bororo Indians' self-
    image, 49, 63–64; cultural
    differences from Indians, ix;
    Indians' incorporation of
    discourse of, 19–20; as reference
    points, 47. *See also* National
    society; Whites
Nostalgic discourse, 31, 35, 36
Nuclear energy, 102
Nudity: and barbarism, ix; of Bororo
    Indians, 76, 86, 107
Nuer Indians, 52–53

Ochoa, Father Gonçalo, 43, 69, 122–
    125, 132–133, 136
Ofaié Indians, 3
Oliveira Filho, João Pacheco, 5, 131
Orientalism, 26, 149n.2
Orlandi, Eni, 19–20, 21
Other: and action, 14; and
    anthropology, xv; and belief, 74,
    84–85; imitation of, 35; and
    psychoanalytical theories, 12;
    representation of, ix, xv–xvi; in

ritual, 143; role playing before,
    xiii; and self, 13, 118; and self-
    awareness, xiv; and self-image,
    xiii, 45, 46; and social self, 143;
    and value systems, 47
Oti Indians, 3

Paese (village), 77
Paganism, and Roman Catholic
    Church, 80, 82, 112, 113
Paiaguá Indians, 58, 59
Pai-Pirá, 58
Pakistanis, in London, 7
Palikur Indians, 24
Paoli, Maria Céllia, xii–xiii
Parecim, Camilo, 126
Pastoral Land Commission, 106, 107
Paulista village, 136, 152n.7
Pedro II (emperor of Brazil), 70
Periera, João Gonçalo, 59
Perigara village, 41, 136, 152n.7
Perimetral Norte, 102
Person, notion of, xiv–xv, xvi, 8, 47,
    145n.4
Personality studies, 11
Piebaga village, 41, 152n.7
Pires de Campos, Antonio, 58
Plantel Company, 103
Play of mirrors: and anthropological
    literature, 37–44; and Bororo
    Indians' self-image, 47–54; and
    contact relationships, xiv; Eco on,
    148n.2; and identity, 46, 144; and
    representations of self, 47; and
    self-image, xiii, xvii, 15, 45; and
    simulation, 23
Pobojari village, 36, 38, 137
Pobori village, 101, 136, 152n.7
Polamazônia Program, 103
Politics: and anthropologists, 41, 43;
    and Bororo Indians' government,
    55; and Bororo Indians' need for
    legal protection, 56, 137; and
    contact relationships, xvi; and
    group identity, xi, xiii; and
    Kayapó Indians, 39; and land
    ownership, 101; and religion, 4;

and rituals, 142–143; and Roman Catholic Church, 106; and Salesian missionaries' image of Bororo Indians, 68; and simulacrum, 25; and structural distance, 52–63; and young Bororo Indians, 34
POLONOROESTE Project, 42, 43
Population of villages, 77, 100, 101, 136, 152n.7
Population segments, Bororo Indians' identification with, 47
Porogi village, 101
Poverty: of Bororo Indians, 54–56, 61; of Indians of Brazil, 67; and Roman Catholic Church's mission, 104–107, 131; and Salesian missionaries, 132; and symbolic meaning of Christ, 106
Power: of *bari*, 54, 85; and Bororo Indians' dependency, 56; and culture, xiii, 6; and interethnic relations, 131, 138; and Roman Catholic Church, 65; of Salesian missionaries, 67
Primeiro Encontro dos Povos Indígenas no Brasil, 18
Primitive societies, 1–2, 17, 61–62
Pro-Bororo Festival, 94
Pro-Bororo Vestiary, 94
Processual analysis, xiv, 33, 129–130
Protestant religious movements, 106
Psychoanalysis, 8, 12
Psychology: and anthropology, 7–16, 146n.14; and self, 8, 46; and self-awareness, xiv; and social changes, 146n.12

Radar na Amazônia (RADAM), 102
Radcliffe-Brown, A. R., 1
Rationality, and value systems, 33–34
Reality: dereferentialization of, 19; fabrication of, 17; and identity, xi, 21, 23; and interdependent relationships, ix–x; and sign, 89, 93

Reciprocity (*mori*), 76
Redfield, Robert, xv
Reflected images, and action, 46, 47
Regional markets, and funeral ceremonies, 33, 147n.2
Religion: changes in, 31–32; and citizenship, 89; and contact relationships, 3; separation of tribal religion from Christianity, 30; and social structure, 4. *See also* Protestant religious movements; Roman Catholic Church
Religious education: boarding schools, 85, 95, 97, 100, 114–115; and Bororo Indians' culture, 110–111, 116; and Bororo Indians' self-image, 54; and Bororo-Salesian relationship, 118; and Gregory I, 113; and Just Wars, 59; mobile Christian instruction, 100; and rituals, 82; of Salesian missionaries, 79–82, 84, 95, 114–115; and Salesian missionaries' image of Bororo Indians, 68, 69; subsistence activity's interference with, 71
Representation: collective representation, 8; and men's house removal, 93; of other, ix, xv–xvi; of self, ix–x, xiii, xv–xvi, 7–8, 47; and simulation, 89–90, 141; system of, xi
Resistance strategy: and conformity, 63; dependence transformed into, 64; of Kayapó Indians, 39; and national society, 43; process of, 38; of young Bororo Indians, 34, 91
Ribeiro, Darcy, 3, 41, 42, 105
Ribeiro, Elza, 126
Richards, I. A., 129–130
Rio de Janeiro, 87–89, 94
Rituals: Christian ceremony introduction, 83; and clans, 143–144; and farming, 63, 82; male initiation ceremonies, 37, 85–86,

120–122; and mass attendance, 83, 85; and men's house, 92, 93; and music, 86, 122; naming rituals, 83, 114; other in, 143; and political conflicts, 4; and politics, 142–143; recording of, 115, 116, 122, 123, 127–129, 139–141; ritual symbols, 130; and subsistence activity, 62, 63; wailing during, 121, 122, 126, 139. *See also* Funeral ceremonies

Rodrigues de Carvalho, Manuel, 59

Role playing, before the other, xiii

Roman Catholic Church: individual's role in, 118; mission of, 66–67, 80, 92, 104–106; and national society, 143; and poverty, 104–107, 131; role of, 43, 112, 133–135; support for Indians of Brazil, 105; and unity, 118–119, 135, 144; and Vatican II, 104–105; and Xavante Indians, 65. *See also* Bororo-Salesian relationship; Jesuits; Salesian missionaries

Rondonópolis, 52, 101

Royce, Anya Peterson, 7, 138

Rua, Reverend, 73, 77, 79, 81–83, 91–92

Saake, Fr. Guilherme, 2, 30–31, 37, 38

Sacilotti, Father, 95, 148n.6

Sagrado Coração de Jesus mission: Bororo band of, 87; cemetery of, 82; Colbacchini as director of, 90–91; establishment of, 75; malaria epidemic of, 72–73; population of, 77

Said, Edward W., 26, 149n.2

Salesian missionaries: and Brazilian government, 67, 75, 78; and Christian names, 83; fundraising efforts of, 86; generation of Christians created by, 30; health care of, 59, 72–74, 75, 79, 84, 110, 135; history of Brazilian settlement, 69–75; image of

Indians of Brazil, 66–69; and Marques, 29; motives of, 80; pacifying role of, 88–89; publications of, 65–66; recruitment efforts of, 74–75; redemption and, 17; representation of self, x; role of, 75, 104, 110; self-image of, 67, 131–135; and Vatican II changes, 68, 107–113; and Xavante Indians, 65–66. *See also* Bororo-Salesian relationship; Religious education

Sangradouro: and Baldus, 27; census of, 136; epidemics of, 73; and FUNAI, 103; success of, 98, 100; transfers to, 77; and Viertler, 32, 38

São José colony, 77, 100

São Lourenço Valley, 70, 77, 78

São Marcos mission, 65, 103

São Paulo, 70, 94

Sapir, Edward, 10

Sarco, Antônio, 126

Sarno, Geraldo, 127–128

Scarcity, and labor, 61

Scarification, 122, 123, 124, 126, 133

Schaden, Egon, 2, 30

Second Vatican Council. *See* Vatican II

Security, and Salesian missionaries, 78

Self: Bateson on, 14–15; and identity, 146–147n.18; objective nature of, 12–13; and other, 13, 118; as process, 12; in psychology, 8, 46; representation of, ix–x, xiii, xv–xvi, 7–8, 47; social self, 143

Self-awareness, and psychology, xiv, 12–13

Self-image: ambiguity of, 51; of Bororo Indians, xvi, 47–54, 59–60, 63–64, 104; and contact relationships, xiv, 6; and identity, xiii–xiv; and linguistics, 8; and other, xiii, 45, 46; and play of mirrors, xiii, xvii, 15; of Salesian missionaries, 67, 131–135; of

social groups, ix; of society, ix
Semiotics, 16, 18, 20
Semiurgy, 19
Serpa, Paulo, 63
Serviço de Proteção dos Indios (SPI), 2, 41, 64, 100
Settlement movement, 102–103
Sign: definition of, 147n.1 (chapter 2); and identity, 25; in linguistics, 8; and men's house removal, 93, 115–116; and reality, 89, 93; referential function of, 19
Signified and signifiers, in linguistics, 8, 19, 147n.1 (chapter 2)
Simão (Bororo Indian): assassination of, 53, 103; as martyr, 124–125, 132–133; rituals held in honor of, 115, 139
Simulacrum: cross as, 93; and image, 89–93; in linguistics, 8; referential simulacrum, 27; and simulation, 23, 141; as strategy, 24–25
Simulation: and identity, 21, 23; and representation, 89–90, 141
Social changes: acculturation studies of, 2; Baldus' view on, 27–30, 38; Bororo Indians' resistance to, 27–28; and contact relationships, xv, xvi; Crocker's views on, 36–37, 38; and cultural disintegration, 3, 5, 38; cultural expressions of, 29; Geertz on, 4–5; Huestis's views on, 31–32, 38; and identity, xv; and orientalism, 26–27; and psychology, 146n.12; Saake's views on, 30–31, 38; Viertler's views on, 32–36, 38
Social drama, 129, 130, 133
Social groups: and contact relationships, xv; and identity, xi–xiii; interaction between, 6; interdependent relationships of, x; minority status of, xi; and representation of self, x; self-images of, ix, 46–47; structural

distance between, 52–53
Socialization standards, 10
Social sciences, xvii, 7
Social self, 143–144
Social situation, 130–131
Social structure, 4–5, 29, 106
Social visibility, xi–xii, 137, 138, 141
Societies: and contact relationships, xiv, xv; disappearance of, 1–2; field research on, 17; functionalist perspective of, 3; imposition of western standards on, 17; primitive societies, 1–2, 17, 61–62; self-images of, ix, 45–46; and social groups, x, 46–47
Sociology, 2
Spatial organization, 92, 97
Specular image, 46
SPI (Serviço de Proteção dos Indios), 2, 41, 64, 100
Spiritism, 32
Spiritual culture, 29
Squatters, 103
Structural distance, between social groups, 52–53
Structural relativity, 53
Subsistence activities: and Bororo funeral ceremonies, 37; interference with religious education, 71; misconceptions concerning, 62; persistence of, 63, 70; restriction of, 32, 60, 61
Suez Canal, 68
Superstitions, 79–80
Symbolic self, 46
Symbols: blood as, 133–135; and concept of culture, 14; in linguistics, 8; mothers as, 132–134; multivocal symbols, 129–130; ritual symbols, 130; symbol systems, 130; symbolic meaning of Christ, 106

Taboos, 9, 10
Tadarimana village, 32, 38, 41, 54, 136, 152n.7

Tax incentives, 102
Television, and ceremony, 141
Terena Indians, 19
Teresa Cristina colony, 59, 66, 70–75
Territorial issues: Bororo Indians' defense of, 58–59, 64, 115; and Bororo Indians' self-image, 48, 54; and boundaries, 42, 53, 148n.11; and contact relationships, 56–58; invasion of territory, 18; land demarcation, 103; land occupation, 100–101; land plotting, 57; land protection, 59; land struggle movement, 34, 132; Mato Grosso land conflicts, 69, 103; and military rule, 102; and national society, 38, 56–58, 131; reduction in territory, 32, 61
Third World countries, 104, 105
Thomas, Father, 125, 127–128
Thurnwald, Richard Christian, 30
Ticuna Indians, 131
Tori-Paru village, 27, 101
Totemism, 9, 32, 108
Totó (*bari*), 72–73
Trans-Amazonian Highway, 103
Tugarege moiety, 121, 123, 143
Tupi Indians, 2
Tupinambá Indians, 3
Turin, Italy, 67
Turner, Terence, 38–40
Turner, Victor, xiv, 129–130, 133–134
Tylor, Sir Edward Burnett, 9, 11, 29

Unconscious, in psychoanalysis, 8
Unconscious nature of language, in linguistics, 8
União das Nações Indígenas (UNI), 18
Union of Indian Nations, 18
United States: acculturation studies in, 2; anthropology in, 9–10; Bororo Indians' support in, 137; Freud's influence in, 9; research projects of, 17; social visibility of groups in, xii

Upper Negro River missions, 2, 66
Urban context: and ethnicity, 7; and Roman Catholic Church, 106, 112, 118

Vale do Rio São Lourenço, 42
Value systems: and ambiguity of images, 51; of Bororo Indians, 69, 84–85, 93, 110, 142; Christian values, 49, 67, 68, 84, 91, 110; and creeds, 74; and culture, 11; and dominating society, 17; environmental values, 40; and rationality, 33–34; and representation of self, 47–48; of Salesian missionaries, 73, 84–85, 142; and self-image, xiii, 6; and structural distance, 53; work as virtue, 69, 79–80, 110, 115, 125
Vangelista, Chiara, 92, 97
Van Velsen, J., xiv, 11, 130–131
Varese, Stefano, 105
Vatican II: and Bororo-Salesian relationship, 113–119; and Roman Catholic Church's mission, 104–105; and Salesian missionaries, 68, 107–113
Venturelli, J. A., 66, 69, 94, 106
Vermelho River, 77
Viertler, Renate, xv, 32–36, 145n.4, 147n.1, 149n.1
Villages (*paese*), 77, 100, 101, 136. *See also specific villages*
Viveiros de Castro, Eduardo, 118, 147n.3

Wallon, Henry, 13
Weber, Max, 16
Whites: Bororo Indian alliances with, 58–59, 138; Bororo Indian conflicts with, 78–79; and Bororo Indians' dependence, 60; and Bororo Indians' poverty, 55; and São José colony, 100. *See also* Non-Indians
Wicklund, R. A., 12
Women: and Christian morality, 107; feminist movement of, xii–

xiii; in funeral ceremonies, 28, 120–122; and men's house, 150–151n.8; representation of self, x; and simulacrum, 24; social status of, 27–28

Work habits: and acculturation studies, 30; Bororo Indians' dislike of work, 67, 70, 77, 88; and chit system, 60–61, 110; and citizenship, 108; and cultural integration, 31; work as virtue, 69, 79–80, 110, 115, 125. *See also* Labor organization; Subsistence activities

World expositions, 68

Wundt, Wilhelm, 9

Xavante Indians: Bororo Indians' image of, 49–52; Bororo Indians' relationship with, xvii, 47–49, 51–54, 65, 100; and Bororo Indians' self-image, 48–49; demographic density of, 50; and FUNAI, 103; and Lunkenbein's assassination, 104; recognition of, 137–138; representation of self, x; rice produced by, 19; Roman Catholic Church's influence on, 65; and Salesian missionaries, 65–66, 95, 111, 148n.6; self-image of, 52, 54

Xavantina, 95

Xet· Indians, 3

Xingu Indians, 52

Xingu River, 2

Young Bororo Indians: alliances of, 34; and Bororo funeral ceremony, 37; and Bororo-Salesian relationship, 85–86; and interethnic relations, 43; transformation of, 35. *See also* Children

Youth movements, of Roman Catholic Church, 104

Zanetti, Elza, 126

Zavattaro, Father, 113

Zulu history, 131